Persian Heritage Series No 2

MASNAVI I MA'NAVI

THE SPIRITUAL COUPLETS

OF

MAULÁNA JALÁLU-'D-DÍN MUHAMMAD I RÚMÍ

TRANSLATED AND ABRIDGED

BY

E. H. WHINFIELD, M.A.

YASSAVOLI
PUBLICATIONS

MASNAVI I MA'NAVI
Jalálu-' d- Dín Rúmí
Translated and abridged by : E.H. WHINFIELD
Second Edition: 1999
Printed and bound in the Islamic Republic of Iran
Published by Yassavoli Publications
Bazzarcheh Ketab, Enqelab Ave. 13146, Tehran, Iran.
Tel: (9821) 6461003 Fax: (9821) 6411913
ISBN : 964-306-030-6

Internet Address. www.yassavoliran.com

CONTENTS

BOOK II

BOOK III

BOOK IV

BOOK V.

BOOK VI.

Introduction

Jalal-e-dîn Rûmi was born at Balkh (Khorassan) in 1207 A.D. The city at that time flourished under the rule of Muhammad the Shah of Khwarazm. The family to which our mystical poet belonged had been settled in Balkh for several generations; it was highly respected and, according to his biographers, had produced a notable succession of jurists and divines.

In 1219, Bahâ-e-dîn Walad, the father of Jalal-e-dîn Rûmi, suddenly departed from Balkh with his family and journeyed westward. There can be no doubt that Bahâ-e-dîn fled before the terrible Mongol hordes which were already approaching his native city. Zarandeh was their first home in Rûm (Turkey) and Konia, the capital of the western Seljuk empire, their final residence. Jalal-e-dîn, under the influence of Burhân-e-dîn Tirmidhi, became imbued with enthusiasm for the discipline and doctrine of Sufism. He devoted himself to imitation of his guide (*pir*) and passed through all the stages of the mystical life until the death of Burhân-e-dîn (1240). He in turn assumed the rank of *shaykh* and his ardent personality attracted disciples in Rûm. In 1244, a wandering dervish, known to posterity by the name of Shams Tabrizi, arrived in Konia. Jalal-e-dîn found in the stranger that perfect image of the Divine Beloved which he had long been seeking. He took him away to his house and for two years they remained inseparable. Meanwhile the disciples of Rûmi, entirely cut off from their master's teaching and bitterly resenting his continued devotion to Shams alone, assailed the intruder with abuse and threats of violence. At last the dervish fled to Damascus but was brought back in triumph by the son of Jalal-e-dîn, Sultan Walad.

Jalal-e-dîn, deeply agitated by the loss of his bosom friend, sent out people in search of him. Thereupon the disciples "repented" (*towbé*) and were forgiven. Soon, however, a renewed outburst of jealousy on their part caused Shams to take refuge in Damascus for the second time and again Sultan Walad was called upon to restore the situation. Finally, in 1247, the man of mystery vanished without leaving a trace behind. After the disappearance of Shams, Rûmi composed an immense collection of mystical odes in the name of Shams and dedicated to his memory (Divân Shams Tabrizi).

The next period (1252 - 1261) in Rûmi's spiritual life is a fainter repetition of the last. For many years, Jalal-e-dîn devoted himself to Salah-e-dîn Zarkûb, who as his deputy (Khalifeh) was charged with the duty of instructing the Rûmi's followers.

On the death of Salah-e-dîn, the poet's enthusiasm found a new and abundant source of inspiration in another disciple Husam-e-dîn ibn Akhi turk, whose name he has mystically associated with his greatest work, the celebrated "Mathnavi". During the last ten years of the poet's life this last beloved follower acted as his deputy, and upon his death in 1273 succeeded him as Head of the Mewlevi order.

We must note that a platonic type of mystical love had been cultivated by sufis long before Rûmi declared that he and Shams Tabrizi were "two bodies with one soul". In this union of loving souls all distinctions vanish: nothing remains but the essential unity of love in which "lover" and "beloved" have merged their separate identities. In calling his lyrics the Divân of Shams, Rûmi of course uses the name Shams as though Shams and himself had become identical and were the same person. The forms in which he clothes his religious philosophy had been fashioned before him by two great sufi poets, Sanâ'i and Attâr. Though he makes no secret of his debt to them both, his flight takes a wider range, his materials are richer and his method of handling the subject is so original that we can say the Rûmi's literary works have a 'new style'. In Jalal-e-dîn, the Persian mystical genius found its supreme expression. The words used by Dante in reference to the "Divine Commedia" would serve excellently as a description of the "Mathnavi": "The poem belongs to the moral or ethical branch of philosophy, its quality is not speculative but practical, and its ultimate end is to lead into the state of felicity, those now enduring the miserable life of man". Rûmi's mysticism is not doctrinal but experimental. He appeals to the heart more than to the mind.

Jamâl Âl Ahmad

THE MASNAVI.

Book I.

PROLOGUE.

Hearken to the reed-flute, how it complains,
Lamenting its banishment from its home :—
"Ever since they tore me from my osier bed,
My plaintive notes have moved men and women to tears.
I burst my breast, striving to give vent to sighs,
And to express the pangs of my yearning for my home.
He who abides far away from his home
Is ever longing for the day he shall return.
My wailing is heard in every throng,
In concert with them that rejoice and them that weep.
Each interprets my notes in harmony with his own feelings,
But not one fathoms the secrets of my heart.
My secrets are not alien from my plaintive notes,
Yet they are not manifest to the sensual eye and ear.
Body is not veiled from soul, neither soul from body,
Yet no man hath ever seen a soul."
This plaint of the flute is fire, not mere air.
Let him who lacks this fire be accounted dead!
'Tis the fire of love that inspires the flute,[1]
'Tis the ferment of love that possesses the wine.
The flute is the confidant of all unhappy lovers;

[1] Love signifies the strong attraction that draws all creatures back to reunion with their Creator.

Yea, its strains lay bare my inmost secrets.
Who hath seen a poison and an antidote like the flute?
Who hath seen a sympathetic consoler like the flute?
The flute tells the tale of love's bloodstained path,
It recounts the story of Majnun's love toils.
None is privy to these feelings save one distracted,
As ear inclines to the whispers of the tongue.
Through grief my days are as labour and sorrow,
My days move on, hand in hand with anguish.
Yet, though my days vanish thus, 'tis no matter,
Do thou abide, O Incomparable Pure One! [1]

But all who are not fishes are soon tired of water;
And they who lack daily bread find the day very long;
So the "Raw" comprehend not the state of the "Ripe;" [2]
Therefore it behoves me to shorten my discourse.

Arise, O son! burst thy bonds and be free!
How long wilt thou be captive to silver and gold?
Though thou pour the ocean into thy pitcher,
It can hold no more than one day's store.
The pitcher of the desire of the covetous never fills,
The oyster-shell fills not with pearls till it is content;
Only he whose garment is rent by the violence of love
Is wholly pure from covetousness and sin.

Hail to thee, then, O LOVE, sweet madness!
Thou who healest all our infirmities!
Who art the physician of our pride and self-conceit!
Who art our Plato and our Galen!
Love exalts our earthly bodies to heaven,
And makes the very hills to dance with joy!
O lover, 'twas love that gave life to Mount Sinai,
When "it quaked, and Moses fell down in a swoon."
Did my Beloved only touch me with his lips,
I too, like the flute, would burst out in melody.

[1] Self-annihilation leads to eternal life in God—the universal Noumenon, by whom all phenomena subsist. See Gulshan i Raz, l. 400.

[2] "Raw" and "Ripe" are terms for "Men of externals" and "Men of heart" or Mystics.

[3] Alluding to the giving of the law on Mount Sinai. Koran vii. 139.

But he who is parted from them that speak his tongue,
Though he possess a hundred voices, is perforce dumb.
When the rose has faded and the garden is withered,
The song of the nightingale is no longer to be heard.
The BELOVED is all in all, the lover only veils Him; [1]
The BELOVED is all that lives, the lover a dead thing.
When the lover feels no longer LOVE'S quickening,
He becomes like a bird who has lost its wings. Alas!
How can I retain my senses about me,
When the BELOVED shows not the light of His countenance?

LOVE desires that this secret should be revealed,
For if a mirror reflects not, of what use is it?
Knowest thou why thy mirror reflects not?
Because the rust has not been scoured from its face.
If it were purified from all rust and defilement,
It would reflect the shining of the SUN of GOD.[2]

O friends, ye have now heard this tale,
Which sets forth the very essence of my case.

[1] All phenomenal existences (man included) are but "veils" obscuring the face of the Divine Noumenon, the only real existence, and the moment His sustaining presence is withdrawn they at once relapse into their original nothingness. See Gulshan i Raz, l. 165.

[2] So Bernard of Clairvaux. See Gulshan i Raz, l. 435.

Story I. *The Prince and the Handmaid* (p. 5).

A prince, while engaged on a hunting excursion, espied a fair maiden, and by promises of gold induced her to accompany him. After a time she fell sick, and the prince had her tended by divers physicians. As, however, they all omitted to say, "*God willing*,[1] we will cure her," their treatment was of no avail. So the prince offered prayer, and in answer thereto a physician was sent from heaven. He at once condemned his predecessors' view of the case, and by a very skilful diagnosis, discovered that the real cause of the maiden's illness was her love for a certain goldsmith of Samarcand. In accordance with the physician's advice, the prince sent to Samarcand and fetched the goldsmith, and married him to the lovesick maiden, and for six months the pair lived together in the utmost harmony and happiness. At the end of that period the physician, by divine command, gave the goldsmith a poisonous draught, which caused his strength and beauty to decay, and he then lost favour with the maiden, and she was reunited to the king. This Divine command was precisely similar to God's command to Abraham to slay his son Ishmael, and to the act of the angel in slaying the servant of Moses,[2] and is therefore beyond human criticism.

[1] As enjoined in Koran xviii. 23. One cannot converse with a strict Musulman for five minutes without hearing the formula, "*In sha Allah Ta'alla*," or *D. V.*

[2] Koran xviii. 73.

Description of Love (p. 7).

A true lover is proved such by his pain of heart;
No sickness is there like sickness of heart.
The lover's ailment is different from all ailments;
Love is the astrolabe of God's mysteries.
A lover may hanker after this love or that love,
But at the last he is drawn to the King of love.
However much we describe and explain love,
When we fall in love we are ashamed of our words.
Explanation by the tongue makes most things clear,
But love unexplained is clearer.
When pen hasted to write,
On reaching the subject of love it split in twain.
When the discourse touched on the matter of love,
Pen was broken and paper torn.
In explaining it Reason sticks fast, as an ass in mire;
Naught but Love itself can explain love and lovers!
None but the sun can display the sun,
If you would see it displayed, turn not away from it.
Shadows, indeed, may indicate the sun's presence,
But only the sun displays the light of life.
Shadows induce slumber, like evening talks,
But when the sun arises the "moon is split asunder."[1]
In the world there is naught so wondrous as the sun,
But the Sun of the soul sets not and has no yesterday.
Though the material sun is unique and single,
We can conceive similar suns like to it.
But the Sun of the soul, beyond this firmament,—
No like thereof is seen in concrete or abstract.[2]
Where is there room in conception for His essence,
So that similitudes of Him should be conceivable?

[1] Koran liv. 1.

[2] There is a tradition, "I know my Lord by my Lord."

Shamsu-'d-Din of Tabriz importunes Jalalu-'d-Din to compose the Masnavi (p. 7).

The sun (*Shams*) of Tabriz is a perfect light,
A sun, yea, one of the beams of God!
When the praise was heard of the "Sun of Tabriz,"
The sun of the fourth heaven bowed its head.
Now that I have mentioned his name, it is but right
To set forth some indications of his beneficence.
  That precious Soul caught my skirt,
Smelling the perfume of the garment of Yusuf;
And said, "For the sake of our ancient friendship,
Tell forth a hint of those sweet states of ecstasy,
That earth and heaven may be rejoiced,
And also Reason and Spirit, a hundredfold."
  I said, "O thou who art far from 'The Friend,'
Like a sick man who has strayed from his physician,
Importune me not, for I am beside myself;
My understanding is gone, I cannot sing praises.
Whatsoever one says, whose reason is thus astray,
Let him not boast; his efforts are useless.
Whatever he says is not to the point,
And is clearly inapt and wide of the mark.
What can I say when not a nerve of mine is sensible?
Can I explain 'The Friend' to one to whom He is no Friend?
Verily my singing His praise were dispraise,
For 'twould prove me existent, and existence is error.[1]
Can I describe my separation and my bleeding heart?
Nay, put off this matter till another season."
  He said, "Feed me, for I am an hungred,
And at once, for 'the time is a sharp sword.'
O comrade, the Sufi is 'the son of time present.'[2]
It is not the rule of his canon to say, 'To-morrow.'
Can it be that thou art not a true Sufi?
Ready money is lost by giving credit."
  I said, "'Tis best to veil the secrets of 'The Friend.'
So give good heed to the morals of these stories.
That is better than that the secrets of 'The Friend'
Should be noised abroad in the talk of strangers."
  He said, "Without veil or covering or deception,
Speak out, and vex me not, O man of many words!
Strip off the veil and speak out, for do not I
Enter under the same coverlet as the Beloved?"
  I said, "If the Beloved were exposed to outward view,
Neither wouldst thou endure, nor embrace, nor form.
Press thy suit, yet with moderation;
A blade of grass cannot pierce a mountain.
If the sun that illumines the world
Were to draw nigher, the world would be consumed.[1]
Close thy mouth and shut the eyes of this matter,
That the world's life be not made a bleeding heart.
No longer seek this peril, this bloodshed;
Hereafter impose silence on the 'Sun of Tabriz.'"
  He said, "Thy words are endless. Now tell forth
All thy story from its beginning."

STORY II. *The Oilman and his Parrot* (p. 10).

An oilman possessed a parrot which used to amuse him with its agreeable prattle, and to watch his shop when he went out. One day, when the parrot was alone in the shop, a cat upset one of the oil-jars. When the

[1] See Gulshan i Ras, l. 400. In the state of union self remains not.

[2] The Sufi is the "son of the time present," because he is an Energumen, or passive instrument moved by the divine impulse of the moment. "The time present is a sharp sword," because the divine impulse of the moment dominates the Energumen, and executes its decrees sharply. See Sohravardi quoted in *Notices et Extraits des MSS.*, xii. 371 note.

[1] "When its Lord appears in glory
to the Mount of existence,
Existence is laid low, like the
dust of the road."
—Gulshan i Raz, l. 195.

Hearken to this Reed forlorn,
Breathing, even since 'twas torn

oilman returned home he thought that the parrot had done this mischief, and in his anger he smote the parrot such a blow on the head as made all its feathers drop off, and so stunned it that it lost the power of speech for several days. But one day the parrot saw a bald-headed man passing the shop, and recovering its speech, it cried out, "Pray, whose oil-jar did you upset?" The passers-by smiled at the parrot's mistake in confounding baldness caused by age with the loss of its own feathers due to a blow.

Confusion of saints with hypocrites (p. 12).

Worldly senses are the ladder of earth,
Spiritual senses are the ladder of heaven.
The health of the former is sought of the leech,
The health of the latter from "The Friend."
The health of the former arises from tending the body,
That of the latter from mortifying the flesh.
The kingly soul lays waste the body,
And after its destruction he builds it anew.
Happy the soul who for love of God
Has lavished family, wealth, and goods!—
Has destroyed its house to find the hidden treasure,
And with that treasure has rebuilt it in fairer sort;
Has dammed up the stream and cleansed the channel,
And then turned a fresh stream into the channel;—
Has cut its flesh to extract a spear-head,[1]
Causing a fresh skin to grow again over the wound;—
Has razed the fort to oust the infidel in possession,
And then rebuilt it with a hundred towers and bulwarks.
Who can describe the unique work of Grace?
I have been forced to illustrate it by these similes.
Sometimes it presents one appearance, sometimes another.
Yea, the affair of religion is only bewilderment.
Not such as occurs when one turns one's back on God,
But such as when one is drowned and absorbed in Him.
The latter has his face ever turned to God,
The former's face shows his undisciplined self-will.
Watch the face of each one, regard it well,
It may be by serving thou wilt recognise Truth's face.
As there are many demons with men's faces,
It is wrong to join hand with every one.
When the fowler sounds his decoy whistle,
That the birds may be beguiled by that snare,
The birds hear that call simulating a bird's call,
And, descending from the air, find net and knife.
So vile hypocrites steal the language of Darveshes,
In order to beguile the simple with their trickery.
The works of the righteous are light and heat,
The works of the evil treachery and shamelessness.
They make stuffed lions to scare the simple,
They give the title of Muhammad to false Musailima.
But Musailima retained the name of "Liar,"
And Muhammad that of "Sublimest of beings."
That wine of God (the righteous) yields a perfume of musk;
Other wine (the evil) is reserved for penalties and pains.

[1] These are all figures and types of self-annihilation in order to the acquisition of eternal life in God.

STORY III. *The Jewish King, his Vazir, and the Christians* (pp. 12–22).

A certain Jewish king used to persecute the Christians, desiring to exterminate their faith. His Vazir persuaded him to try a stratagem, namely, to mutilate the Vazir himself, and expel him from his court, with the intent that he might take refuge with the Christians, and stir up mutual dissensions amongst them. The Vazir's suggestion was adopted.[1] He fled to the Christians, and found no difficulty in persuading them that he had been treated in that barbarous way on account of his attachment to the Chistian faith. He soon gained

[1] Compare the story of Zopyrus, Herodotus, iii. 155.

complete influence over them, and was accepted as a saintly martyr and a divine teacher. Only a few discerning men divined his treachery; the majority were all deluded by him. The Christians were divided into twelve legions, and at the head of each was a captain. To each of these captains the Vazir gave secretly a volume of religious directions, taking care to make the directions in each volume different from and contradictory to those in the others. One volume enjoined fasting, another charity, another faith, another works, and so on. Afterwards the Vazir withdrew into a cave, and refused to come out to instruct his disciples, in spite of all their entreaties. Calling the captains to him, he gave secret instructions to each to set himself up as his successor, and to be guided by the instructions in the volume secretly confided to him, and to slay all other claimants of the apostolic office. Having given these directions, he slew himself. In the event each captain set himself up as the Vazir's successor, and the Christians were split up into many sects at enmity with one another, even as the Vazir had intended. But the malicious scheme did not altogether succeed, as one faithful band cleaved to the name of "Ahmad," mentioned in the Gospel,[1] and were thus saved from sharing the ruin of the rest.

The Vazir's Teaching (p. 13).

Myriads of Christians flocked round him,
One after another they assembled in his street.
Then he would preach to them of mysteries,—
Mysteries of the Gospel, of stoles, of prayers.
He would preach to them with eloquent words
Concerning the words and acts of the Messiah.
Outwardly he was a preacher of religious duties,
But within a decoy call and a fowler's snare.

[1] John xiv. 26: "But the Comforter (*parakletos*) shall teach you all things." Musulmans read *periklytos*, "praised" = Muhammad.

Therefore the followers of the Prophet ('Isa)
Were beguiled by the fraud of that demon soul.
He mingled in his discourses many secret doctrines
Concerning devotion and sincerity of soul.
He taught them to make a fair show of devotion,
But to say of secret sins, "What do they matter?"
Hair by hair and jot by jot they learned of him
Fraud of soul, as roses might learn of garlic.
Hair-splitters and all their disciples
Are darkened by similar preaching and discourse.
The Christians gave their hearts to him entirely,
For the blind faith of the vulgar has no discernment.
In their inmost breasts they planted love of him,
And fancied him to be the Vicar of Christ;—
Yea, him, that one-eyed and cursed Dajjál![1]
Save us, O God! who art our only defender!
O God, there are hundreds of snares and baits,
And we are even as greedy and foolish birds;
Every moment our feet are caught in a fresh snare;
Yea, each one of us, though he be a falcon or Simurgh!
Thou dost release us every moment, and straightway
We again fly into the snare, O Almighty One!

Sleep of the body the soul's awaking (p. 14).

Every night Thou freest our spirits from the body
And its snare, making them pure as rased tablets.
Every night spirits are released from this cage,
And set free, neither lording it nor lorded over.
At night prisoners are unaware of their prison,
At night kings are unaware of their majesty.
Then there is no thought or care for loss or gain,
No regard to such an one or such an one.
The state of the "Knower" is such as this, even when awake.

[1] Dajjál, *i.e.*, Antichrist. Sale, Prelim. Discourse, p. 57.

God says,[1] "Thou wouldst deem him awake though
asleep,
Sleeping to the affairs of the world, day and night,
Like a pen in the directing hand of the writer.
He who sees not the hand which effects the writing
Fancies the effect proceeds from the motion of the pen.
If the "Knower" revealed the particulars of this state,
'Twould rob the vulgar of their sensual sleep.
His soul wanders in the desert that has no similitude;
Like his body, his spirit is enjoying perfect rest;—
Freed from desire of eating and drinking,
Like a bird escaped from cage and snare.
But when he is again beguiled into the snare,
He cries for help to the Almighty.

Laila and the Khalifa (p. 14).

The Khalifa said to Laila, "Art thou really she
For whom Majnun lost his head and went distracted?
Thou art not fairer than many other fair ones."
She replied, "Be silent; thou art not Majnun!"
If thou hadst Majnun's eyes,
The two worlds would be within thy view.
Thou art in thy senses, but Majnun is beside himself.
In love to be wide awake is treason.
The more a man is awake, the more he sleeps (to love);
His (critical) wakefulness is worse than slumbering.
Our wakefulness fetters our spirits,
Then our souls are a prey to divers whims,
Thoughts of loss and gain and fears of misery.
They retain not purity, nor dignity, nor lustre,
Nor aspiration to soar heavenwards.
That one is really sleeping who hankers after each
whim
And holds parley with each fancy.

[1] Said of the Seven Sleepers in the cave. Koran xviii. 17; "Knower" = the Gnostic who through ecstasy beholds divine verities.

The twelve volumes of theology (p. 16).

He drew up a separate scroll to the address of each,
The contents of each scroll of a different tenor;
The rules of each of a different purport,
This contradictory of that, from beginning to end.
In one the road of fasting and asceticism
Was made the pillar and condition of right devotion.
In one 'twas said, "Abstinence profits not;
Sincerity in this path is naught but charity."
In one 'twas said, "Thy fasting and thy charity
Are both a making thyself equal with God;
Save faith and utter resignation to God's will
In weal and woe, all virtues are fraud and snares."
In one 'twas said, "Works are the one thing needful;
The doctrine of faith without works is a delusion."
In one 'twas said, "Commands and prohibitions are
Not for observance, but to demonstrate our weakness,
That we may see our own weakness (to carry them out),
And thereby recognise and confess God's power."[1]
In one 'twas said, "Reference to thine own weakness
Is ingratitude for God's mercies towards us.
Rather regard thy power, for thou hast power from God.
Know thy power to be God's grace, for 'tis of Him."
In one 'twas said, "Leave power and weakness alone;
Whatever withdraws thine eyes from God is an idol."
In one 'twas said, "Quench not thy earthy torch,[2]
That it may be a light to lighten mankind.
If thou neglectest regard and care for it,
Thou wilt quench at midnight the lamp of union."
In one 'twas said, "Quench that torch without fear,
That in lieu of one thou may'st see a thousand joys,
For by quenching the light the soul is rejoiced,
And thy Laila is then as bold as her Majnun.

[1] This was the doctrine of the Jabriyan or extreme predestinarians.

[2] *i.e.*, Hide not thy light (of good works or of self-denial) under a bushel.

Whoso to display his devotion renounces the world,
The world is ever with him, before and behind."
In one 'twas said, "Whatsoever God has given thee
In His creation, that He has made sweet to thee;
Yea, pleasant to thee and allowable. Take it, then,
And cast not thyself into the pangs of abstinence."
In one 'twas said, "Give up all thou possessest,
For to be ruled by covetousness is grievous sin."
(Ah! how many diverse roads are pointed out,
And each followed by some sect for dear life!
If the right road were easily attainable,
Every Jew and Gueber would have hit on it!)
In one 'twas said, "The right road is attainable,
For the heart's life is the food of the soul.
Whatever is enjoyed by the carnal man
Yields no fruit, even as salt and waste land.
Its result is naught but remorse,
Its traffic yields only loss.
It is not profitable in the long run;
Its name is called 'bankrupt' in the upshot.
Discern, then, the bankrupt from the profitable,
Consider the eventual value of this and that."
In one 'twas said, "Choose ye a wise Director,
But foresight of results is not found in dignities."
(Each sect looked to results in a different way,
And so, perforce, became captive to errors.
Real foresight of results is not simple jugglery,
Otherwise all these differences would not have arisen.)
In one 'twas said, "Thyself art thy master,
Inasmuch as thou art acquainted with the Master of all;
Be a man, and not another man's beast of burden!
Follow thine own way and lose not thy head!"
In one 'twas said, "All we see is One.
Whoever says 'tis two is suffering from double vision."
In one 'twas said, "A hundred are even as one."[1]
But whoso thinks this is a madman.

[1] Alluding to the doctrine of the Trinity.

Each scroll had its contrary piece of rhetoric,
In form and substance utterly opposed to it;
This contrary to that, from first to last,
As if each was compounded of poison and antidotes.

STORY IV. *Another Tyrannical Jewish King* (p. 22).

A certain Jewish king, the same who is referred to in the Sura "Signs of the Zodiac,"[1] made up his mind to utterly exterminate the Christian faith, and with that view he set up a huge idol, and issued commands that all who refused to worship it should be cast into the fire. Thereupon his officers seized a Christian woman with her babe, and as she refused to worship it, they cast the babe into the fire. But the babe cried out to its mother, "Be not afraid, the fire has no power to burn me; it is as cool as water!" Hearing this, the rest of the Christians leapt into the fire, and found that it did not burn them. The king reproached the fire for failing to do its office, but the fire replied that it was God's servant, and that its consuming properties were not to be used for evil purposes. It then blazed up and consumed the king, and all his Jews with him.

Second causes only operate in subordination to, and from the impulsion of, the First Cause (p. 25).

Air, earth, water, and fire are God's servants.
To us they seem lifeless, but to God living.
In God's presence fire ever waits to do its service,
Like a submissive lover with no will of its own.
When you strike steel on flint fire leaps forth;
But 'tis by God's command it thus steps forth.
Strike not together the flint and steel of wrong,
For the pair will generate more, like man and woman.

[1] Koran lxxxv.

The flint and steel are themselves causes, yet
Look higher for the First Cause, O righteous man!
For that Cause precedes this second cause.
How can a cause exist of itself without precedent cause?
That Cause makes this cause operative,
And again helpless and inoperative.
That Cause, which is a guiding light to the prophets,
That, I say, is higher than these second causes.
Men's minds recognise these second causes,
But only prophets perceive the action of the First
Cause.

Praise compared to vapour drawn upwards, and then descending in rain (p. 25).

Though water be enclosed in a reservoir,
Yet air will absorb it, for 'tis its supporter;
It sets it free and bears it to its source,
Little by little, so that you see not the process.
In like manner this breath of ours by degrees
Steals away our souls from the prison-house of earth.
"The good word riseth up to Him,"[1]
Rising from us whither He knoweth.
Our breathings are lifted up in fear of God,
Offerings from us to the throne of Eternity.
Then come down to us rewards for our praises,
The double thereof, yea, mercies from the King of Glory.
Therefore are we constrained to utter these praises,
That slaves may attain the height of God's gifts.
And so this rising and descent go on evermore,
And cease not for ever and aye.
To speak in plain Persian, this attraction
Comes from the same quarter whence comes this sweet
savour.[2]

[1] Koran, xxxv. 11.
[2] Sweet savour, *i.e.*, the joy of heart experienced by the offerer of prayer when his prayer is accepted of God. See Book II. Story XVII.

STORY V. *The Lion and the Beasts* (p. 26).

In the book of Kalila and Damna a story is told of a lion who held all the beasts of the neighbourhood in subjection, and was in the habit of making constant raids upon them, to take and kill such of them as he required for his daily food. At last the beasts took counsel together, and agreed to deliver up one of their company every day, to satisfy the lion's hunger, if he, on his part, would cease to annoy them by his continual forays. The lion was at first unwilling to trust to their promise, remarking that he always preferred to rely on his own exertions; but the beasts succeeded in persuading him that he would do well to trust Providence and their word. To illustrate the thesis that human exertions are vain, they related a story of a man who got Solomon to transport him to Hindustan to escape the angel of death, but was smitten by the angel the moment he got there. Having carried their point, the beasts continued for some time to perform their engagement. One day it came to the turn of the hare to be delivered up as a victim to the lion; but he requested the others to let him practise a stratagem. They scoffed at him, asking how such a silly beast as he could pretend to outwit the lion. The hare assured them that wisdom was of God, and God might choose weak things to confound the strong. At last they consented to let him try his luck. He took his way slowly to the lion, and found him sorely enraged. In excuse for his tardy arrival he represented that he and another hare had set out together to appear before the lion, but a strange lion had seized the second hare, and carried it off in spite of his remonstrances. On hearing this the lion was exceeding wroth, and commanded the hare to show him the foe who had trespassed on his preserves. Pretending to be afraid, the hare got the lion to take him upon his back, and directed him to a well. On looking down the well, the lion saw in the water the reflection of himself and of the hare on his back; and thinking that he saw his foe with the stolen hare, he plunged in to attack him, and was drowned, while the hare sprang off his back and escaped. This folly on the part of the lion was predestined to punish him for denying God's ruling providence. So Adam, though he knew the names of all things, in accordance with God's predestination, neglected to obey a single prohibition, and his disobedience cost him dearly.

Trust in God, as opposed to human exertions (p. 26).

The beasts said, "O enlightened sage,
Lay aside caution; it cannot help thee against destiny;
To worry with precaution is toil and moil;
Go, trust in Providence, trust is the better part.
War not with the divine decree, O hot-headed one,
Lest that decree enter into conflict with thee.
Man should be as dead before the commands of God,
Lest a blow befall him from the Lord of all creatures."
He said, "True; but though trust be our mainstay,
Yet the Prophet teaches us to have regard to means.
The Prophet cried with a loud voice,
'Trust in God, yet tie the camel's leg.'[1]
Hear the adage, 'The worker is the friend of God;'[2]
Through trust in Providence neglect not to use means.
Go, O Quietists, practise trust with self-exertion,
Exert yourself to attain your objects, bit by bit.
In order to succeed, strive and exert yourselves;
If ye strive not for your objects, ye are fools."
They said, "What is gained from the poor by exertions
Is a fraudulent morsel that will bring ill luck.
Again, know that self-exertion springs from weakness;
Relying on other means is a blot upon perfect trust.
Self-exertion is not more noble than trust in God.

[1] "Trust in God and keep your powder dry."
[2] "Laborare est orare."

What is more lovely than committing oneself to God?
Many there are who flee from one danger to a worse;
Many flee from a snake and meet a dragon.
Man plans a stratagem, and thereby snares himself;
What he takes for life turns out to be destruction.
He shuts the door after his foe is in the house.
After this sort were the schemes of Pharaoh.
That jealous king slew a myriad babes,
While Moses, whom he sought, was in his house.
Our eyes are subject to many infirmities;
Go! annihilate your sight in God's sight.
For our foresight His foresight is a fair exchange;
In His sight is all that ye can desire.
So long as a babe cannot grasp or run,
It takes its father's back for its carriage.
But when it becomes independent and uses its hands,
It falls into grievous troubles and disgrace.
The souls of our first parents, even before their hands,
Flew away from fidelity after vain pleasure.
Being made captives by the command, 'Get down hence,'[1]
They became bond-slaves of enmity, lust, and vanity.
We are the family of the Lord and His sucking babes.
The Prophet said, 'The people are God's family;'
He who sends forth the rain from heaven,
Can He not also provide us our daily bread?"
The lion said, "True; yet the Lord of creatures
Sets a ladder before our feet.
Step by step must we mount up to the roof!
The notion of fatalism is groundless in this place.
Ye have feet—why then pretend ye are lame?
Ye have hands—why then conceal your claws?
When a master places a spade in the hand of a slave,
The slave knows his meaning without being told.
Like this spade, our hands are our Master's hints to us;
Yea, if ye consider, they are His directions to us.
When ye have taken to heart His hints,

[1] Koran ii. 341.

Ye will shape your life in reliance on their direction;
Wherefore these hints disclose His intent,
Take the burden from you, and appoint your work.
He that bears it makes it bearable by you,
He that is able makes it within your ability.
Accept His command, and you will be able to execute it;
Seek union with Him, and you will find yourselves united.
Exertion is giving thanks for God's blessings;
Think ye that your fatalism gives such thanks?
Giving thanks for blessings increases blessings,
But fatalism snatches those blessings from your hands.
Your fatalism is to sleep on the road; sleep not
Till ye behold the gates of the King's palace.
Ah! sleep not, O unreflecting fatalists,
Till ye have reached that fruit-laden Tree of Life
Whose branches are ever shaken by the wind,
And whose fruit is showered on the sleepers' heads.
Fatalism means sleeping amidst highwaymen.
Can a cock who crows too soon expect peace?
If ye cavil at and accept not God's hints,
Though ye count yourselves men, see, ye are women.
The quantum of reason ye possessed is lost,
And the head whose reason has fled is a tail.
Inasmuch as the unthankful are despicable,
They are at last cast into the fiery pit.
If ye really have trust in God, exert yourselves,
And strive, in constant reliance on the Almighty."

Wisdom is granted oftentimes to the weak (p. 29).

He said, "O friends, God has given me inspiration.
Oftentimes strong counsel is suggested to the weak.
The wit taught by God to the bee
Is withheld from the lion and the wild ass.
It fills its cells with liquid sweets,
For God opens the door of this knowledge to it.
The skill taught by God to the silkworm
Is a learning beyond the reach of the elephant.
The earthly Adam was taught of God names,[1]
So that his glory reached the seventh heaven.
He laid low the name and fame of the angels,[2]
Yet blind indeed are they whom God dooms to doubt!
The devotee of seven hundred thousand years (Satan)
Was made a muzzle for that yearling calf (Adam),[3]
Lest he should suck milk of the knowledge of faith,
And soar on high even to the towers of heaven.
The knowledge of men of external sense is a muzzle
To stop them sucking milk of that sublime knowledge.
But God drops into the heart a single pearl-drop
Which is not bestowed on oceans or skies!"

"How long regard ye mere form, O form-worshippers?
Your souls, void of substance, rest still in forms.
If the form of man were all that made man,
Ahmad and Abu Jahl would be upon a par.
A painting on a wall resembles a man,
But see what it is lacking in that empty form.
'Tis life that is lacking to that mere semblance of man.
Go! seek for that pearl it never will find.
The heads of earth's lions were bowed down
When God gave might to the Seven Sleepers' dog.[4]
What mattered its despised form
When its soul was drowned in the sea of light?"

Human wisdom the manifestation of divine (p. 31).

On his way to the lion the hare lingered,
Devising a stratagem with himself.
He proceeded on his way after delaying long,
In order to have a secret or two for the lion.

What worlds the principle of Reason embraces!
How broad is this ocean of Reason!

[1] "And He taught Adam the names of all things" (Koran ii. 29).

[2] The angels said, "We have no knowledge but what thou hast given us to know" (Koran ii. 30).

[3] See Gulshan i Raz, l. 543.

[4] Koran xviii. 17.

Yea, the Reason of man is a boundless ocean.
O son, that ocean requires, as it were, a diver.[1]
On this fair ocean our human forms
Float about, like bowls on the surface of water;
Yea, like cups on the surface, till they are filled;
And when filled, these cups sink into the water.
The ocean of Reason is not seen; reasoning men are seen;
But our forms (minds) are only as waves or spray thereof.
Whatever form that ocean uses as its instrument,
Therewith it casts its spray far and wide.[2]
Till the heart sees the Giver of the secret,
Till it espies that Bowman shooting from afar,
It fancies its own steed lost, while in bewilderment
It is urging that steed hither and thither;[3]
It fancies its own steed lost, when all the while
That swift steed is bearing it on like the wind.
In deep distress that blunderhead
Runs from door to door, searching and inquiring,
"Who and where is he that hath stolen my steed?"
They say, "What is this thou ridest on, O master?"
He says, "True, 'tis a steed; but where is mine?"
They say, "Look to thyself, O rider; thy steed is there."
The real Soul is lost to view, and seems far off;[4]
Thou art like a pitcher with full belly but dry lip;
How canst thou ever see red, green, and scarlet
Unless thou see'st the light first of all?
When thy sight is dazzled by colours,

[1] See Gulshan i Raz, l. 575: The ocean of Reason is the same as what is elsewhere called the ocean of Being, viz., the Noumenon, or Divine substratum of all phenomenal being and thought.

[2] "Those arrows were God's, not yours" (Koran viii. 17); *i.e.*, Man's reason proceeds from God, the "Only Real Agent."

[3] Alluding to the "Believer's lost camel" (Book II. Story XII., *infra*). Men seek wisdom, and do not know that in themselves is the reflected wisdom of God (Gulshan i Raz, l. 435).

[4] The real Soul, *i.e.*, the spirit which God "breathed into man" (Koran xv. 29). "In yourselves are signs; will ye not behold them?" (Koran li. 21).

These colours veil the light from thee.
But when night veils those colours from thee,
Thou seest that colours are seen only through light.
As there is no seeing outward colours without light,
So it is with the mental colours within.
Outward colours arise from the light of sun and stars,
And inward colours from the Light on high.
The light that lights the eye is also the heart's Light;
The eye's light proceeds from the Light of the heart.
But the light that lights the heart is the Light of God,
Which is distinct from the light of reason and sense.
At night there is no light, and colours are not seen;
Hence we know what light is by its opposite, darkness.
At night no colours are visible, for light is lacking.
How can colour be the attribute of dark blackness?
Looking on light is the same as looking on colours;
Opposite shows up opposite, as a Frank a Negro.
The opposite of light shows what is light,
Hence colours too are known by their opposite.
God created pain and grief for this purpose,
To wit, to manifest happiness by its opposites.[1]
Hidden things are manifested by their opposites;
But, as God has no opposite, He remains hidden.
God's light has no opposite in the range of creation
Whereby it may be manifested to view.
Perforce "Our eyes see not Him, though He sees us."[2]
Behold this in the case of Moses and Mount Sinai.[3]
Discern form from substance, as lion from desert,
Or as sound and speech from the thought they convey.
The sound and speech arise from the thought;
Thou knowest not where is the Ocean of thought;
Yet when thou seest fair waves of speech,

[1] See Gulshan i Raz, l. 92. Mr. Mansel (Bampton Lectures, p. 49) says: "A thing can be known as that which it is only by being distinguished from that which it is not." But the Infinite Deity *ex hypothesi* includes all things; so there is nothing to contrast Him with.

[2] Koran vi. 103.

[3] Koran vii. 139: "He said, 'Thou shalt not see me.'"

Thou knowest there is a glorious Ocean beneath them.
When waves of thought arise from the Ocean of Wisdom,
They assume the forms of sound and speech.
These forms of speech are born and die again,
These waves cast themselves back into the Ocean.
Form is born of That which is without form,
And goes again, for, "Verily to Him do we return."[1]
Wherefore to thee every moment come death and "return."
Mustafa saith, "The world endureth only a moment."
So, thought is an arrow shot by God into the air.
How can it stay in the air? It returns to God.
  Every moment the world and we are renewed,[2]
Yet we are ignorant of this renewing for ever and aye.
Life, like a stream of water, is renewed and renewed,
Though it wears the appearance of continuity in form.
That seeming continuity arises from its swift renewal,
As when a single spark of fire is whirled round swiftly.[3]
If a single spark be whirled round swiftly,
It seems to the eye a continuous line of fire.
This apparent extension, owing to the quick motion,
Demonstrates the rapidity with which it is moved.
If ye seek the deepest student of this mystery,
Lo! 'tis Husamu-'d-Din, the most exalted of creatures!

STORY VI. *'Omar and the Ambassador* (p. 38).

The hare, having delivered his companions from the tyranny of the lion, in the manner just described, proceeds to improve the occasion by exhorting them to engage in a greater and more arduous warfare, viz., the struggle against their inward enemy, the lusts of the flesh. He illustrates his meaning by the story of an ambassador who was sent by the Emperor of Rum to the Khalifa 'Omar. On approaching Medina this ambassador inquired for 'Omar's palace, and learned that 'Omar dwelt in no material palace, but in a spiritual tabernacle, only visible to purified hearts. At last he discerned 'Omar lying under a palm-tree, and drew near to him in fear and awe. 'Omar received him kindly, and instructed him in the doctrine of the mystical union with God. The ambassador heard him gladly, and asked him two questions, first, How can souls descend from heaven to earth? and secondly, With what object are souls imprisoned in the bonds of flesh and blood? 'Omar responded, and the ambassador accepted his teaching, and became a pure-hearted Sufi. The hare urged his companions to abjure lust and pride, and to go and do likewise.

[1] Koran ii. 151.
[2] See Gulshan i Raz, l. 645: All phenomena are every moment renewed by fresh effluxes of being from the Divine Noumenon.
[3] See Gulshan i Raz, l. 710.

God's agency reconciled with man's freewill (p. 39).

The ambassador said, "O Commander of the faithful,
How comes the soul down from above to earth?
How can so noble a bird be confined in a cage?"
  He said, "God speaks words of power to souls,—
To things of naught, without eyes or ears,
And at these words they all spring into motion;
At His words of power these nothings arise quickly,
And strong impulse urges them into existence.
Again, He speaks other spells to these creatures,
And swiftly drives them back again into Not-being.
He speaks to the rose's ear, and causes it to bloom;
He speaks to the tulip, and makes it blossom.
He speaks a spell to body, and it becomes soul;
He speaks to the sun, and it becomes a fount of light.
Again, in its ear He whispers a word of power,
And its face is darkened as by a hundred eclipses.
What is it that God says to the ear of earth,
That it attends thereto and rests steadfast?
What is it that Speaker says to the cloud,
That it pours forth rain-water like a water-skin?

Whosoever is bewildered by wavering will,[1]
In his ear hath God whispered His riddle,
That He may bind him on the horns of a dilemma;
For he says, 'Shall I do this or its reverse?'
Also from God comes the preference of one alternative;
'Tis from God's impulsion that man chooses one of the two.
If you desire sanity in this embarrassment,
Stuff not the ear of your mind with cotton.
Take the cotton of evil suggestions from the mind's ear,[2]
That the heavenly voice from above may enter it,
That you may understand that riddle of His,
That you may be cognisant of that open secret.
Then the mind's ear becomes the sensorium of inspiration;
For what is this Divine voice but the inward voice?[3]
The spirit's eye and ear possess this sense,
The eye and ear of reason and sense lack it.
The word 'compulsion' makes me impatient for love's sake;
'Tis he who loves not who is fettered by compulsion.
This is close communion with God, not compulsion,
The shining of the sun, and not a dark cloud.
Or, if it be compulsion, 'tis not common compulsion,
It is not the domination of wanton wilfulness.
O son, they understand this compulsion
For whom God opens the eyes of the inner man.
Things hidden and things future are plain to them;
To speak of the past seems to them despicable.
They possess freewill and compulsion besides,[4]
As in oyster-shells raindrops are pearls.
Outside the shell they are raindrops, great and small;
Inside they are precious pearls, big and little.
These men also resemble the musk deer's bag;
Outside it is blood, but inside pure musk;
Yet, say not that outside 'twas mere blood,
Which on entering the bag becomes musk.
Nor say that outside the alembic 'twas mere copper,
And becomes gold inside, when mixed with elixir.
In you freewill and compulsion are vain fancies,
But in them they are the light of Almighty power.
On the table bread is a mere lifeless thing,
When taken into the body it is a life-giving spirit.
This transmutation occurs not in the table's heart,
'Tis soul effects this transmutation with water of life.
Such is the power of the soul, O man of right views!
Then what is the power of the Soul of souls? (God).
Bread is the food of the body, yet consider,
How can it be the food of the soul, O son?
Flesh-born man by force of soul
Cleaves mountains with tunnels and mines.
The might of Ferhad's soul cleft a hill;
The might of the Soul's soul cleaves the moon.[1]
If the heart opens the mouth of mystery's store,
The soul springs up swiftly to highest heaven.
If tongue discourses of hidden mysteries,
It kindles a fire that consumes the world.

Behold, then, God's action and man's action;
Know, action does belong to us; this is evident.
If no actions proceeded from men,
How could you say, 'Why act ye thus?'
The agency of God is the cause of our action,
Our actions are the signs of God's agency;
Nevertheless our actions are freely willed by us,
Whence our recompense is either hell or 'The Friend.'"

[1] The poet's insistence on the doctrine of God being the *Fá'il i Hakiki*, or Only Real Agent, without whose word no being and no action can be, leads him to the question of freewill and compulsion of man's will (see Gulshan i Raz, l. 555).

[2] So Gulshan i Raz, l. 442.

[3] The leading principle of all mysticism is that, independently of sense and reason, man possesses an inward sense, or intuition, which conveys to him a knowledge of God by direct apprehension (see Gulshan i Raz, l. 431).

[4] Their wills are identified with God's will, as in the case of the saint Daquqi (*infra*, Book III. Story XII.)

[1] As a sign of the last day (Koran liv. 1).

STORY VII. *The Merchant and his Clever Parrot* (p. 42).

There was a certain merchant who kept a parrot in a cage. Being about to travel to Hindustan on business, he asked the parrot if he had any message to send to his kinsmen in that country, and the parrot desired him to tell them that he was kept confined in a cage. The merchant promised to deliver this message, and on reaching Hindustan, duly delivered it to the first flock of parrots he saw. On hearing it one of them at once fell down dead. The merchant was annoyed with his own parrot for having sent such a fatal message, and on his return home sharply rebuked his parrot for doing so. But the parrot no sooner heard the merchant's tale than he too fell down dead in his cage. The merchant, after lamenting his death, took his corpse out of the cage and threw it away; but, to his surprise, the corpse immediately recovered life, and flew away, explaining that the Hindustani parrot had only feigned death to suggest this way of escaping from confinement in a cage.

Saints are preserved from all harm[1] (p. 43).

As to a "man of heart," he takes no hurt,
Even though he should eat deadly poison.
He who gains health from practising abstinence is safe;
The poor disciple is safe in the midst of fever.
The prophet said, "O disciple, though you be bold,
Yet enter not into conflict with every foe."
Within you is a Nimrod; enter not his fire;
But if you must do so, first become an Abraham.[2]
If you are neither swimmer nor seaman,
Cast not yourself into the sea out of self-conceit.
A swimmer brings pearls from the deep sea;
Yea, he plucks gain from the midst of perils.
If the saint handles earth, it becomes gold;
If a sinner handles gold, it turns to dust.
Whereas the saint is well-pleasing to God,
In his actions his hand is the hand of God.
But the sinner's hand is the hand of Satan and demons,
Because he is ensnared in falsity and fraud.
If folly meets him, he takes it for wisdom;
Yea, the learning gained by the wicked is folly.
Whatever a sick man eats is a source of sickness,
But if a saint imbibe infidelity it becomes faith.
Ah! footman who contendest with horsemen,
Thou wilt not succeed in carrying the day!

1 This is a comment on the saying of Faridu-'d-Din Attar, "Thou art a man of lusts, O fool! In dust eat blood! but if a man of heart eats poison, 'tis as honey."

2 See Koran xxi. 68, and Rodwell's note.

The jealousy of God[1] (p. 46).

The whole world is jealous for this cause,
That God surpasseth the world in jealousy.
God is as a soul and the world as a body,
And bodies derive their good and evil from souls.
He to whom the sanctuary of true prayer is revealed
Deems it shameful to turn back to mere formal religion.
He who is master of the robes of a king
Brings shame on his lord by petty huckstering.
He who is admitted to the king's presence-chamber
Would show disrespect by tarrying at the doorway.
If the king grants him license to kiss his hand,
He would err were he to kiss merely the king's foot.
Though to lay head at the king's feet is due obeisance,
In the case supposed it would be wrong to kiss the feet.
The king's jealousy would be kindled against him
Who, after he had seen his face, preferred his mere perfume.

1 This is a comment on the Hadis, "Verily Sa'd is a jealous man, and I am more jealous than he, and God is more jealous than I, and of His jealousy He prohibits 'All pollutions, both outward and inward.'" (Koran vi. 152.)

God's jealousy may be likened to a grain of wheat,
But man's jealousy is but empty chaff.
For know ye that the source of jealousy is in God,
And man's jealousy is only an offshoot from God's.
But let me now quit this subject, and make complaint
Of the severity of That Fickle Fair One.

Complaints of God's harsh dealings with His adoring slaves (p. 47).

" Wherefore dost thou abandon thy creed and faith?
What matters it if it be heathen or true?
Why hast thou forsaken thy Beloved?
What matters it if she be fair or ugly?" [1]

Let me then, I say, make complaint
Of the severity of That Fickle Fair One.
I cry, and my cries sound sweet in His ear;
He requires from the two worlds cries and groans.
How shall I not wail under His chastening hand?
How shall I not be in the number of those bewitched by Him?
How shall I be other than night without His day?
Without the vision of His face that illumes the day?
His bitters are very sweets to my soul,
My sad heart is a lively sacrifice to my Beloved.
I am enamoured of my own grief and pain,
For it makes me well-pleasing to my peerless King.
I use the dust of my grief as salve for my eyes,
That my eyes, like seas, may teem with pearls.
The tears which are shed because of His chastening
Are very pearls, though men deem them mere tears.
'Tis "The Soul of souls" of whom I am making complaint;
Yet I do not complain;—I merely state my case.

[1] This is a quotation from Hakim Sanai, and forms the text of the following discourse.

My heart says, "He has injured me,"
But I laugh at these pretended injuries.
Do me justice, O Thou who art the glory of the just,
Who art the throne, and I the lintel of Thy door!
But, in sober truth, where are throne and doorway?
Where are "We" and "I?" There where our Beloved is!
O Thou, who art exempt from "Us" and "Me,"—
Who pervadest the spirits of all men and women;
When man and woman become one, Thou art that One!
When their union is dissolved, lo! Thou abidest!
Thou hast made these "Us" and "Me" for this purpose,
To wit, to play chess with them by Thyself.[1]
When Thou shalt become one entity with "Us" and "You."
Then wilt Thou show true affection for these lovers.
When these "We" and "Ye" shall all become one Soul,
Then they will be lost and absorbed in the "Beloved."
These are plain truths. Come then, O Lord!
Who art exalted above description and explanation!
Is it possible for the bodily eye to behold Thee?
Can mind of man conceive Thy frowns and Thy smiles?
Are hearts, when bewitched by Thy smiles and frowns,[2]
In a fit state to see the vision of Thyself?
When our hearts are bewitched by Thy smiles and frowns,
Can we gain life from these two alternating states?
The fertile garden of love, as it is boundless,
Contains other fruits besides joy and sorrow.
The true lover is exalted above these two states,
He is fresh and green independently of autumn or spring!
Pay tithe on Thy beauty, O Beauteous One!
Tell forth the tale of the Beloved, every whit!

[1] See Gulshan i Raz, l. 140, and Omar Khayyam Quatr., 270.

[2] See Gulshan i Raz, l. 745: Frowns are the occultation of the Beloved by the veil of phenomena; smiles, the revelation of Absolute Being to its votaries. Sa'di (Gulistan, Book II. Story XI.) says: "The vision of God to the pious consists of manifestation and occultation; He shows Himself, and again withdraws Himself from our sight."

Last night our Sheikh was going round the town with a lantern Saying he was tired of all the wild beasts around him

For through coquetry His glances
Are still inflicting fresh wounds on my heart.
I gave Him leave to shed my blood, if He willed it;
I only said, "Is it right?" and He forsook me.
Why dost Thou flee from the cries of us on earth?
Why pourest Thou sorrow on the heart of the sorrowful?
O Thou who, as each new morn dawns from the east,
Art seen uprising anew, like a bright fountain!
What excuse makest Thou for Thy witcheries?
O Thou whose lips are sweeter than sugar,
Thou that ever renewest the life of this old world,
Hear the cry of this lifeless body and heart!
  But, for God's sake, leave off telling of the Rose;
Tell of the Bulbul who is severed from his Rose.
My ardour arises not from joy or grief,
My sense mates not with illusion and fancy.
My condition is different, for it is strange.
Deny it not! God is all-powerful.
Argue not from the condition of common men,
Stumble not at severity and at mercy.
For mercy and severity, joy and sorrow, are transient,
And transient things die; "God is heir of all."[1]
  "Tis dawn! O Protector and Asylum of the dawn!
Make excuse for me to my lord Husamu-'d-Din!
Thou makest excuses for "Universal Reason and Soul;"[2]
Soul of souls and Gem of life art Thou!
The light of my dawn is a beam from Thy light,
Shining in the morning draught of Thy protection!
Since Thy gift keeps me, as it were, intoxicated,
What is this spiritual wine that causes me this joy?
Natural wine lacks the ferment in my breast,
The spheres lag behind me in revolutions!
Wine is intoxicated with me, not I with it!

[1] Koran xv. 23.

[2] *i.e.*, the Logos, and First Soul, upposed to be referred to in the text: "O men, fear your Lord, who hath created you from one Soul, and of him created his wife" (Koran iv. 1). See Gulshan i Raz, l. 203.

The world takes its being from me, not I from it!
I am like bees, and earthly bodies like wax,[1]
I build up these bodies as with my own wax!

Story VIII. *The Harper* (p. 50).

In the time of the Khalifa 'Omar there lived a harper, whose voice was as sweet as that of the angel Isráfil, and who was in great request at all feasts. But he grew old, and his voice broke, and no one would employ him any longer. In despair he went to the burial-ground of Yathrub, and there played his harp to God, looking to Him for recompense. Having finished his melody he fell asleep, and dreamed he was in heaven. The same night a divine voice came to 'Omar, directing him to go to the burial-ground, and relieve an old man whom he should find there. 'Omar proceeded to the place, found the harper, and gave him money, promising him more when he should need it. The harper cast away his harp, saying that it had diverted him from God, and expressed great contrition for his past sins. 'Omar then instructed him that his worldly journey was now over, and that he must not give way to contrition for the past, as he was now entered into the state of ecstasy and intoxication of union with God, and in this exalted state regard to past and future should be swept away. The harper acted on his instructions, and sang no more.

Apology for applying the term "Bride" to God (p. 52).

Mustafa became beside himself at that sweet call,
His prayer failed on "the night of the early morning halt."
He lifted not head from that blissful sleep,"[2]
So that his morning prayer was put off till noon.

[1] *I.e.*, in his spiritual exaltation he feels himself as the Logos, wherefrom the whole material creation emanates.

[2] The night of his marriage with Safiyya.

On that, his wedding night, in presence of his bride,
His pure soul attained to kiss her hands.
Love and mistress are both veiled and hidden,
Impute it not as a fault if I call Him "Bride."
I would have kept silence from fear of my Beloved,
If He had granted me but a moment's respite.
But He said, "Speak on, 'tis no fault,
'Tis naught but the necessary result of the hidden decree,
'Tis a fault only to him who only sees faults.
How can the Pure Hidden Spirit notice faults?"
Faults seem so to ignorant creatures,
Not in the sight of the Lord of Benignity.
Blasphemy even may be wisdom in the Creator's sight,
Whereas from our point of view it is grievous sin.
If one fault occur among a hundred beauties,
'Tis as one dry stick in a garden of green herbs.
Both weigh equally in the scales,
For the two resemble body and soul.
Wherefore the sages have said not idly,
"The bodies of the righteous are as pure souls."
Their words, their actions, their praises,
Are all as a pure soul without spot or blemish.

'Omar rebukes the Harper for brooding over and bewailing the past (p. 57).

Then 'Omar said to him, "This wailing of thine
Shows thou art still in a state of 'sobriety.'"
Afterwards he thus urged him to quit that state,
And called him out of his beggary to absorption in God:
"Sobriety savours of memory of the past;
Past and future are what veil God from our sight.
Burn up both of them with fire! How long
Wilt thou be partitioned by these segments as a reed?
So long as a reed has partitions 'tis not privy to secrets,
Nor is it vocal in response to lip and breathing.
While circumambulating the house thou art a stranger;
When thou enterest in thou art at home.
Thou whose knowledge is ignorance of the Giver of knowledge,
Thy wailing contrition is worse than thy sin.
The road of the 'annihilated' is another road;
Sobriety is wrong, and a straying from that other road.
O thou who seekest to be contrite for the past,
How wilt thou be contrite for this contrition?
At one time thou adorest the music of the lute,
At another embracest wailing and weeping."
While the "Discerner" reflected these mysteries,
The heart of the harper was emancipated.
Like a soul he was freed from weeping and rejoicing,
His old life died, and he was regenerated.
Amazement fell upon him at that moment,
For he was exalted above earth and heaven,
An uplifting of the heart surpassing all uplifting;—
I cannot describe it; if you can, say on!
Ecstasy and words beyond all ecstatic words;—
Immersion in the glory of the Lord of glory!
Immersion wherefrom was no extrication,—
As it were identification with the Very Ocean!
Partial Reason is as naught to Universal Reason,
If one impulse dependent on another impulse be naught;
But when *that* impulse moves *this* impulse,
The waves of *that* sea rise to *this* point.[1]

Story IX. *The Arab and his Wife* (p. 58).

An Arab lived with his wife in the desert in extreme poverty, so that they became a reproach to their neighbours. The wife at last lost patience, and began to abuse her husband, and to urge him to improve their condition. The Arab rebuked her for her covetousness, reminding her that the Prophet had said, "Poverty is my glory," and

[1] *I.e.*, he is possessed by the Deity as an "Energumen," and the Deity works these ecstatic states in him.

showing her how poverty was a better preparation for death than riches, and finally threatening to divorce her if she persisted in her querulous ways. The wife, however, by blandishments reduced her husband to obedience, as wives always do, and made him promise to carry out her wishes. She directed him to go and represent their case to the Khalifa at Bagdad, and to make him an offering of a pot of water, that being the only present they could afford to make. Accordingly the Arab travelled to Bagdad, and laid his offering at the feet of the Khalifa, who received it graciously, and in return filled the pot with pieces of gold, and then sent him back to his home in a boat up the river Tigris. The Arab was lost in wonder at the benignity of the Khalifa, who had recompensed him so bountifully for his petty offering of a drop of water. The story contains several digressions, on Pharaoh, on the prophet Salih, and on Adam and the angels, and the poet, *apropos* of its disconnectedness, compares it to eternity, as it has no beginning and no end.

Men subdued by women's wiles (p. 62).

In this manner she pleaded with gentle coaxing,
The while her tears fell upon her cheeks.
How could his firmness and endurance abide
When even without tears she could charm his heart?
That rain brought forth a flash of lightning
Which kindled a spark in the heart of that poor man.
Since the man was the slave of her fair face,
How was it when she stooped to slavish entreaties?
When she whose airs set thy heart a-quaking,—
When she weeps, how feelest thou then?
When she whose coquetry makes thy heart bleed
Condescends to entreaties, how is it then?
She who subdues us with her pride and severity,
What plea is left us when she begins to plead?
When she who traded in naught but bloodshed
Submits at last, ah! what a profit she makes!
God has adorned them "fair in the sight of men;"[1]
From her whom God has adorned how can man escape?
Since He created him "to dwell together with her,"[2]
How can Adam sever himself from his Eve?
Though he be Rustum, son of Zal, and braver than Hamza,
Yet he is submissive to the behests of his dame.
He by whose preaching the world was entranced
Was he who spake the two words, "O Humaira!"[3]
Though water prevails over fire in might,
Yet it boils by fire when in a cauldron.
When the cauldron intervenes between these two,
Air (desire) makes as naught the action of the water.
Apparently thou art the ruler of thy wife, like water;
In reality thou art ruled by and suppliant to her.
Such is the peculiarity of man,
He cannot withstand animal desire; that is his failing.
The Prophet said that women hold dominion
Over sages and over men of heart,
But that fools, again, hold the upper hand over women,
Because fools are violent and exceedingly froward.
They have no tenderness or gentleness or amity,
Because the animal nature sways their temperament.
Love and tenderness are qualities of humanity,
Passion and lust are qualities of animality.
Woman is a ray of God, not a mere mistress,
The Creator's self, as it were, not a mere creature!

Moses and Pharaoh, alike doers of God's will, as Light and Darkness, Poison and Antidote (p. 63).

Verily, both Moses and Pharaoh walked in the right way,
Though seemingly the one did so, and the other not.
By day Moses wept before God,
At midnight Pharaoh lifted up his cry,

[1] Koran iii. 12.
[2] Koran iii. 189.
[3] Muhammad said these words to his wife, Ayísha.

Saying, "What a yoke is this upon my neck, O God!
Were it not for this yoke who would boast, 'I am?'
Because Thou hast made Moses' face bright as the moon,
And hast made the moon of my face black in the face.
Can my star ever shine brighter than the moon?
If it be eclipsed, what remedy have I?
Though princes and kings beat drums,
And men beat cymbals because of my eclipse,[1]
They beat their brass dishes and raise a clamour,
And make my moon ashamed thereby,
I, who am Pharaoh, woe is me! The people's clamour
Confounds my boast, 'I am Lord Supreme!'[2]
Moses and I are Thy nurslings both alike,
Yet Thy axe cuts down the branches in Thy woods.
Some of these branches Thou plantest in the ground,
Others Thou castest away as useless.
Can branch strive against axe? Not so.
Can branch elude the power of the axe? Nay,
O Lord of the power that dwells in Thy axe,
In mercy make these crooked things straight!"

Man and wife types of the spirit and the flesh (p. 67).

The dissension of this husband and wife is a parable;
They are types of thy animal and rational souls.
This husband and wife are the reason and the flesh,
A couple joined together for good and for evil.
And in this earthly house this linked pair
Day and night are ever at variance and strife.
The wife is ever seeking dainties for domestic needs,
Namely, bread and meat and her own dignity and position.
Like the wife, the animal soul seeks comfort,
Sometimes carnal, sometimes ambitious;
Reason has no care for these matters,
In its mind is naught but regard to Allah.

[1] Compare the ancient custom of ringing bells to still thunder.

[2] Koran lxxix. 24. Pharaoh's boast.

Though the secret moral hereof is a bait and snare,
Hear its outward form to the end.
If spiritual manifestations had been sufficient,
The creation of the world had been needless and vain.
If spiritual thought were equivalent to love of God,
Outward forms of temples and prayers would not exist.
Presents which friends make one to another
Are naught but signs and indications,
To give outward testimony and witness
Of the love concealed within the heart.
Because outward attentions are evidence
Of secret love, O beloved!
The witness may be true or false,—
Now drunk with real wine, now with sour whey;
He who drinks fermented whey displays drunkenness,
Makes a noise, and reels to and fro.
That hypocrite in prayers and fasts
Displays exceeding diligence,
That men may think him drunk with love of God;
But if you look into the truth, he is drowned in hypocrisy.
In fine, outward actions are guides
To show the way to what is concealed within.
Sometimes the guide is true, sometimes false,
Sometimes a help, and at other times a hindrance.
O Lord, grant, in answer to my prayers, discernment,
That I may know such false signs from the true!
Know you how discernment accrues to the sense?
'Tis when sense "sees by the light of Allah."
If effects are obscure, still causes testify;
Kindred, for instance, shows that there is love.
But he to whom God's light is the guide
Is no longer a slave to effects and causes.
When the light of Allah illumes his senses,
A man is no longer a slave to effects.
When love of God kindles a flame in the inward man,
He burns, and is freed from effects.
He has no need of signs to assure him of love,

For love casts its own light up to heaven.
Other details are wanting to complete this subject,
But take this much, and all hail to you!
Though reality is exposed to view in this form,
Form is at once nigh to and far from reality.
For instance, these two resemble water and a tree;
When you look to their essence they are far apart;
Yet see how quickly a seed becomes a high tree
Out of water, along with earth and sunshine!
If you turn your eyes to their real essence,
These two are far, far apart from each other!
But let us quit this talk of essences and properties,
And return to the story of those two wealth-seekers.

How God made Adam superior to the Angels in wisdom and honour (p. 68).

He said, "By Allah, who knoweth hidden secrets,
Who created pure Adam out of dust;—
In the form, three cubits high, which he gave him,
He displayed the contents of all spirits, all decrees!—
Communicated to him the indelible tablet of existence,[1]
That he might know all that is written on those tablets,
All that should be first and last to endless eternity
He taught him, with the knowledge of his own 'names,'[2]
So that the angels were beside themselves at his instruction,
And gained more sanctity from his sanctification.
The expansion of their minds, which Adam brought about,
Was a thing unequalled by the expansion of the heavens.
For the wide expanse of that pure mind
The wide space of the seven heavens was not enough."
The Prophet said that God has declared,
"I am not contained in aught above or below,
I am not contained in earth or sky, or even

[1] The tablet on which God writes His eternal decrees.
[2] Koran ii. 29.

In highest heaven. Know this for a surety, O beloved!
Yet am I contained in the believer's heart!
If ye seek me, search in such hearts!"
He said also, "Enter the hearts of my servants[1]
To gain the paradise of beholding Me, O fearer of God."
Highest heaven, with all its light and wide expanse,
When it beheld Adam, was shaken from its place!
Highest heaven is greatness itself revealed;
But what is form when reality draws nigh?
Every angel declared, "In times of yore
We bore friendship to the plains of earth;
We were wont to sow the seed of service on the earth,
Wherefore we bore a wondrous attachment to it.
What was this attachment to that house of earth
When our own natures are heavenly?
What was the friendship of lights like us to darkness?
How can light dwell together with darkness?
O Adam! that friendship arose from the scent of thee,
Because the earth is the warp and weft of thy body.
Thy earthly body was taken from *there*,
Thy pure spirit of light was shed down from *here!*
But our souls were enlightened by thy spirit[2]
Long, long before earth had diverted it to itself.
We used to be on earth, ignorant of the earth,—
Ignorant of the treasure buried within it.
When we were commanded to depart from that place,
We felt sorrow at turning our steps away from it.
So that we raised many questions, saying,
'O Lord! who will come to take our place?
Wilt Thou barter the glory of our praises and homage
For the vain babble (of men)?'
The commands of God then diffused joy upon us; He said,
'What are ye saying at such length?
What ye give tongue to so foolishly
Is as the words of spoiled children to their father.

[1] Koran lxxxix. 29.
[2] The Logos, the first of created beings, was afterwards embodied in Adam, the "Perfect Man," or Microcosm.

I knew of myself what ye thought,
But I desired that ye should speak it;
As this boasting of yours is very improper,
So shall my mercy be shown to prevail over my wrath:
O angels, in order to show forth that prevailing,
I inspired that pretension to cavil and doubt;
If you say your say, and I forbear to punish you,
The gainsayers of my mercy must hold their peace.
My mercy equals that of a hundred fathers and mothers;
Every soul that is born is amazed thereat.
Their mercy is as the foam of the sea of my mercy;
It is mere foam of waves, but the sea abides ever!
What more shall I say? In that earthly shell
There is naught but foam of foam of foam of foam!'"
God is that foam; God is also that pure sea,
For His words are neither a temptation nor a vain boast.

Plurality and Partial Evil, though seemingly opposed to Unity, subserve Good (p. 73).

The story is now concluded, with its ups and downs,
Like lovers' musings, without beginning or ending.
It has no beginning, even as eternity,
Nor ending, for 'tis akin to world without end.
Or like water, each drop whereof is at once
Beginning and end, and also has no beginning or end.
But God forbid! This story is not a vain fable,
'Tis the ready money of your state and mine, be sure!
Before every Sufi who is enlightened
Whatever is past is never mentioned.
When his whole thoughts are absorbed in present ecstasy,
No thought of consequences enters his mind.[1]
Arab, water-pot, and angels are all ourselves!
"Whatsoever turneth from God is turned from Him."[2]
Know the husband is reason, the wife lust and greed;
She is vested with darkness and a gainsayer of reason.
Learn now whence springs the root of this circumstance,
From this, that the Whole has parts of divers kinds.
These parts of the Whole are not parts in relation to it,—
Not in the way that rose's scent is a part of the rose.
The beauty of the green shoot is part of the rose's beauty,
But the turtle-dove's cooing is a part of *that* Bulbul's
music.
But if I engage in doubts and answers,
How can I give water to thirsty souls?
Yet, if you are perplexed by Whole and finite parts,
Have patience, for "patience is the key of joy."
Be abstinent,—abstinent from vague thoughts,
Since there are lions in that desert (of thoughts).
Abstinence is the prince of medicines,
As scratching only aggravates a scab.
Abstinence is certainly the root of medicine;
Practise abstinence, see how it invigorates thy soul!
Accept this counsel and give ear thereto,
That it may be to thee as an earring of gold!
Nay, not a mere earring, but that thou mayest be a mine
of gold,
Or that thou mayest surpass moon and Pleiades.
First, know creation is in various forms;
Souls are as various as the letters from *Alif* to *Yá*.
In this variety of letters there seems disorder,
Though in fact they agree in an integral unity.
In one aspect they are opposed, in another united;
In one aspect capricious, in another serious.
The day of judgment is the day of the great review;
Whoso is fair and enlightened longs for that review;
Whoso, like a Hindoo, is black (with sin),
The day of review will sound the knell of his disgrace.
Since he has not a face like a sun,
He desires only night like to a veil!
If his thorn puts not forth a single rosebud,
The spring in disclosing him is his foe.

[1] He is the "son of the time present and instant," as said above.
[2] Koran li. 9.

But he who is from head to foot a perfect rose or lily,
To him spring brings rejoicing.
The useless thorn desires the autumn,
That autumn may associate itself with the garden;
And hide the rose's beauty and the thorn's shame,
That men may not see the bloom of the one and the other's shame,
That common stone and pure ruby may appear all as one.
True, the Gardener knows the difference even in autumn,
But the sight of *One* is better than the world's sight.
That *One* Person is Himself the world, as He is the sun,
And every star in heaven is a part of the sun.
That *One* Person is Himself the world, and the rest
Are all His dependents and parasites, O man!
He is the perfect world, yet He is single;
He holds in hand the writing of the whole of existence.
Wherefore all forms and colours of beauty cry out,
"Good news! good news! Lo! the spring is at hand!"
If the blossoms did not shine as bright helmets,
How could the fruits display their globes?
When the blossoms are shed the fruits come to a head,
When the body is destroyed the soul lifts up its head.
The fruit is the substance, the blossom only its form,
Blossom the good news, and fruit the promised boon.
When the blossoms fall the fruit appears,
When the former vanish the fruit is tasted.
Till bread is broken, how can it serve as food?
Till the grapes are crushed, how can they yield wine?
Till citrons be pounded up with drugs,
How can they afford healing to the sick?

Story X. *The Man who was Tattooed* (p. 74).

It was the custom of the men of Qazwin to have various devices tattooed upon their bodies. A certain coward went to the artist to have such a device tattooed on his back, and desired that it might be the figure of a lion. But when he felt the pricks of the needles he roared with pain, and said to the artist, "What part of the lion are you now painting?" The artist replied, "I am doing the tail." The patient cried, "Never mind the tail; go on with another part." The artist accordingly began in another part, but the patient again cried out and told him to try somewhere else. Wherever the artist applied his needles, the patient raised similar objections, till at last the artist dashed all his needles and pigments on the ground, and refused to proceed any further.

The Prophet's counsels to 'Ali to follow the direction of the Pir or Spiritual Guide, and to endure his chastisements patiently (p. 75).

The Prophet said to 'Ali, "O 'Ali,
Thou art the Lion of God, a hero most valiant;
Yet confide not in thy lion-like valour,
But seek refuge under the palm-trees of the 'Truth.'
Whoso takes obedience as his exemplar
Shares its proximity to the ineffable Presence.
Do thou seek to draw near to Reason; let not thy heart
Rely, like others, on thy own virtue and piety.
Come under the shadow of the Man of Reason,[1]
Thou canst not find it in the road of the traditionists.
That man enjoys close proximity to Allah;
Turn not away from obedience to him in any wise;
For he makes the thorn a bed of roses,
And gives sight to the eyes of the blind.
His shadow on earth is as that of Mount Qáf,
His spirit is as a Simurgh soaring on high.
He lends aid to the slaves of the friends of God,
And advances to high place them who seek him.
Were I to tell his praises till the last day,

[1] *I.e.*, the Pir, or Perfect Shaikh, or Spiritual Director. So St. John of the Cross and St. Theresa enjoin obedience to the Director (Vaughan, xii. 122).

My words would not be too many nor admit of curtailment,
He is the sun of the spirit, not that of the sky,
For from his light men and angels draw life.
That sun is hidden in the form of a man,
Understand me! Allah knows the truth.
O 'Ali, out of all forms of religious service
Choose thou the shadow of that dear friend of God!
Every man takes refuge in some form of service,
And chooses for himself some asylum;
Do thou seek refuge in the shadow of the wise man,
That thou mayest escape thy fierce secret foes.
Of all forms of service this is fittest for thee;
Thou shalt surpass all who were before thee.
Having chosen thy Director, be submissive to him,
Even as Moses submitted to the commands of Khizr.[1]
Have patience with Khizr's actions, O sincere one!
Lest he say, 'There is a partition between us.'
Though he stave in thy boat, yet hold thy peace;
Though he slay a young man, heave not a sigh.
God declares his hand to be even as God's hand,
For He saith, 'The hand of God is over their hands.'[2]
The hand of God impels him and gives him life;
Nay, not life only, but an eternal soul.
A friend is needed; travel not the road alone,
Take not thy own way through this desert!
Whoso travels this road alone
Only does so by aid of the might of holy men.
The hand of the Director is not weaker than theirs;
His hand is none other than the grasp of Allah!
If absent saints can confer such protection,
Doubtless present saints are more powerful than absent.
If such food be bestowed on the absent,
What dainties may not the guest who is present expect?
The courtier who attends in the presence of the king
Is served better than the stranger outside the gate.
The difference between them is beyond calculation;
One sees the light, the other only the veil.
Strive to obtain entrance within,
If thou wouldst not remain as a ring outside the door.
Having chosen thy Director, be not weak of heart,
Nor yet sluggish and lax as water and mud;
But if thou takest umbrage at every rub,
How wilt thou become a polished mirror?"

STORY XI. *The Lion who Hunted with the Wolf and the Fox* (p. 76).

A lion took a wolf and a fox with him on a hunting excursion, and succeeded in catching a wild ox, an ibex, and a hare. He then directed the wolf to divide the prey. The wolf proposed to award the ox to the lion, the ibex to himself, and the hare to the fox. The lion was enraged with the wolf because he had presumed to talk of "I" and "Thou," and "My share" and "Thy share," when it all belonged of right to the lion, and he slew the wolf with one blow of his paw. Then, turning to the fox, he ordered him to make the division. The fox, rendered wary by the fate of the wolf, replied that the whole should be the portion of the lion. The lion, pleased with his self-abnegation, gave it all up to him, saying, "Thou art no longer a fox, but myself."

Till man destroys "self" he is no true friend of God (p. 77).

Once a man came and knocked at the door of his friend.
His friend said, "Who art thou, O faithful one?"
He said, "'Tis I." He answered, "There is no admittance.
There is no room for the 'raw' at my well-cooked feast.
Naught but fire of separation and absence

[1] See Koran xviii. 77 for the story of Moses and Khizr. It is also given in Parnell's 'Hermit.'

[2] Koran xlviii. 10.

Can cook the raw one and free him from hypocrisy!
Since thy 'self' has not yet left thee,
Thou must be burned in fiery flames."
The poor man went away, and for one whole year
Journeyed burning with grief for his friend's absence.
His heart burned till it was cooked; then he went again
And drew near to the house of his friend.
He knocked at the door in fear and trepidation
Lest some careless word might fall from his lips.
His friend shouted, "Who is that at the door?"
He answered, "'Tis Thou who art at the door, O Beloved!"
The friend said, "Since 'tis I, let me come in,
There is not room for two 'I's' in one house."

STORY XII. *Joseph and the Mirror* (p. 80).

An old friend came to pay his respects to Joseph, and, after some remarks upon the bad behaviour of his brethren, Joseph asked him what present he had brought to show his respect. The friend replied that he had long considered what gift would be most suitable to offer, and at last had fixed upon a mirror, which he accordingly produced from his pocket and presented to Joseph, at the same time begging him to admire his own beauteous face in it.

Defect and Not-being the Mirror wherein Absolute Perfect Being is reflected[1] (p. 81).

He drew forth a mirror from his side
A mirror is what Beauty busies itself with.
Since Not-being is the mirror of Being,
If you are wise, choose Not-being (self-abnegation).
Being may be displayed in that Not-being,
Wealthy men show their liberality on the poor.
He who is an hungered is the clear mirror of bread,
The tinder is the mirror of the flint and steel.
Not-being and Defect, wherever they occur,
Are the mirrors of the Beauty of all beings.
Because Not-being is a clear filtered essence,
Wherein all these beings are infused.
When a garment is made by a good tailor,
'Tis an evidence of the tailor's art.
Logs of wood would not be duly shaped
Did not the carpenter plan outline and detail.
The leech skilled in setting bones goes
Where lies the patient with a broken leg.
If there were no sick and infirm,
How could the excellence of the leech's art be seen?
If vile base copper were not mingled,
How could the alchemist show his skill?
Defects are the mirrors of the attributes of Beauty,
The base is the mirror of the High and Glorious One,
Because one contrary shows forth its contrary,[1]
As honey's sweetness is shown by vinegar's sourness.
Whoso recognises and confesses his own defects
Is hastening in the way that leads to perfection!
But he advances not towards the Almighty
Who fancies himself to be perfect.
No sickness worse than fancying thyself perfect
Can infect thy soul, O arrogant misguided one!
Shed many tears of blood from eyes and heart,
That this self-satisfaction may be driven out.
The fault of Iblis lay in saying, "I am better than he,"[2]
And this same weakness lurks in the soul of all creatures.

[1] Compare the parallel passage in Gulshan i Raz, l. 135, and the notes thereon.

[1] Cp. "Religio Medici," Sect. 35: "Herein is divinity conformant unto philosophy, and not only generation founded on contrarieties, but also creation. God, being all things, is contrary unto nothing; out of which were made all things, and so nothing became something, and Omneity informed nullity into existence."

[2] Koran vii. 11.

Story XIII. *The Prophet's Scribe* (p. 81).

The Prophet had a scribe who used to write down the texts that fell from his lips. At last this scribe became so conceited that he imagined all this heavenly wisdom proceeded from his own wit, and not from the Prophet. Puffed up with self-importance, he fancied himself inspired, and his heart was hardened against his master, and he became a renegade, like the fallen angels Harut and Marut. He took his own foolish surmises to be the truth, whereas they were all wide of the mark, as those of the deaf man who went to condole with a sick neighbour, and answered all his remarks at cross purposes.

How philosophers deceive themselves (p. 32).

On the last day,[1] "when Earth shall quake with quaking,"
This earth shall give witness of her condition.
For she "shall tell out her tidings openly,"
Yea, earth and her rocks shall tell them forth!
The philosopher reasons from base analogies
(True reason comes not out of a dark corner);
The philosopher (I say) denies this in his pride of intellect.
Say to him, "Go, dash thy head against a wall!"
The speech of water, of earth, of mire,
Is audible by the ears of men of heart!
The philosopher, who denies Divine Providence,
Is a stranger to the perceptions of saints.
He says that the flashes of men's morbid imaginations
Instil many vain fancies into men's minds.
But, on the contrary, 'tis his perverseness and want of faith
Which implant in himself this vain fancy of negation.
The philosopher denies the existence of the Devil;
At the same time he is the Devil's laughing-stock.

[1] Koran xcix. 1–4.

If thou hast not seen the Devil, look at thyself,
Without demon's aid how came that blue turban[1] on thy brow?
Whosoever has a doubt or disquietude in his heart
Is a secret denier and philosopher.
Now and then he displays firm belief,
But that slight dash of philosophy blackens his face.
Beware, O believers! That lurks in you too;
You may develop innumerable states of mind.
All the seventy and two heresies lurk in you;
Have a care lest one day they prevail over you!
He in whose breast the leaf of true faith is grown
Must tremble as a leaf from fear of such a catastrophe.
Thou makest a mock of Iblis and the Devil,
Because thou art a fine man in thy own sight;
But when thy soul shall tell thy wretched faults,
What lamentation thou wilt cause to the faithful!
The sellers of base gold sit smiling in their shops,
Because the touchstone is not as yet in their sight.
O Veiler of sins! strip not the veil from us;
Lend us aid on the day of trial!

Story XIV. *The Chinese and the Greek Artists* (p. 86).

The Chinese and the Greeks disputed before the Sultan which of them were the better painters; and, in order to settle the dispute, the Sultan allotted to each a house to be painted by them. The Chinese procured all kinds of paints, and coloured their house in the most elaborate way. The Greeks, on the other hand, used no colours at all, but contented themselves with cleansing the walls of their house from all filth, and burnishing them till they were as clear and bright as the heavens. When the two houses were offered to the Sultan's inspection, that painted by the Chinese was much admired; but the Greek house

[1] Blue turbans were considered a sign of hypocrisy (Hafiz, Ode 5).

carried off the palm, as all the colours of the other house were reflected on its walls with an endless variety of shades and hues.

Knowledge of the heart preferable to the knowledge of the schools (p. 86).

The knowledge of men of heart bears them up,
The knowledge of men of the body weighs them down.
When 'tis knowledge of the heart, it is a friend;
When knowledge of the body, it is a burden.
God saith, "As an ass bearing a load of books,"[1]
The knowledge which is not of Him is a burden.
Knowledge which comes not immediately from Him
Endures no longer than the rouge of the tirewoman.
Nevertheless, if you bear this burden in a right spirit
'Twill be removed, and you will obtain joy.
See you bear not that burden out of vainglory,
Then you will behold a store of true knowledge within.
When you mount the steed of this true knowledge,
Straightway the burden will fall from your back.
If you drink not His cup, how will you escape lusts?
You, who seek no more of Him than to name His name?
What do His name and fame suggest? The idea of Him.
And the idea of Him guides you to union with Him.
Know you a guide without something to which it guides?
Were there no roads there would be no *ghouls*.
Know you a name without a thing answering to it?
Have you ever plucked a rose (*Gul*) from *Gáf* and *Lám*?
You name His name; go, seek the reality named by it!
Look for the moon in heaven, not in the water!
If you desire to rise above mere names and letters,
Make yourself free from self at one stroke!
Like a sword be without trace of soft iron;
Like a steel mirror, scour off all rust with contrition;
Make yourself pure from all attributes of self,

[1] Koran lxii. 5.

That you may see your own pure bright essence!
Yea, see in your heart the knowledge of the Prophet,
Without book, without tutor, without preceptor.
The Prophet saith, "He is one of my people,
Whoso is of like temper and spirit with me.
His soul beholds me by the selfsame light
Whereby I myself behold him,—
Without traditions and scriptures and histories,
In the fount of the water of life."
Learn the mystery, "I was last night a Kurd,
And this morning am become an Arab."[1]
This mystery of "last night" and "this morning"
Leads you into the road that brings you to God.
But if you want an instance of this secret knowledge,
Hear the story of the Greeks and the Chinese.

STORY XV. *Counsels of Reserve given by the Prophet to his Freedman Zaid* (p. 87).

At dawn the Prophet said to Zaid,
"How is it with thee this morning, O pure disciple?"
He replied, "Thy faithful slave am I." Again he said,
"If the garden of faith has bloomed, show a token of it."
He answered, "I was athirst many days,
By night I slept not for the burning pangs of love;
So that I passed by days and nights,
As the point of a spear glances off a shield.
For in that state all faith is one,
A hundred thousand years and a moment are all one;
World without beginning and world without end are one;
Reason finds no entrance when mind is thus lost."

The Prophet again urged Zaid to deliver to him a present from that celestial region, as a token that he had really been there in the spirit. Zaid answered that he had seen

[1] Syad Abu'l Wafa, an unlettered Kurd, found a paper with the words *Bismillah* upon it, and, after spending the night in prayer, found himself able to understand Arabic (Lucknow Commentator).

the eight heavens and the seven hells, and the destinies of all men, whether bound to heaven or hell. The body, he said, is as a mother, and the soul as her infant, and death is the time of parturition, when it becomes manifest to what class the infant soul belongs. As, on the day of judgment it will be manifest to all men whether a soul belongs to the saved or to the lost, so now it was plain and manifest to him. He went on to ask the Prophet if he should publish this secret knowledge of his to all men, or hold his peace. The Prophet told him to hold his peace. Zaid, however, proceeded to detail the vision of the last judgment, which he had seen when in the spirit; and the Prophet again commanded him to pause, adding that "God is never ashamed to say the truth,"[1] and allows His Prophet to speak forth the truth, but that for Zaid to blab forth the secrets seen in ecstatic vision would be wrong. Zaid replied that it was impossible for one who had once beheld the Sun of "The Truth" to keep his vision a secret. But the Prophet in reply instructed him that all men are masters of their own wills, and that he must not reveal what God has determined to keep secret till the last day, in order to leave men till then under the stimulus of hope and fear, and to give them the credit of "believing what is not seen."[2] More honour is given to the warder of a castle who faithfully executes his trust at a distance from the court than to those courtiers who serve constantly under the king's own eye. Zaid submitted to the Prophet's injunctions, and remained self-contained in his ecstatic visions. Anecdotes of the sage Luqman, of King Solomon, and of a conflagration in the days of the Khalifa 'Omar complete the section.

The Prophet's final counsels of "Reserve" (p. 91).

The Prophet said, "My companions are as the stars,
Lights to them that walk aright, missiles against Satan.
If every man had strength of eyesight

[1] Koran xxxiii. 53. [2] Koran ii. 2.

To look straight at the light of the sun in heaven,
What need were there of stars, O humble one,
To one who was guided by the light of the sun?
Neither moon nor planets would be needed
By one who saw directly the Sun of 'The Truth.'
The Moon[1] declares, as also the clouds and shadows,
'I am a man, yet it hath been revealed to me.'[2]
Like you, I was naturally dark,
'Twas the Sun's revelation that gave me such light.
I still am dark compared to the Sun,
Though I am light compared to the dark souls of men.
Therefore is my light weak, that you may bear it,
For you are not strong enough to bear the dazzling Sun.
I have, as it were, mixed honey with vinegar,
To succour the sickness of your hearts.
When you are cured of your sickness, O invalid,
Then leave out the vinegar and eat pure honey.
When the heart is garnished and swept clear of lust,
Therein 'The God of Mercy sitteth on His throne.'[3]
Then God rules the heart immediately,
When it has gained this immediate connection with Him.
This subject is endless; but where is Zaid,
That I may tell him again not to seek notoriety?
'Tis not wise to publish these mysteries,
Since the last day is approaching to reveal all things."
Now you will not find Zaid, for he is fled,
He sprang from the place where the shoes were left,[4]
Scattering the shoes in his hurry.
If you had been Zaid, you too would have been lost,
As a star is lost when the sun shines on it;
For then you see no trace or sign of it,
No place or track of it in the milky way.
Our senses and our endless discourses
Are annihilated in the light of the knowledge of our King.
Our senses and our reason within us

[1] *I.e.*, the Prophet.
[2] Koran xviii. 110.
[3] Koran xx. 4.
[4] *I.e.*, the vestibule of the house.

If you sit next to Shams of Tabriz
From that moon a sun will burst onto you.

Are as waves on waves "assembled before us."[1]
When night returns and 'tis the time of the sky's levée,
The stars that were hidden come forth to their work.
The people of the world lie unconscious,
With veils drawn over their faces, and asleep;
But when the morn shall burst forth and the sun arise
Every creature will raise its head from its couch;
To the unconscious God will restore consciousness;
They will stand in rings as slaves with rings in ears;
Dancing and clapping hands with songs of praise,
Singing with joy, "Our Lord hath restored us to life!"
Shedding their old skins and bones,
As horsemen stirring up a cloud of dust.
All pressing on from Not-being to Being,
On the last day, as well the thankful as the unthankful.

[1] Koran xxxvi. 53.

STORY XVI. *'Ali's Forbearance* (p. 92).

'Ali, the "Lion of God," was once engaged in conflict with a Magian chief, and in the midst of the struggle the Magian spat in his face. 'Ali, instead of taking vengeance on him, at once dropped his sword, to the Magian's great astonishment. On his inquiring the reason of such forbearance, 'Ali informed him that the "Lion of God" did not destroy life for the satisfaction of his own vengeance, but simply to carry out God's will, and that whenever he saw just cause, he held his hand even in the midst of the strife, and spared the foe. The Prophet, 'Ali continued, had long since informed him that he would die by the hand of his own stirrup-bearer (Ibn Maljun), and the stirrup-bearer had frequently implored 'Ali to kill him, and thus save him from the commission of that great crime; but 'Ali said he always refused to do so, as to him death was as sweet as life, and he felt no anger against his destined assassin, who was only the instrument of God's eternal purpose. The Magian chief, on hearing 'Ali's discourse, was so much affected that he embraced Islam, together with all his family, to the number of fifty souls.

How the Prophet whispered to 'Ali's stirrup-bearer that he would one day assassinate his master (p. 90).

"The Prophet whispered in the ear of my servant
That one day he would sever my head from my neck.
The Prophet also warned by inspiration me, his friend,
That the hand of my servant would destroy me.
My servant cried, "O kill me first,
That I may not become guilty of so grievous a sin!"
I replied, "Since my death is to come from thee,
How can I balk the fateful decree?"
He fell at my feet and cried, "O gracious lord,
For God's sake cleave now my body in twain,
That such an evil deed may not be wrought by me,
And my soul burn with anguish for its beloved."
I replied, "What God's pen has written, it has written;
In presence of its writings knowledge is confounded;
There is no anger in my soul against thee,
Because I attribute not this deed to thee;
Thou art God's instrument, God's hand is the agent.
How can I chide or fret at God's instrument?"
He said, "If this be so, why is there retaliation?"[1]
I answered, "'Tis from God, and 'tis God's secret;
If He shows displeasure at His own acts,
From His displeasure He evolves a Paradise;
He feels displeasure at His own acts,
Because He is a God of vengeance as of mercy.
In this city of events He is the Lord,
In this realm He is the King who plans all events.
If He crushes His own instruments,
He makes those crushed ones fair in His sight.

[1] *I.e.*, why is the rule "an eye for an eye" enjoined in the Koran, ii. 173?

Know the great mystery of 'Whatever verses we cancel,
Or cause you to forget, we substitute better for them.'[1]
Whatever law God cancels, He makes as a weed,
And in its stead He brings forth a rose.
So night cancels the business of the daytime,
When the reason that lights our minds becomes inanimate.
Again, night is cancelled by the light of day,
And inanimate reason is rekindled to life by its rays.
Though darkness produces this sleep and quiet,
Is not the 'water of life' in the darkness?[2]
Are not spirits refreshed in that very darkness?
Is not that silence the season of heavenly voices?
For from contraries contraries are brought forth,
Out of darkness was created light.
The Prophet's wars brought about the present peace,
The peace of these latter days resulted from those wars.
That conqueror of hearts cut off a thousand heads,
That the heads of his people might rest in peace."

God's rebuke to Adam for scorning Iblis (p. 9).

To whomsoever God's order comes,
He must smite with his sword even his own child.
Fear then, and revile not the wicked,
For the wicked are impotent under God's commands.
In presence of God's commands bow down the neck of pride.
Scoff not nor chide even them that go astray!
One day Adam cast a look of contempt and scorn
Upon Iblis, thinking what a wretch he was.
He felt self-important and proud of himself,
And he smiled at the actions of cursed Iblis.
God Almighty cried out to him, "O pure one,
Thou art wholly ignorant of hidden mysteries.
If I were to blab the faults of the unfortunate,

[1] Koran ii, 100.
[2] Alluding to the "water of life" in the land of darkness discovered by Khizr.

I should root up the mountains from their bases,
And lay bare the secrets of a hundred Adams,
And convert a hundred fresh Iblises into Musulmans."
Adam answered, "I repent me of my scornful looks;
Such arrogant thoughts shall not be mine again.
O Lord, pardon this rashness in Thy slave;
I repent; chastise me not for these words!"
O Aider of aid-seekers, guide us,
For there is no security in knowledge or wealth;
"Lead not our hearts astray after Thou hast guided us,"[1]
And avert the evil that the "Pen" has written.
Turn aside from our souls the evil written in our fates,
Repel us not from the tables of purity!
O God, Thy grace is the proper object of our desire;
To couple others with Thee is not proper.
Nothing is bitterer than severance from Thee,
Without Thy shelter there is naught but perplexity.
Our worldly goods rob us of our heavenly goods,
Our body rends the garment of our soul.
Our hands, as it were, prey on our feet;
Without reliance on Thee how can we live?
And if the soul escapes these great perils,
It is made captive as a victim of misfortunes and fears,
Inasmuch as when the soul lacks union with the Beloved,
It abides for ever blind and darkened by itself.
If Thou showest not the way, our life is lost;
A life living without Thee esteem as dead!
If Thou findest fault with Thy slaves,
Verily it is right in Thee, O Blessed One!
If Thou shouldst call sun and moon obscure,
If Thou shouldst call the straight cypress crooked,
If Thou shouldst declare the highest heaven base,
Or rich mines and oceans paupers,—
All this is the truth in relation to Thy perfection!
Thine is the dominion and the glory and the wealth!

[1] Koran iii. 6.

For Thou art exempt from defect and not-being,
Thou givest existence to things non-existent, and again
Thou makest them non-existent.

Epilogue to Book I. (p. 99).

Alas! the forbidden fruits were eaten,
And thereby the warm life of reason was congealed.
A grain of wheat eclipsed the sun Of Adam,[1]
Like as the Dragon's tail[2] dulls the brightness of the moon.
Behold how delicate is the heart, that a morsel of dust
Clouded its moon with foul obscurity!
When bread is "substance," to eat it nourishes us;
When 'tis empty "form," it profits nothing.
Like as the green thorn which is cropped by the camel,
And then yields him pleasure and nutriment;
When its greenness has gone and it becomes dry,—
If the camel crops that same thorn in the desert,
It wounds his palate and mouth without pity,
As if conserve of roses should turn to sharp swords.
When bread is "substance," it is as a green thorn;
When 'tis "form," 'tis as the dry and coarse thorn.
And thou eatest it in the same way as of yore
Thou wert wont to eat it, O helpless being,—
Eatest this dry thing in the same manner,
After the real "substance" is mingled with dust;
It has become mingled with dust, dry in pith and rind.
O camel, now beware of that herb!
The Word is become foul with mingled earth;
The water is become muddy; close the mouth of the well,
Till God makes it again pure and sweet;
Yea, till He purifies what He has made foul.
Patience will accomplish thy desire, not haste.
Be patient, God knows what is best.

[1] Muhammadans think the forbidden fruit to have been wheat.

[2] The descending node of the moon (see Gulshan i Raz, l. 233).

Book II.

PROLOGUE.

The composition of this Masnavi has been delayed for a season.[1]
Time is needed for blood to become milk.
Till thy fortune comes forth as a new-born babe,
Blood becomes not milk, sweet and pleasant to the mind.
When that light of God, Husámu-'d-Din
Turned his course down from the summit of heaven,—
While he had ascended to sublimest verities,
In the absence of his spring the buds blossomed not,—
But when out of that sea he came to shore,
The lute of the poesy of the Masnavi sounded again.
This Masnavi, which is the polisher of spirits,—
Its recommencement occurred on the day of "Opening."
The commencement date of this precious work
Was the year six hundred and sixty-two of the Flight.
The Bulbul started on this date and became a hawk;
Yea, a hawk to hunt out these mysteries.
May the wrist of the King be the resting-place of this hawk,
And may this door be open to the people for ever!

[1] The delay was caused by the grief of Husam for the death of his wife.

Sufis. In the course of this story there occur anecdotes of God consulting with the angels as to the creation of man, of a king who lost his hawk and found it again in the house of a poor old man, and of Shaikh Ahmad Khizrawíya buying sweetmeats for his creditors.

Story I. *The Sufi's Beast* (p. 103).

After anecdotes of the man, in the time of 'Omar, who mistook his eyelash for the new moon, of one who stole a snake and got bitten by it, and of 'Isa's foolish disciple who besought the Lord to teach him the spell whereby he raised the dead, comes the following story.

A certain Sufi, after a long day's journey, arrived at a monastery, where he put up for the night, and strictly enjoined his servant to groom his ass carefully and give him plenty of litter and fodder. The servant assured him that his minute directions were superfluous, and promised to attend to the ass most carefully; but when his master's back was turned he neglected the ass, and the poor animal remained all night without water or food. Consequently he was weak and unfit to travel next morning, and in spite of the blows and kicks that were showered on him, could not carry his master, but had to be led. The other Sufis who were travelling with his owner thought that the ass was useless, and when they arrived at the place where they halted for the night, they sold the ass to a traveller, and with the proceeds of the sale bought delicate viands and torches, and made a feast. The owner of the ass, who was ignorant of this transaction, shared the feast, and joined in the chorus sung by the others, "The ass is gone, the ass is gone," without attaching any sense to the words, and blindly following their example. Next morning he asked his servant what had become of the ass, and the servant told him it had been sold, adding that he thought he had known it overnight, because he had heard him singing "The ass is gone" along with the other

Why the poet veils his doctrines in fables (p. 104).

What is it hinders me from expounding my doctrines
But this, that my hearers' hearts incline elsewhere.
Their thoughts are intent on that Sufi guest;
They are immersed in his affairs neck deep.
So I am compelled to turn from my discourse
To that story, and to set forth his condition.
But, O friend, think not this Sufi a mere outward form,
As children see in a vine nothing but raisins.
O son, our bodies are as dried grapes and raisins;
If you are a man, cast away these things.
If you pass on to the pure mysteries of God,
You will be exalted above the nine heavenly spheres.
Now hear the outward form of my story,
But yet separate the grain from the chaff.

Why the prophets were sent (p. 106).

God sent the prophets for this purpose,
Namely, to sever infidelity from faith.
God sent the prophets to mankind
That they might gather the pure grain on their tray.
Infidel and faithful, Musulman and Jew,
Before the prophets came, seemed all as one.
Before they came we were all alike,
No one knew whether he was right or wrong.
Genuine coin and base coin were current alike;
The world was a night, and we travellers in the dark,
Till the sun of the prophets arose, and cried,
"Begone, O slumber; welcome, O pure light!"

Now the eye sees how to distinguish colours,
It sees the difference between rubies and pebbles.
The eye distinguishes jewels from dust,
Hence it is dust makes the eyes smart.
Makers of base coin hate the daylight,
Coins of pure gold love the daylight,
Because daylight is the mirror that reflects them,
So that they see their own perfect beauty.

Mystical Meaning of "Daylight" (p. 106).

God has named the resurrection "that day;"
Day shows off the beauty of red and yellow.
Wherefore "Day" in truth is the mystery of the saints;
One day of their moons is as whole years.
Know, "Day" is the reflection of the mystery of the saints,
Eye-closing night that of their hidden secrets.
Therefore hath God revealed the chapter "Daylight,"[1]
Which daylight is the light of the heart of Mustafa.
On the other view, that daylight means "The Friend,"
It is also a reflection of the same prophet.
For, as it is wrong to swear by a transitory being,
How can we suppose a transitory being spoken of by God?
The Friend of God said, "I love not them that set?"[2]
How, then, could Allah have meant a transitory being?
Again, the words "by the night" mean Muhammad's veiling,
Namely, the fair earthly body that he bore;
When his sun proceeded from heaven on high
Into that body's night, it said, "He hath not forsaken thee;"
Union with God arose out of the depth of that disgrace;
That boon was the word, "He hath not been displeased."

[1] Koran xciii: "By the daylight and by the night thy Lord hath not forsaken thee nor been displeased."

[2] Koran vi. 76: "And when the night overshadowed Abraham, he beheld a star, and he said, 'This is my Lord;' but when it set he said, 'I love not Gods which set.'"

Expressions of religious or other feeling derive their only value from the state of mind from which they proceed (p. 107).

Every expression is the sign of a state of mind;
That state is a hand, the expression an instrument.
A goldsmith's instruments in the hand of a cobbler
Are as grains of wheat sown on sand.
The tools of a cobbler in the hand of a cultivator
Are as grass before a dog or bones before an ass.
The words, "I am the Truth" were light in Mansur's[1] mouth,
In the mouth of Pharaoh "I am Lord Supreme" was blasphemy.
The staff in the hand of Moses was a witness,
In the hands of the magicians it was naught.
For this cause 'Isa taught not to that foolish man
The words of power whereby he raised the dead.
For he who is ignorant misuses the instrument;
If you strike flint on mud you will get no fire.
Hand and instrument resemble flint and steel;
You must have a pair; a pair is needed to generate.
He who has no peer or member is the "One,"
An uneven number, One without dispute!
Whoso says "one" and "two," and so on,
Confesses thereby the existence of the "One."
When the illusion of seeing double is swept away,
They who say "one" and "two" are even as they who say "One."
If you take "One" as your ball in his tennis-field,
It is made to revolve by the strokes of his bat.[2]
Yea, the ball that is even and without fault
Is made to revolve by the strokes of the King's hand.
O man of double vision,[3] hearken with attention,

[1] Mansur Hallaj, a celebrated Sufi who was put to death at Bagdad in 309 A.H. for using these words

[2] *I.e.*, unity is made to appear as plurality (see Gulshan i Raz, l. 710).

[3] See Gulshan i Raz, l. 104.

Seek a cure for your defective sight by listening.
Many are the holy words that find no entrance
Into blind hearts, but they enter hearts full of light.
But the deceits of Satan enter crooked hearts,
Even as crooked shoes fit crooked feet.
Though you repeat pious expressions again and again,
If you are a fool, they affect you not at all;—
Nay, not though you set them down in writing,
And though you proclaim them vauntingly;
Wisdom averts its face from you, O man of sin,
Wisdom breaks away from you and takes to flight!

On Taqlíd, blind imitation or cant (p. 112).

"O wretch, why did you not come and say to me,
'Such and such a disastrous affair has occurred?'"
The servant replied, "By Allah, I came again and again,
That I might acquaint you with the matter.
You were always saying, 'The ass is gone, my lad!'
Along with the others in high excitement;
So I went away, thinking you knew all about it,
And were pleased at the transaction, being a wise man."
The Sufi said, "They were all singing the same words,
So I felt impelled to sing them as well.
Blind imitation of them has undone me.
Cursed be that blind imitation!"
The effect of blindly imitating unprofitable conduct
Is that men cast away honour for a morsel of bread.
The ecstasy of that company cast a reflection,
Whereby that Sufi's heart became ecstatic like them.
You need many reflections from your associates
In order to draw water from the peerless Ocean.
The first reflection cast is mere blind imitation;
After it has been often repeated you may test its truth.
Till it is thus verified, take it not from your friends;
The drop, not yet become pearl, sever not from its shell.

Evil influence of covetousness (p. 112).

Would you have eyes and ears of reason clear,
Tear off the obstructing veil of greed!
The blind imitation of that Sufi proceeded from greed;
Greed closed his mind to the pure light.
Yea, 'twas greed that led astray that Sufi,
And brought him to loss of property and ruin.
Greed of victuals, greed of that ecstatic singing
Hindered his wits from grasping the truth.
If greed stained the face of a mirror,
That mirror would be as deceitful as we men are.[1]
If a pair of scales were greedy of riches,
Would they tell truly the weight of anything?
The Prophet saith, "O people, through singleness of mind,
I ask of you no recompense for my prophesying;[2]
I am a guide; God buyeth my guidance for you,
God giveth you my guidance in both worlds.
True, a guide deserves his wages;
Wages are due to him for directing you aright.
But what are my wages? The vision of The Friend.
Abu Bakr indeed offered me forty thousand pieces of gold,
But his forty thousand pieces were no wages for me.[3]
How could I take brass beads for pearls of Aden?"
I will tell you a tale; hearken attentively,
That you may know how greed closes up the ears.
Every man subject to greed is a miser.
Can eyes of hearts clouded with greed see clearly?
The illusion of rank and riches blinds his sight,
Like hair dropping down before his eyes.

[1] The Turkish commentator translates thus. The Lucknow copy reads *Ba sati* for *Ma sti*.
[2] Koran xi. 53.
[3] Abu Bakr made over all his goods to the Prophet in aid of the expedition to Syria.

Story II. *The Pauper and the Prisoners* (p. 113).

A certain pauper obtained admittance to a prison, and annoyed the prisoners by eating up all their victuals and leaving them none. At last they made a formal complaint to the Qázi, and prayed him to banish the greedy pauper from the prison. The Qázi summoned the pauper before him, and asked him why he did not go to his own house instead of living on the prisoners. The pauper replied that he had no house or means of livelihood except that supplied by the prison; whereupon the Qázi ordered him to be carried through the city, and proclamation to be made that he was a pauper, that no one might be induced to lend him money or trade with him. Accordingly the attendants sought for a camel whereon to carry him through the city, and at last induced a Kurd who sold firewood to lend his camel for the purpose. The Kurd consented from greed of reward, and the pauper, being seated on the camel, was carried through the city from morning till evening, proclamation being made in Persian, Arabic, and Kurdish that he was a pauper. When evening came the Kurd demanded payment, but the pauper refused to give him anything, observing that if he had kept his ears open he must have heard the proclamation. Thus the Kurd was led by greed to spend the day in useless labour.

Satan's office in the world (p. 114).

The pauper said, "Your beneficence is my sustenance;
To me, as to aliens, your prison is a paradise.
If you banish me from your prison in reprobation,
I must needs die of poverty and affliction."
Just so Iblis said to Allah, "O have compassion;
Lord! respite me till the day of resurrection.[1]
For in this prison of the world I am at ease,—

[1] Koran vii. 13.

That I may slay the children of my enemies.
From every one who has true faith for food,
And as bread for his provisions by the way,
I take it away by fraud or deceit,
So that they raise bitter cries of regret.
Sometimes I menace them with poverty,[1]
Sometimes I blind their eyes with tresses and moles."
In this prison the food of true faith is scarce,
And by the tricks of this dog what there is is lost.
In spite of prayers and fasts and endless pains,
Our food is altogether devoured by him.
Let us seek refuge with Allah from Satan.
Alas! we are perishing by his insolence.
The dog is one, yet he enters a thousand forms;[2]
Whatever he enters straight becomes himself.
Whatever makes you shiver, know he is in it,—
The Devil is hidden beneath its outward form.
When he finds no form at hand, he enters your thoughts,
To cause them to draw you into sin.
From your thoughts proceeds destruction,
When from time to time evil thoughts occur to you.
Sometimes thoughts of pleasure, sometimes of business,
Sometimes thoughts of science, sometimes of house and home.
Sometimes thoughts of gain and traffic,
Sometimes thoughts of merchandise and wealth.
Sometimes thoughts of money and wives and children,
Sometimes thoughts of wisdom or of sadness.
Sometimes thoughts of household goods and fine linen,
Sometimes thoughts of carpets, sometimes of sweepers.
Sometimes thoughts of mills, gardens, and villas,
Sometimes of clouds and mists and jokes and jests.
Sometimes thoughts of peace and war,
Sometimes thoughts of honour and disgrace.
Ah! cast out of your head these vain imaginations,

[1] Koran ii. 279.
[2] Cf. Gulshan i Raz, p. 86.

Ah! sweep out of your heart these evil suggestions.
Cry, "There is no power nor strength but in God!"
To avert the Evil One from the world and your own soul.

It is the true Beloved who causes all outward earthly beauty to exist (p. 115).

Whatsoever is perceived by sense He annuls,
But He stablishes that which is hidden from the senses.
The lover's love is visible, his Beloved hidden.
The Friend is absent, the distraction he causes present.
Renounce these affections for outward forms,
Love depends not on outward form or face.
Whatever is beloved is not a mere empty form,
Whether your beloved be of the earth or of heaven.
Whatever be the form you have fallen in love with,—
Why do you forsake it the moment life leaves it?
The form is still there; whence, then, this disgust at it?
Ah! lover, consider well what is really your beloved.
If a thing perceived by outward senses is the beloved,
Then all who retain their senses must still love it;
And since love increases constancy,
How can constancy fail while form abides?[1]
But the truth is, the sun's beams strike the wall,
And the wall only reflects that borrowed light.
Why give your heart to mere stones, O simpleton?
Go! seek the source of light which shineth alway!

. . . . . .

Distinguish well true dawn from false dawn,
Distinguish the colour of the wine from that of the cup;
So that, instead of many eyes of caprice,
One eye may be opened through patience and constancy.
Then you will behold true colours instead of false,
And precious jewels in lieu of stones.
But what is a jewel? Nay, you will be an ocean of pearls;
Yea, a sun that measures the heavens!

[1] This couplet exercises both the Turkish and the Lucknow commentators.

The real Workman is hidden in His workshop,
Go you into that workshop and see Him face to face.
Inasmuch as over that Workman His work spreads a curtain,
You cannot see Him outside His work.
Since His workshop is the abode of the Wise One,
Whoso seeks Him without is ignorant of Him.
Come, then, into His workshop, which is Not-being,[1]
That you may see the Creator and creation at once.
Whoso has seen how bright is the workshop
Sees how obscure is the outside of that shop.
Rebellious Pharaoh set his face towards Being (egoism),
And was perforce blind to that workshop.
Perforce he looked for the Divine decree to change,
And hoped to turn his destiny from his door.
While destiny at the impotence of that crafty one
All the while was secretly mocking.
He slew a hundred thousand guiltless babes
That the ordinance and decree of Allah might be thwarted.
That the prophet Moses might not be born alive,
He committed a thousand murders in the land.
He did all this, yet Moses was born,
And was protected against his wrath.
Had he but seen the Eternal workshop,
He had refrained hand and foot from these vain devices.
Within his house was Moses safe and sound,
While he was killing the babes outside to no purpose.
Just so the slave of lusts who pampers his body
Fancies that some other man bears him ill-will;
Saying this one is my enemy, and this one my foe,
While it is his own body which is his enemy and foe,
He is like Pharaoh, and his body is like Moses,
He runs abroad crying, "Where is my foe?"
While lust is in his house, which is his body,
He bites his finger in spite against strangers.

[1] *I.e.*, annihilation of self and of all phenomenal being, regarding self as naught in the presence of the Deity.

Then follows an anecdote of a man who slew his mother because she was always misconducting herself with strangers, and who excused himself by pleading that if he had not done so he would have been obliged to slay strangers every day, and thus incur blood-guiltiness. Lust is likened to this abandoned mother; when it is once slain, you are at peace with all men. In answer to an objection that if this were so the prophets and saints, who have subdued lust, would not have been hated and oppressed as they were, it is pointed out that they who hated the prophets in reality hated themselves, just as sick men quarrel with the physician or boys with the teacher. Prophets and saints are created to test the dispositions of men, that the good may be severed from the bad. The numerous grades of prophets, of saints, and of holy men are ordained, as so many curtains of the light of God, to tone down its brilliance, and make it visible to all grades of human sight.

Story III. *The King and his Two Slaves* (p. 118).

A king purchased two slaves, one extremely handsome, and the other very ugly. He sent the first away to the bath, and in his absence questioned the other. He told him that the first slave had given a very bad account of him, saying that he was a thief and a bad character, and asked if it was true. The second slave replied that the first was everything that was good, his inward qualities corresponding to the beauty of his outward appearance, and that whatever he had told the king was worthy of credit. The king replied that beauty was only an accident, and that, according to the tradition, accidents "endure only two moments;"—that at death the animal soul is destroyed,—that the text, "Whoso shall present himself with beauty shall receive tenfold reward,"[1] does not refer to outward accidents, but to the "substance," the eternal soul. The slave in reply urged that the accidents of good works and thoughts will in some way bear fruit in the next world, pointing out that thought is always the precursor of the completed work, as the plan of the architect precedes the building, and the gardener's design the perfect fruit resulting from his labours. He added that the world is only the realised thought of "Universal Reason."[1] The king then sent away the slave with whom he had held this discourse, and summoned the other, and told him that his fellow slave had given a bad account of him, and asked what he had to say. He replied that his fellow slave was a liar and a rascal, and the king then dismissed him, observing that, in accordance with the tradition, "Every man is hidden under his own tongue," his tongue had betrayed his inner vileness. "The safety of a man lies in holding his tongue."

[1] Koran vi. 161.

The apostolical succession of the prophets and the saints (p. 120).

With that "brightness of lightning"[2] He kindled their souls
So that Adam acquired knowledge from that light.
That which shone from Adam was gathered by Seth,
Wherefore Adam made him his viceroy when he saw it.
When Noah received the gift of that lustre,
He became a soul bearing pearls in the tempest of the flood.
By that light the soul of Abraham was led,
Without fear he entered Nimrod's fiery furnace.
When Ishmael sought out that light,
He meekly laid his head beneath his father's bright knife.
The soul of David was warmed by its heat,
Iron became pliable by the force of his weaving.[3]

[1] *I.e.*, the Logos as Demiurge.
[2] Koran xxiv. 43. The prophetic inspiration is likened to a light handed on from one to another.
[3] Koran xxi. 80.

When Solomon was nurtured by its fruition,
The devils became the submissive slaves of his will.
When Jacob bowed his head to the Divine decree,
He recovered his sight at the scent of his son.[1]
When moonlike Joseph saw that brilliant sun,
He became so expert as he was in interpreting dreams.
When the staff drew might from the hand of Moses,
It devoured the realm of Pharaoh at a mouthful.
When the soul of Jirjis [2] became privy to its light,
He sacrificed his life seven times, and regained it.
When Zakhariah [3] boasted of his love for it,
He ransomed his life in the hollow of the tree.
When Jonah swallowed a draught from that cup,
He found repose in the belly of the fish.
When John the Baptist became filled with its unction,
He laid his head in the golden charger in ardour for it.
When Jethro became aware of this exaltation,
He risked his life to find it.
Patient Job gave thanks for seven years,
For in his calamities he saw signs of its approach.
When Khizr and Elias boasted of gaining it,
They found the water of life and were no more seen.
When Jesus, Son of Mary, found that ladder of ascent,
He ascended to the height of the fourth heaven.
When Muhammad gained that blessed possession,
In a moment he cleft asunder the disk of the moon.[4]
When Abu Bakr became the exemplar of that grace,
He was companion of that Lord, and a "faithful witness."
When 'Omar was enraptured with that beauty,
Like a mind he discerned true and false.[5]
When Osman viewed those brilliant sights,
He diffused light and became "Lord of the two lights."[6]

[1] Koran lxxvii. 96.
[2] Jirjis or St. George is supposed by Muhammadans to be the same person as Khizr or Elias.
[3] Zakhariah the prophet is said to have taken refuge from his persecutors in the hollow of a tree.
[4] Koran liv. 1.
[5] 'Omar was called "The Discerner."
[6] He bore this name because he had two daughters of Muhammad as his wives.

When Martaza ('Ali) shined with its reflection,
He became the "Lion of God" in the soul's domain.
When his two sons were illumined by this light,
They became the "Pearly earrings of highest heaven;"[1]
One of them losing his life by poison,
The other losing his head as he went about his march.
When Junaid was succoured by the forces of that light,
His ecstatic states exceeded counting.
Báyazíd saw his way to increased fruition thereof,
And gained from God the name "Polestar of Gnostics."
What time King Mansúr became victorious,[2]
He left his throne and hastened to the stake.
When Karkhi of Karkh became its keeper,
He became lord of love and of the breath of Jesus.
Ibrahim son of Adham rode his horse to that point,
And became king of kings of equity.
And that Shakík starting from that junction
Became a sun of wit and acute of genius.
Fazíl from a highway robber became a sage of the way,[3]
When he was regarded with esteem by the King.
To Bishr Hafi the doctrine was announced,
And he set his face towards the desert of inquiry.
When Zu-l-Nún became distraught with care for it,
Egypt (Milk) as sugar became the house of his soul.
When Sari [4] lost his head in seeking the way thereto,
His rank was exalted above the seats of the mighty.
A hundred thousand great (spiritual) kings
Exalted by this divine light approach the world.
Their names remain hidden through God's jealousy;
Every beggar tells not their names.[5]

[1] A tradition gives this title to Hasan and Hussain.
[2] Mansúr Halláj, the celebrated Sufi impaled at Bagdad. Shah or King was a title often assumed by darveshes.
[3] The "way" means the Sufi doctrines.
[4] All these saints lived in the second and third centuries of the Flight.
[5] In the introduction to the Nafahatu-'l Uns, Jami says there are always 4000 saints on the earth who are not even known to one another.

Story IV. *The Falcon and the Owls* (p. 125).

A certain falcon lost his way, and found himself in the waste places inhabited by owls. The owls suspected that he had come to seize their nests, and all surrounded him to make an end of him. The falcon assured them that he had no such design as they imputed to him, that his abode was on the wrist of the king, and that he did not envy their foul habitation. The owls replied that he was trying to deceive them, inasmuch as such a strange bird as he could not be a favourite of the king. The falcon repeated that he was indeed a favourite of the king, and that the king would assuredly destroy their houses if they injured him, and proceeded to give them some good advice on the folly of trusting to outward appearances. He said, "It is true I am not homogeneous with the king, but yet the king's light is reflected in me, as water becomes homogeneous with earth in plants. I am, as it were, the dust beneath the king's feet; and if you become like me in this respect, you will be exalted as I am. Copy the outward form you behold in me, and perchance you will reach the real substance of the king."

The right use of forms (p. 126).

That my outward form may not mislead you,
Digest my sweet advice before copying me.
Many are they who have been captured by form,
Who aimed at form, and found Allah.
After all, soul is linked to body,
Though it in nowise resembles the body.
The power of the light of the eye is mated with fat,
The light of the heart is hidden in a drop of blood.
Joy harbours in the kidneys and pain in the liver,
The lamp of reason in the brains of the head;
Smell in the nostrils and speech in the tongue,
Concupiscence in the flesh and courage in the heart.
These connections are not without a why and a how,
But reason is at a loss to understand the how.
Universal Soul had connection with Partial Soul,[1]
Which thence conceived a pearl and retained it in its bosom.
From that connection, like Mary,
Soul became pregnant of a fair Messiah;—
Not that Messiah who walked upon earth and water,
But that Messiah who is higher than space.[2]
Next, as Soul became pregnant by the Soul of souls,
So by the former Soul did the world become pregnant;
Then the World brought forth another world,
And of this last are brought forth other worlds.
Should I reckon them in my speech till the last day
I should fail to tell the total of these resurrections.[3]

Story V. *The Thirsty Man who threw Bricks into the Water* (p. 126).

A thirsty man discovered a tank of water, but could not drink of it because it was surrounded by a high wall. He took some of the bricks off the top of the wall and cast them over it into the water. The water cried out, "What advantage do you gain by doing this?" He made answer, "The first advantage is this, that I hear your voice; and the second, that the more bricks I pull off the wall, the nearer I approach to you." The moral is, that so long as the wall of the body intervenes, we cannot reach the water of life. The abasement of the body brings men nearer to union with the Deity. Destroy, therefore, the

[1] This is a figurative account of the emanations of Absolute Being, whereby the world of phenomena is constituted (see Gulshan i Raz, p. 21, note, and p. 66).

[2] *I.e.*, the spirit of the Prophet Muhammad, whom the Sufis identify with the Primal Soul.

[3] "Continually is creation born again in a new creation" (Gulshan i Raz, p. 66). By constant effluxes from Absolute Being the world of phenomena is every moment renewed.

fleshly lusts which war against the soul. Then follows another parable to illustrate the folly of procrastination in this important matter.

"*It was not ye who shot, but God shot; and those arrows were God's, not yours*" (p. 130).[1]

'Tis God's light that illumines the senses' light,
That is the meaning of "Light upon light."[2]
The senses' light draws us earthwards,
God's light carries us heavenwards.
As objects of sense are of base condition,
God's light is an ocean, and the senses' light a dewdrop.
But that light which is "upon this light" is not seen,
Save through signs and holy discourses.
Since the senses' light is gross and dense,
It lies hidden in the black pupil of the eye.
When you cannot see the senses' light with the eye,
How can you see with the eye the Light of the mind?
As the senses' light is hidden in these gross veils,
Must not that Light which is pure be also hidden?
Like the senses, this world is ruled by a hidden Power.
It confesses its impotence before that hidden Power,
Which sometimes exalts it and sometimes lays it low,
Sometimes makes it dry and sometimes moist.
The hand is hidden, yet we see the pen writing;
The horse is galloping, yet the rider is hid from view.
The arrow speeds forth, yet the bow is not seen;
Souls are seen, the Soul of souls (God) is hidden.
Break not the arrow, for it is the arrow of the King;
Yea, it is an arrow from the bow of Wisdom.
"Ye shot not when ye shot," was said by God;
God's action has predominance over all actions.
Break your own passion, break not that arrow,
The eye of passion takes milk to be blood.

[1] Koran viii. 17, meaning, "God is the *Fa'il i Hakiki*, or Only Real Agent."
[2] Koran xxiv. 35.

Kiss that arrow and bear it to the King,
Yea, though it be stained with your own blood.
Whatsoever is seen is weak and base and impotent;
What is hidden is equally fierce and headstrong.
We are the captured game; who is the snare?
We are the balls; where is the bat?
He tears and mends; who is this tailor?
He fans and kindles the flame; who is this kindler?
At one time He makes the faithful one an infidel,
At another He makes the atheist a devotee!

Next comes an anecdote of a dirty man who refused to bathe because he was ashamed to go into the water, with the moral that "Shame hinders religion;"[1] and then another of Zu'l Nún, a celebrated Egyptian Sufi of the third century A.H. Zu'l Nún appeared to his ignorant friends to be mad, and they accordingly confined him in a madhouse. After a time they thought that he was not really mad, but had feigned madness for some deep purpose, and they went to the madhouse to inquire into the state of his health. When they arrived there, Zu'l Nún asked them who they were, and they answered that they were his devoted friends, who were now convinced that the story of his being mad was a calumny. Zu'l Nún jumped up and drove them away with sticks and stones, saying that true friendship would have been manifested in sharing his troubles, even as pure gold is tried by fire.

STORY VI. *Luqman's Master examines him and discovers his Acuteness* (p. 132).

Luqman the Sage,[2] who is sometimes identified with Esop, and sometimes with the nephew of the prophet. Job, though "gifted with wisdom by God," was a slave.

[1] Freytag, Arabum Proverbia, vol. ii. pp. 379 and 418, gives two proverbs—one, "Shame is a part of religion;" and the other, "Shame hinders getting a livelihood."
[2] See Koran xxxi. Another anecdote of his wit occurs in Book I.

With each breath, caressing
sounds call to us from afar; Oh we're
heaven- bound; who's coming to watch?

His master, however, discovered his worth, and became extremely attached to him, so that he never received any delicacy without giving Luqman a share of it. One day, having received a water-melon, he gave Luqman the best part of it, and Luqman devoured it with such apparent relish that his master was tempted to taste it. To his surprise he found it very bitter, and asked Luqman why he had not told him of this. Luqman replied that it was not for him, who lived on his master's bounty, to complain if he now and then received disagreeable things at his hands. Thus, though to outward appearance a slave, Luqman showed himself to be a lord.

Love endures hardships at the hands of the Beloved (p. 134).

Through love bitter things seem sweet,
Through love bits of copper are made gold.
Through love dregs taste like pure wine,
Through love pains are as healing balms.
Through love thorns become roses,
And through love vinegar becomes sweet wine.
Through love the stake becomes a throne,
Through love reverse of fortune seems good fortune.
Through love a prison seems a rose bower,
Without love a grate full of ashes seems a garden.
Through love burning fire is pleasing light,
Through love the Devil becomes a Houri.
Through love hard stones become soft as butter,
Without love soft wax becomes hard iron.
Through love grief is as joy,
Through love *Ghouls* turn into angels.
Through love stings are as honey,
Through love lions are harmless as mice.
Through love sickness is health,
Through love wrath is as mercy.
Through love the dead rise to life,
Through love the king becomes a slave.

Even when an evil befalls you, have due regard;
Regard well him who does you this ill turn.
The sight which regards the ebb and flow of good and ill
Opens a passage for you from misfortune to happpiness.
Thence you see the one state moves you into the other,[1]
One opposite state generating its opposite in exchange.
So long as you experience not fears after joys,
How can you look for pleasures after disgusts?
While ye fear the doom of the angel on the left hand,
Men hope for the bliss of the angel on the right.[2]
May you gain two wings![3] A fowl with only one wing
Is impotent to fly, O well-intentioned one!
Now either permit me to hold my peace altogether,
Or give me leave to explain the whole matter.
And if you mislike this and forbid that,
Who can tell what your desire is?
You must have the soul of Abraham in order with light
To see the mansions of Paradise in the fire.
Step by step he ascended above sun and moon,
And so lagged not below, as a ring that fastens a door.
Since the "Friend of God" ascended above the heavens,
And said, "I love not Gods that set;"[4]
So this world of the body is a breeder of misconceptions
In all who have not fled from lust.

STORY VII. *Moses and the Shepherd* (p. 138).

Next follows an anecdote of Bilkis, Queen of Sheba, whose reason was enlightened by the counsels of the Hoopoo sent to her by King Solomon. Outward sense is

[1] The doctrine of Heraclitus, that opposite states generate one another, is discussed by Jelaludin in a passage quoted in Lumsden's Grammar, ii. 323, and is mentioned in the Phædo and the Nicomachæan Ethics.

[2] An anacoluthon (see Koran l. 16).

[3] The two wings are hope and fear, both of which are needed to guide men's religious flight (see Book III. on "Probability the guide of life").

[4] Koran vi. 77.

as opposed to true reason as Abù Jahl was to Muhammad; and when the outward senses are replaced by the true inner reason, man sees that the body is only foam, and the heart the limitless ocean. Afterwards comes an anecdote of a philosopher who was struck blind for cavilling at the verse, "What think ye? If at early morn your waters shall have sunk away, who will then give you clear running water?"[1] This is succeeded by the story of Moses and the shepherd. Moses once heard a shepherd praying as follows: "O God, show me where thou art, that I may become Thy servant. I will clean Thy shoes and comb Thy hair, and sew Thy clothes, and fetch Thee milk." When Moses heard him praying in this senseless manner, he rebuked him, saying, "O foolish one, though your father was a Musulman, you have become an infidel. God is a Spirit, and needs not such gross ministrations as, in your ignorance, you suppose." The shepherd was abashed at his rebuke, and tore his clothes and fled away into the desert. Then a voice from heaven was heard, saying, "O Moses, wherefore have you driven away my servant? Your office is to reconcile my people with me, not to drive them away from me. I have given to each race different usages and forms of praising and adoring me. I have no need of their praises, being exalted above all such needs. I regard not the words that are spoken, but the heart that offers them. I do not require fine words, but a burning heart. Men's ways of showing devotion to me are various, but so long as the devotions are genuine, they are accepted."

Religious forms indifferent (*p.* 139).

A voice came from God to Moses,
"Why hast thou sent my servant away?
Thou hast come to draw men to union with me,
Not to drive them far away from me.

[1] Koran lxvii. 30.

So far as possible, engage not in dissevering;
'The thing most repugnant to me is divorce.'[1]
To each person have I allotted peculiar forms,
To each have I given particular usages.
What is praiseworthy in thee is blameable in him,
What is poison for thee is honey for him.
What is good in him is bad in thee,
What is fair in him is repulsive in thee.
I am exempt from all purity and impurity,
I need not the laziness or alacrity of my people.
I created not men to gain a profit from them,
But to shower my beneficence upon them.
In the men of Hind the usages of Hind are praiseworthy,
In the men of Sind those of Sind.
I am not purified by their praises,
'Tis they who become pure and shining thereby.
I regard not the outside and the words,
I regard the inside and the state of heart.
I look at the heart if it be humble,
Though the words may be the reverse of humble.
Because the heart is substance, and words accidents,
Accidents are only a means, substance is the final cause.
How long wilt thou dwell on words and superficialities?
A burning heart is what I want; consort with burning!
Kindle in thy heart the flame of love,
And burn up utterly thoughts and fine expressions.
O Moses! the lovers of fair rites are one class,
They whose hearts and souls burn with love are another.
Lovers must burn every moment,
As tax and tithe are levied on a ruined village.
If they speak amiss, call them not sinners;
If a martyr be stained with blood, wash it not away.
Blood is better than water for martyrs,
This fault is better than a thousand correct forms.
No need to turn to the Ka'ba when one is in it,
And divers have no need of shoes.

[1] A tradition.

One does not take a drunken man as a guide on the way,
Nor speak of darns to torn garments.
The sect of lovers is distinct from all others,
Lovers have a religion and a faith of their own.
Though the ruby has no stamp, what matters it?
Love is fearless in the midst of the sea of fear.

. . . .

Beware, if thou offerest praises or thanksgivings,
And know them to be even as the babble of that shepherd;
Though thy praises be better compared with his,
Yet in regard to God they are full of defects.
How long wilt thou say, 'They obscure the truth,
For it is not such as they fancy'?
Thy own prayers are accepted only through mercy,
They are suffered as the prayers of an impure woman.
If her prayers are made impure by the flow of blood,
Thine are stained with metaphors and similitudes.
Blood is impure, yet its stain is removed by water;
But that impurity of ignorance is more lasting,
Seeing that without the blessed water of God
It is not banished from the man who is subject to it.
O that thou wouldst turn thy face to thy own prayers,
And become cognisant of the meaning of thy ejaculations,
And say, 'Ah! my prayers are as defective as my being;
O requite me good for evil!'"

Moses questions God as to the reason of the flourishing state of the wicked (p. 140).

Moses said, "O beneficent Creator,
With whom a moment's remembrance is as long ages,
I see Thy plan distorted in this world of earth and water;
My heart, like the angel's, feels a difficulty thereat.
With what object hast thou framed this plan,
And sowed therein the seeds of evil?
Why hast Thou kindled the fire of violence and wrong?
Why burnt up mosques and them who worship therein?

Paradise is attached to requirements unpleasant to us,
Hell is attached to things flattering our lusts.
The branch full of sap is the main fuel of thy fire.
'They that are burnt with fire are near to Kausar.'[1]
Whoso is in prison and acquainted with troubles,
That is in requital for his gluttony and lusts.
Whoso is in a palace and enjoying wealth,
That is in reward for toils and troubles.
Whoso is seen enjoying uncounted gold and silver,
Know that he strove patiently to acquire it.
He, whose soul is exempt from natural conditions,
And who possesses the power of overriding causes,
Can see without causes, like eyes that pierce night;
But thou, who art dependent on sense attend to causes.

. . . .

Having left Jesus, thou cherishest an ass (lust),
And art perforce excluded, like an ass;
The portion of Jesus is knowledge and wisdom,
Not so the portion of an ass, O asinine one!
Thou pitiest thine ass when it complains;
So art thou ignorant, thy ass makes thee asinine.
Keep thy pity for Jesus, not for the ass,
Make not thy lust to vanquish thy reason.
Leave thy natural lusts to whine and howl,
Tear thee from them, escape that snare of the soul!

STORY VIII. *The Man who made a Pet of a Bear* (p. 143).[2]

A kind man, seeing a serpent overcoming a bear, went to the bear's assistance, and delivered him from the serpent. The bear was so sensible of the kindness the man had done him that he followed him about wherever he went, and became his faithful slave, guarding him from everything that might annoy him. One day the man was lying asleep, and the bear, according to his custom, was sitting by him and driving off the flies. The flies

[1] A saying of the Prophet. [2] Anwari Suhaili, i. 27.

became so persistent in their annoyances that the bear lost patience, and seizing the largest stone he could find, dashed it at them in order to crush them utterly; but unfortunately the flies escaped, and the stone lighted upon the sleeper's face and crushed it. The moral is, "Do not make friends with fools." In the course of this story occur anecdotes of a blind man, of Moses rebuking the worshippers of the calf, and of the Greek physician Galen and a madman.

He who needs mercy finds it (p. 143).

Doing kindness is the game and quarry of good men,
A good man seeks in the world only pains to cure.
Wherever there is a pain there goes the remedy,
Wherever there is poverty there goes relief.
Seek not water, only show you are thirsty,
That water may spring up all around you.
That you may hear the words, "The Lord gives them to drink,"[1]
Be athirst! Allah knows what is best for you.
Seek you the water of mercy? Be downcast,
And straightway drink the wine of mercy to intoxication.
Mercy is called down by mercy to the last.
Withhold not, then, mercy from any one, O son!

. . . . . .

If of yourself you cannot journey to the Ka'ba,
Represent your helplessness to the Reliever.
Cries and groans are a powerful means,
And the All-Merciful is a mighty nurse.
The nurse and the mother keep excusing themselves,
Till their child begins to cry.
In you too has God created infant needs;
When they cry out, their milk is brought to them;
God said, "Call on God;" continue crying,
So that the milk of His love may boil up.[2]

[1] Koran lxxvi. 21. [2] Koran xvii. 110.

Moses and the worshipper of the calf (p. 145).

Moses said to one of those full of vain imaginations,
"O malevolent one, through error and heresy
You entertain a hundred doubts as to my prophethood,
Notwithstanding these proofs, and my holy character.
You have seen thousands of miracles done by me,
Yet they only multiply your doubts and cavils.
Through doubts and evil thoughts you are in a strait,
You speak despitefully of my prophethood.
I brought the host out of the Red Sea before all men,
That ye might escape the oppression of the Egyptians.
For forty years meat and drink came from heaven,
And water sprang from the rock at my prayer.
My staff became a mighty serpent in my hand,
Water became blood for my ill-conditioned enemy.
The staff became a snake, and my hand bright as the sun;
From the reflection of that light the sun became a star.
Have not these incidents, and hundreds more like them,
Banished these doubts from you, O cold-hearted one?
The calf lowed through magic,
And you bowed down to it, saying, 'Thou art my God.'[1]

. . . .

The golden calf lowed; but what did it say,
That the fools should feel all this devotion to it?
You have seen many more wondrous works done by me,
But where is the base man who accepts the truth?
What is it that charms vain men but vanity?
What else pleases the foolish but folly?
Because each kind is charmed by its own kind,
Does a cow ever seek the lion?
Did the wolf show love to Joseph,[2]
Or only fraud upon fraud with a view to devour him?
True, if it lose his wolf-like nature it becomes a friend;
Even as the dog of the cave became a son of man.[3]

[1] See Koran xx. 90. [2] Koran xii. 17. [3] Koran xviii. 17.

When good Abu Bakr saw Muhammad,
He recognised his truth, saying, 'This one is true;'
When Abu Bakr caught the perfume of Muhammad,
He said, 'This is no false one.'
But Abu Jahl, who was not one of the sympathisers,
Saw the moon split asunder, yet believed not.
If from a sympathiser, to whom it is well known,
I withhold the truth, still 'tis not hidden from him;
But he who is ignorant and without sympathy,
However much I show him the truth, he sees it not.
The mirror of the heart must needs be polished
Before you can distinguish fair and foul therein."

Story IX. *The Gardener and the Three Friends* (p. 148).

A voice came from heaven to Moses, saying, "O Moses, why didst thou not visit me when I was sick?" Moses inquired the meaning of this dark saying, and the answer was, "When one of God's saints is sick, God regards his sickness as His own; and, therefore, he who desires to hold companionship with God must not forsake the saints."[1] This is illustrated by a story of a gardener who saw three friends walking in his garden, and making free with his fruit. Knowing he could not prevail against them while they remained united, he contrived by tricks to separate them, and then proceeded to chastise them one by one. And this caused one of them to make the reflection that he had acted very foolishly in deserting his friends.

Story X. *Báyazíd and the Saint* (p. 149).

The celebrated Sufi, Abu Yazíd or Báyazíd of Bastám, in Khorasan, who lived in the third century of the Flight, was once making a pilgrimage to Mecca, and visiting all the "Pillars of insight" who lived in the various towns that lay on his route. At last he discovered the "Khizr of the age" in the person of a venerable Darvesh, with whom he held the following conversation:—

The Sage said, "Whither are you going, O Báyazíd?
Where will you bring your caravan to a halt?"
Báyazíd replied, "At dawn I start for the Ka'ba."
Quoth the Sage, "What provision for the way have you?"
He answered, "I have two hundred silver dirhams;
See them tied up tightly in the corner of my cloak."
The Sage said, "Circumambulate me seven times;
Count this better than circumambulating the Ka'ba;
And as for the dirhams, give them to me, O liberal one,
And know you have finished your course and obtained your wish,
You have made the pilgrimage and gained the life to come,
You have become pure, and that in a moment of time.
Of a truth that is God which your soul sees in me,
For God has chosen me to be His house.
Though the Ka'ba is the house of His grace and favours,
Yet my body too is the house of His secret.
Since He made *that* house He has never entered it,
But none but That Living One enters *this* house.[1]
When you have seen me you have seen God,
And have circumambulated the veritable Ka'ba.
To serve me is to worship and praise God;
Think not that God is distinct from me.
Open clear eyes and look upon me,
That you may behold the light of God in a mortal.
The Beloved once called the Ka'ba 'My house,'
But has said to me 'O my servant' seventy times.[1]
O Báyazíd, you have found the Ka'ba,
You have found a hundred precious blessings."
Báyazíd gave heed to these deep sayings,
And placed them as golden earrings in his ears.

[1] Cp. Matthew xxv. 40.

[1] Alluding to the *Hadis*: "Heaven and earth contain me not, but the heart of my faithful servant contains me."

Then follow anecdotes of the Prophet paying a visit to one of his disciples who lay sick, of Shaikh Bahlol, nicknamed "The Madman," who was a favourite at the court of Harunu-'r-Rashid, and of the people of Moses.

The sweet uses of adversity (p. 150).

The sick man said, "Sickness has brought me this boon,
That this Prince (Muhammad) has come to me this morn,
So that health and strength may return to me
From the visit of this unparalleled King.
O blessed pain and sickness and fever!
O welcome weariness and sleeplessness by night!
Lo! God of His bounty and favour
Has sent me this pain and sickness in my old age;
He has given me pain in the back, that I may not fail
To spring up out of my sleep at midnight;
That I may not sleep all night like the cattle,
God in His mercy has sent me these pains.
At my broken state the pity of kings has boiled up,
And hell is put to silence by their threats!"
Pain is a treasure, for it contains mercies;
The kernel is soft when the rind is scraped off.
O brother, the place of darkness and cold
Is the fountain of life and the cup of ecstasy.
So also is endurance of pain and sickness and disease.
For from abasement proceeds exaltation.
The spring seasons are hidden in the autumns,
And autumns are charged with springs; flee them not.
Consort with grief and put up with sadness,
Seek long life in your own death!
Since 'tis bad, whatever lust says on this matter
Heed it not, its business is opposition.
But act contrary thereto, for the prophets
Have laid this injunction upon the world.[1]
Though it is right to take counsel in affairs,
That you may have less to regret in the upshot;—
The prophets have laboured much
To make the world revolve on this pivot stone;[1]
But, in order to destroy the people, lust desires
To make them go astray and lose their heads;—
The people say, 'With whom shall we take counsel?'
The prophets answer, 'With the reason of your chief.'
Again they say, 'Suppose a child or a woman enter,
Who lacks reason and clear judgment;'
They reply, 'Take counsel with them,
And act contrary to what they advise.'
Know your lust to be woman, and worse than woman;
Woman is partial evil, lust universal evil.
If you take counsel with your lust,
See you act contrary to what that base one advises.
Even though it enjoin prayers and fasting,
It is treacherously laying a snare for you.'

. . . . . .

You must abandon and ignore your own knowledge,
And dip your hand in the dish of abnegation of knowledge.
Whatever seems profitable, flee from it,
Drink poison and spill the water of life.
Contemn whatever praises you,
Lend to paupers your wealth and profits!
Quit your sect and be a subject of aversion,
Cast away name and fame and seek disgrace!"

God the Author of good and evil (p. 156).

If you seek the explanation of God's love and favour,
In connection therewith read the chapter "Brightness."[2]
And if you say evil also proceeds from Him,
Yet what damage is that to His perfection?

[1] Freytag quotes a saying of 'Omar, "A fool may indicate the right course" (Arabum Proverbia, i. p. 566).

[1] The law defining the right course.

[2] Koran xciii.: "By the noonday brightness, and by the night when it darkeneth, thy Lord hath not forsaken thee nor been displeased."

To send that evil is one of His perfections.
I will give you an illustration, O arrogant one;
The heavenly Artist paints His pictures of two sorts,
Fair pictures and pictures the reverse of fair.
Joseph he painted fair and made him beautiful;
He also painted ugly pictures of demons and *'afrits.*
Both sorts of pictures are of His workmanship,
They proceed not from His imperfection, but His skill,
That the perfection of His wisdom may be shown,
And the gainsayers of His art be put to shame.
Could He not paint ugly things He would lack art,
And therefore He creates Guebers as well as Moslems.
Thus, both infidelity and faith bear witness to Him,
Both alike bow down before His almighty sway.
But know, the faithful worship Him willingly,
For they seek and aim at pleasing Him;
While Guebers worship Him unwillingly,
Their real aim and purpose being quite otherwise.

Evil itself is turned into good for the good (p. 157).

The Prophet said to that sick man,
"Pray in this wise and allay your difficulties;
'Give us good in the house of our present world,
And give us good in the house of our next world.[1]
Make our path pleasant as a garden,
And be Thou, O Holy One, our goal!'"
The faithful will say on the last day, "O King!
Was not Hell on the route all of us travelled?
Did not faithful as well as infidels pass through it?
Yet on our way we perceived not the smoke of the fire;
Nay, it seemed Paradise and the mansion of the blessed."
Then the King will answer, "That green garden,
As it appeared to you on your passage through it,
Was indeed Hell and the place of dread torment;

[1] "O Lord, give us good in this world and good in the next, and save us from the torment of the fire." (Koran ii. 197).

Yet for you it became a garden green with trees.
Since you have laboured to make hellish lusts,
And the fire of pride that courts destruction,—
To make these, I say, pure and clean,—
And, to please God, have quenched those fires,
So that the fire of lust, that erst breathed flame,
Has become a holy garden and a guiding light,—
Since you have turned the fire of wrath to meekness,
And the darkness of ignorance to shining knowledge,
Since you have turned the fire of greed into bounty,
And the vile thorns of malice into a rose-garden;
Since you have quenched all these fires of your own
For my sake, so that those poisons are now pure sweets;—
Since you have made fiery lust as a verdant garden,
And have sowed therein the seed of fidelity,
So that nightingales of prayer and praise
Ever warble sweetly around this garden;—
Since you have responded to the call of God,
And have drawn water out of the hell of lust,—
For this cause my hell also, for your behoof,
Becomes a verdant garden and yields leaves and fruit."
What is the recompense of well-doing, O son?
It is kindness and good treatment and rich requital.
Have ye not said, "We are victims,
Mere nothings before eternal Being?
If we are drunkards or madmen,
'Tis *that* Cup-bearer and *that* Cup which make us so.
We bow down our heads before His edict and ordinance,
We stake precious life to gain His favour.
While the thought of the Beloved fills our hearts,
All our work is to do Him service and spend life for Him.
Wherever He kindles His destructive torch,
Myriads of lovers' souls are burnt therewith.
The lovers who dwell within the sanctuary
Are moths burnt with the torch of the Beloved's face."
O heart haste thither,[2] for God will shine upon you,

[1] *I.e.*, to annihilation of self in God, as a moth in the flame.

And seem to you a sweet garden instead of a terror.
He will infuse into your soul a new soul,
So as to fill you, like a goblet, with wine.
Take up your abode in His soul!
Take up your abode in heaven, O bright full moon!
Like the heavenly Scribe,[1] He will open your heart's book
That He may reveal mysteries unto you.
Abide with your Friend, since you have gone astray,
Strive to be a full moon; you are now a fragment thereof.
Wherefore this shrinking of the part from its whole?
Why this association with its foes?
Behold Genus become Species in due course,
Behold secrets become manifest through his light!
So long as woman-like you swallow blandishments,
How, O wise man, can you get relief from false flatteries?
These flatteries and fair words and deceits (of lust)
You take, and swallow, just like women.
But the reproaches and the blows of Darveshes
Are really better for you than the praises of sinners.
Take the light blows of Darveshes, not the honey of sinners,
And become, by the fortune of good, good yourself.
Because from them the robe of good fortune is gained,
In the asylum of the spirit blood becomes life.

STORY XI. *Mo'avia and Iblis* (p. 158).

Mo'avia, the first of the Ommiad Khalifas, was one day lying asleep in his palace, when he was awakened by a strange man. Mo'avia asked him who he was, and he replied that he was Iblis. Mo'avia then asked him why he had awakened him, and Iblis replied that the hour of prayer was come, and he feared Mo'avia would be late. Mo'avia answered, "Nay! it could never have been your intention to direct me in the right way. How can I trust a thief like you to guard my interests?" Iblis answered, "Remember that I was bred up as an angel of light, and that I cannot quite abandon my original occupation. You may travel to Rome or Cathay, but still you retain the love of your fatherland. I still retain my love of God, who fed me when I was young; nay, even though I revolted from Him, that was only from jealousy (of Adam), and jealousy proceeds from love, not from denial of God. I played a game of chess with God at His own desire, and though I was utterly checkmated and ruined, in my ruin I still experience God's blessings." Mo'avia answered, "What you say is not credible. Your words are like the decoy calls of a fowler, which resemble the voices of the birds, and so lure them to destruction. You have caused the destruction of hundreds of mortals, such as the people of Noah, the tribe of 'Ad,[1] the family of Lot, Nimrod, Pharaoh, Abu Jahl, and so on." Iblis retorted, "You are mistaken if you suppose me to be the cause of all the evil you mention. I am not God, that I should be able to make good evil, or fair foul. Mercy and vengeance are twin divine attributes, and they generate the good and evil seen in all earthly things. I am, therefore, not to blame for the existence of evil, as I am only a mirror, which reflects the good and evil existing in the objects presented to it." Mo'avia then prayed to God to guard him against the sophistries of Iblis, and again adjured Iblis to cease his arguments and tell plainly the reason why he had awakened him. Iblis, instead of answering, continued to justify himself, saying how hard it was that men and women should blame him when they did anything wrong, instead of blaming their own evil lusts. Mo'avia, in reply, reproached him with concealing the truth, and ultimately brought him to confess that the true reason why he had awakened him was this, that if he had overslept himself, and so missed the hour of prayer, he would have felt deep sorrow and have heaved many sighs, and each of these sighs would, in the sight of God, have counted for as many as two hundred ordinary prayers.

[1] Atarid or Mercury.

[1] See Koran xi. 63.

The value of sighs (p. 162).

A certain man was going into the mosque,
Just as another was coming out.
He inquired of him what had occurred to the meeting,
That the people were coming out of the mosque so soon.
The other told him that the Prophet
Had concluded the public prayers and mysteries.
"Whither go you," said he, "O foolish one,
Seeing the Prophet has already given the blessing?"
The first heaved a sigh, and its smoke ascended;
That sigh yielded a perfume of his heart's blood.
The other, who came from the mosque, said to him,
"Give me that sigh, and take my prayers instead."
The first said, "I give it, and take your prayers."
The other took that sigh with a hundred thanks.
He went his way with deep humility and contrition,
As a hawk who had ascended in the track of the falcon.
That night, as he lay asleep, he heard a voice from heaven,
"Thou hast bought the water of life and healing;
The worth of what thou hast chosen and possessed
Equals that of all the people's accepted prayers."

To illustrate the treachery of wolves in sheep's clothing,—of Satans rebuking sin and preaching religion—an anecdote is told of a master of a house who caught a thief, but was induced to let him escape by the stratagem of the thief's confederate, who cried that he had got the real thief elsewhere. *Apropos* of the same theme, the poet next relates the story of "those who built a mosque for mischief," as recorded in the Koran.[1] The tribe of Bani Ganim built a mosque, and invited the Prophet to dedicate it. The Prophet, however, discovered that their real motive was jealousy of the tribe of Bani Amru Ibn Auf, and of the mosque at Kuba, near Medina, and a treacherous understanding with the Syrian monk Abu Amir, and therefore he refused their request, and ordered the mosque to be razed to the ground.

[1] Koran ix. 108.

Wisdom the believer's lost camel (p. 165).

My people adopt my law without obeying it,
They take that coin without assaying it.
The Koran's wisdom is like the "believer's lost camel,'[1]
Every one is certain his camel is lost.
You have lost your camel and seek it diligently;
Yet how will you find it if you know not your own?
What was lost? Was it a female camel that you lost?
It escaped from your hand, and you are in a maze.
The caravan is come to be loaded,
Your camel is vanished from the midst of it.
You run here and there, your mouth parched with heat;
The caravan moves on, and night approaches.
Your goods lie on the ground in a dangerous road,
You hurry after your camel in all directions.
You cry "O Moslems, who has seen a camel,
Which escaped from its stable this morning?
To him who shall give me news of my camel
I will give a reward of so many dirhems."
You go on seeking news of your camel from every one,
And every lewd fellow flatters you with a fresh rumour,
Saying, "I saw a camel; it went this way;
'Twas red, and it went towards this pasture."
Another says, "Its ear was cropped."
Another says, "Its cloth was embroidered."
Another that it had only one eye,
Another that it had lost its hair from mange.
To gain the reward every base fellow
Mentions a hundred marks without any foundation.

[1] This is a proverb ascribed to Ali. It means, people are always losing wisdom and seeking it like a lost camel (Freytag, Arabum Proverbia, i. p. 385).

All false doctrines contain an element of truth (p. 165).

Just so every one in matters of doctrine
Gives a different description of the hidden subject.
A philosopher expounds it in one way,
And a critic at once refutes his propositions.
A third censures both of them;
A fourth spends his life in traducing the others.
Every one mentions indications of this road,
In order to create an impression that he has gone it.
This truth and that truth cannot be all true,
And yet all of them are not entirely astray in error.
Because error occurs not without some truth,
Fools buy base coins from their likeness to real coins.
If there were no genuine coins current in the world,
How could coiners succeed in passing false coins?
If there were no truth, how could falsehood exist?
Falsehood derives its plausibility from truth.
'Tis the desire of right that makes men buy wrong;
Let poison be mixed with sugar, and they eat it at once.
If wheat were not valued as sweet and good for food,
The cheat who shows wheat and sells barley would make no profit!
Say not, then, that all these creeds are false,
The false ones ensnare hearts by the scent of truth.
Say not that they are all erroneous fancies,
There is no fancy in the universe without some truth.
Truth is the "night of power"[1] hidden amongst other nights,
In order to try the spirit of every night.
Not every night is that of power, O youth,
Nor yet is every night quite void of power.
In the crowd of rag-wearers there is but one Faqir;[2]
Search well and find out that true one.

[1] The night on which the Koran was revealed.

[2] So in the Phædo, "Many are the wandbearers, but few the Mystics."

Tell the wary and discerning believer
To distinguish the king from the beggar.
If there were no bad goods in the world,
Every fool might be a skilful merchant;
For then the hard art of judging goods would be easy.
If there were no faults, one man could judge as well as another.
Again, if all were faulty, skill would be profitless.
If all wood were common, there would be no aloes.
He who accepts everything as true is a fool,
But he who says all is false is a knave.

STORY XII. *The Four Hindustanis who censured one another* (p. 167).

Four Hindustanis went to the mosque to say their prayers. Each one duly pronounced the *Takbír*, and was saying his prayers with great devotion, when the Mu'azzin happened to come in. One of them immediately called out, "O Mu'azzin, have you yet called to prayer? It is time to do so." Then the second said to the speaker, "Ah! you have spoken words unconnected with worship, and therefore, according to the *Hadis*, you have spoiled your prayers."[1] Thereupon the third scolded the last speaker, saying, "O simpleton, why do you rebuke him? Rather rebuke yourself." Last of all, the fourth said, "God be praised that I have not fallen into the same ditch as my three companions." The moral is, not to find fault with others, but rather, according to the proverb,[2] to be admonished by their bad example. *Apropos* of this proverb, a story is told of two prisoners captured by the tribe of Ghuz. The Ghuzians were about to put one of them to death, to frighten the other, and make him confess where the treasure was concealed, when the doomed man discovered their object, and said, "O noble sirs, kill my companion, and frighten me instead."

[1] Mishkát ul Masábih, by Matthews, i. 205.

[2] Freytag, Arabum Proverbia, i. 628.

STORY XIII. *The Old Man and the Physician* (p. 169).

An old man complained to his physician that he suffered from headache. The physician replied, "That is caused by old age." The old man next complained of a defect in his sight, and the physician again told him that his malady was due to old age. The old man went on to say that he suffered from pain in the back, from dyspepsia, from shortness of breath, from nervous debility, from inability to walk, and so on; and the physician replied that each of these ailments was likewise caused by old age. The old man, losing patience, said, "O fool, know you not that God has ordained a remedy for every malady?" The physician answered, "This passion and choler are also symptoms of old age. Since all your members are weak, you have lost the power of self-control, and fly into a passion at every word."

Bad principles always produce bad acts (p. 169).

Fools laud and magnify the mosque,
While they strive to oppress holy men of heart.
But the former is mere form, the latter spirit and truth.
The only true mosque is that in the hearts of saints.
The mosque that is built in the hearts of the saints
Is the place of worship of all, for God dwells there.
So long as the hearts of the saints are not afflicted,
God never destroys the nation.
Our forefathers lifted their hands against the prophets;
Seeing their bodies, they took them for ordinary men.
In you also abide the morals of those men of old;
How can you avoid fearing that you will act like them?
The morals of those unthankful ones dwell in you,
Your urn will not always return unbroken from the well.
Seeing that all these bad symptoms are seen in you,
And that you are one with those men, how can you escape?

STORY XIV. *The Arab Carrier and the Scholar* (p. 171).

An Arab loaded his camel with two sacks, filling one with wheat and the second with sand, in order to balance the first. As he was proceeding on his way he met a certain tradition-monger, who questioned him about the contents of his sacks. On learning that one contained nothing but sand, he pointed out that the object might be attained much better by putting half the wheat in one sack and half in the other. On hearing this the Arab was so struck by his sagacity that he conceived a great respect for him, and mounted him on his camel. Then he said, "As you possess such great wisdom, I presume that you are a king or a Vazir, or at least a very rich and powerful noble." The theologian replied, "On the contrary, I am a very poor man; all the riches my learning has brought me are weariness and headaches, and I know not where to look for a loaf of bread." The Arab said, "In that case get off my camel and go your way, and suffer me to go mine, for I see your learning brings ill luck." The moral of the story is the worthlessness of mere human knowledge, and its inferiority to the divine knowledge proceeding from inspiration. This thesis is further illustrated by an account of the mighty works which were done by the saint Ibrahim bin Adham, through the divine knowledge that God had given him. Ibrahim was originally prince of Balkh, but renounced his kingdom and became a saint. One day he was sitting by the shore mending his cloak, when one of his former subjects passed by and marvelled to see him engaged in such a mean occupation. The saint at once, by inspired knowledge, read his thoughts, and thus corrected his false impressions. He took the needle with which he was mending his cloak and cast it into the sea. Then with a loud voice he cried out, "O needle, rise again from the midst of the sea, and come back again into my hands." Without a moment's delay thousands of fishes rose to the surface of the sea, each bearing in its mouth a golden needle, and cried out, "O Shaikh, take these needles of God!" Ibrahim then turned to the noble, saying, "Is not the kingdom of the heart better than the contemptible earthly kingdom I formerly possessed? What you have just seen is a very trifling sign of my spiritual power—as it were, a mere leaf plucked to show the beauty of a garden. You have now caught the scent of this garden, and it ought to attract your soul to the garden itself, for you must know that scents have great influence, *e.g.*, the scent of Joseph's coat,[1] which restored Jacob's sight, and the scents which were loved by the Prophet."[2]

STORY XV. *The Man who boasted that God did not punish him for his sins, and Jethro's answer to him* (p. 175).

That person said in the time of Shu'aib (Jethro),
"God has seen many faults done by me;
Yea, how many sins and faults of mine has He seen,
Nevertheless of His mercy He punishes me not."
God Almighty spake in the ear of Shu'aib,
Addressing him with an inner voice in answer thereto,
"Why hast thou said I have sinned so much,
And God of His mercy has not punished my sins?"
Thou sayest the very reverse of the truth, O fool!
Wandering from the way and lost in the desert!
How many times do I smite thee, and thou knowest not?
Thou art bound in my chains from head to foot.
On thy heart is rust on rust collected,
So thou art blind to mysteries.
Thy rust, layer on layer, O black kettle!
Makes the aspect of thy inner parts foul.
If that smoke touched a new kettle,
It would show the smut, were it only as a grain of barley;
For everything is made manifest by its opposite,
In contrast with its whiteness that black shows foul.
But when the kettle is black, then afterwards
Who can see on it the impression of the smoke?
If the blacksmith be a negro,
His face agrees in colour with the smoke.
But if a man of Rum does blacksmith's work,
His face becomes grimed by the smoke fumes;
Then he quickly perceives the impression of his fault,
So that he wails and cries 'O Allah!'
When he is stubborn and follows his evil practices,
He casts dust in the eyes of his discernment.
He recks not of repentance, and, moreover, that sin
Becomes dear to his heart, so that he becomes without faith,
Old shame for sin and calling on God quit him,
Rust five layers deep settles on his mirror,
Rust spots begin to gnaw his iron,
The colour in his jewel grows less and less.
When you write on white paper,
What is written is read at a glance;
But when you write on the face of a written page,
It is not plain, reading it is deceptive;
For that black is written on the top of other black,
Both the writings are illegible and senseless.
Or if, in the third place, you write on the page,
And then blacken it like an infidel's soul,
Then what remedy but the aid of the Remedier?
Despair is copper and sight its elixir.
Lay your despair before Him,
That you may escape from pain without medicine."
When Shu'aib spoke these aphorisms to him,
From that breath of the soul roses bloomed in his heart,
His soul heard the revelations of heaven;
He said, "If He has punished me, where is the sign of it?"
Shu'aib said, "O Lord, he repels my arguments,
He seeks for a sign of that punishment."

[1] Koran xii. 93.
[2] There is a *Hadis*: "The Prophet loved perfumes and fair women and brightness of eyes in prayer."

When Jesus had heard the pleas of the young man
He pointed to the bone and invoked the sacreds word,

The Veiler of sins replied, "I will tell him no secrets,
Save only one, in order to try him.
One sign that I punish him is this,
That he observes obedience and fasting and prayer,
And devotions and almsgiving, and so on,
Yet never feels the least expansion of soul.
He performs the devotions and acts enjoined by law,
Yet derives not an atom of relish from them.
Outward devotion is sweet to him, spirit is not sweet,
Nuts in plenty, but no kernel in any of them.
Relish is needed for devotions to bear fruit,
Kernels are needed that seeds may yield trees.
How can seeds without kernels become trees?
Form without soul (life) is only a dream."

STORY XVI. *The Gluttonous Sufi* (p. 178).

In a certain convent there lived a Sufi whose conduct gave just offence to the brethren. They brought him before their Shaikh and thus accused him, "This Sufi has three very bad qualities; he babbles exceedingly like a bell, at his meals he eats more than twenty men, and when he sleeps he is as one of the Seven Sleepers." The Shaikh then admonished him, insisting on the obligation of keeping to the golden mean, and reminding him that even the prophet Moses[1] was once rebuked by Khizr for speaking to excess. But the delinquent excused himself on the grounds that the mean is relative, what is excess in one man being moderation in another, that he who is led by the spirit is no longer subject to the outward law, and that the "inner voice," which rules such an one's conduct, is its own evidence.

[1] Koran xviii. 77.

The mean is relative (p. 178).

He said, "Though the path of the mean is wisdom,
Yet is this same mean also relative.
The water which is insufficient for a camel
Is like an ocean to a mouse.
Whoso has four loaves as his daily allowance,
Whether he eat two or three, he observes the mean.
But if he eat all four he transgresses the mean,
A very slave to greed, and voracious as a duck.
Whoso has an appetite for ten loaves,
Know, though he eat six, he observes the mean.
If I have an appetite for fifty loaves,
While you can manage only six, we are not on a par.
You are wearied with ten prostrations in prayer,
Whilst I can endure five hundred.
Such an one goes barefoot to the Ka'ba,
Whilst another faints with going to the mosque."

The ecstatic state which exalts the subject of it above law (p. 179).

"At times my state resembles a dream,
My dreaming seems to them infidelity.
Know my eyes sleep, but my heart is awake;
My body, though torpid, is instinct with energy.
The Prophet said, 'Mine eyes sleep,
But my heart is awake with the Lord of mankind.'
Your eyes are awake and your heart fast asleep,
My eyes are closed, and my heart at the 'open door.'
My heart has other five senses of its own;
These senses of my heart view the two worlds.
Let not a weakling like you censure me,
What seems night to you is broad day to me;
What seems a prison to you is a garden to me,
Busiest occupation is rest to me.

Your feet are in the mire, to me mire is rose,
What to you is funeral wailing is marriage drum to me.
While I seem on earth, abiding with you in the house,
I ascend like Saturn to the seventh heaven.
'Tis not I who companion with you, 'tis my shadow;
My exaltation transcends your thoughts,
Because I have transcended thought,
Yea, I have sped beyond reach of thought.
I am lord of thought, not overlorded by thought,
As the builder is lord of the building.
All creatures are enslaved to thought;
For this cause are they sad at heart and sorrowful.
I send myself on an embassy to thought,
And, at will, spring back again from thought.
I am as the bird of heaven and thought as the fly,
How can the fly lend a helping hand to me?

. . . . . .

Whoso has in him a spark of the light of Omnipotence,
However much he eats, say 'Eat on;' 'tis lawful to him."

To the spiritual man the "inner voice" is its own evidence, and needs no other proof (p. 179).

"If you are a true lover of my soul,
This truth-fraught saying of mine is no vain pretence,—
'Though I talk half the night I am superior to you;'
And again, 'Fear not the night; here am I, your kinsman.'
These two assertions of mine will both seem true to you
The moment you recognise the voice of your kinsman.
Superiority and kinsmanship are both mere assertions,
Yet both are recognised for truth by men of clear wit.
The nearness of the voice proves to such an one
That the voice proceeds from a friend who is near.
The sweetness of the kinsman's voice, too, O beloved,
Proves the veracity of that kinsman.
But the uninspired fool who from ignorance
Cannot tell the voice of a stranger from a friend's,—
To him the friend's saying seems a vain pretension,
His ignorance is the material cause of his disbelief.
To the wise, whose hearts are enlightened,
The mere sound of that voice proves its truth."

. . . . . .

"When you say to a thirsty man, 'Come quickly;
This is water in the cup, take and drink it,'
Does the thirsty man say, 'This is a vain pretension;
Go, remove yourself from me, O vain pretender,
Or proceed to give proofs and evidence
That this is generic water, and concrete water thereof'?
Or when a mother cries to her sucking babe,
'Come, O son, I am thy mother,'
Does the babe answer, 'O mother, show a proof
That I shall find comfort from taking thy milk'?
In the hearts of every sect that has a taste of the truth
The sight and the voice of prophets work miracles.
When the prophets raise their cry to the outward ear,
The souls of each sect bow in devotion within;—
Because never in this world hath the soul's ear
Heard from any man the like of that cry.
That poor man in that strange sweet voice
Recognises the voice of God, 'Verily I am nigh.'"[1]

STORY XVII. *The Tree of Life* (p. 180).

The preceding story is followed by a short anecdote of the infants of the Virgin Mary and the mother of John the Baptist leaping in their mothers' wombs,[2] and in reply to matter of fact cavillers and questioners of this anecdote, the poet says we must look at its spirit and essential basis rather than its outward form. This introduces the story of the tree of life. A certain wise man related that in

[1] "And when my servants ask thee concerning me, then will I be nigh unto them. I will answer the cry of him that crieth, when he crieth unto me" (Koran ii. 182).

[2] Luke i. 41.

Hindustan there was a tree of such wonderful virtue that whosoever ate of its fruit lived for ever. Hearing this, a king deputed one of his courtiers to go in quest of it. The courtier accordingly proceeded to Hindustan, and travelled all over that country, inquiring of every one he met where this tree was to be found. Some of these persons professed their entire ignorance, others joked him, and others gave him false information; and, finally, he had to return to his country with his mission unaccomplished. He then, as a last resource, betook himself to the sage who had first spoken of the tree, and begged for further information about it, and the sage replied to him as follows:—

The Shaikh laughed, and said to him, " O friend,
This is the tree of knowledge, O knowing one;
Very high, very fine, very expansive,
The very water of life from the circumfluent ocean.
Thou hast run after *form*, O ill-informed one,
Wherefore thou lackest the fruit of the tree of *substance*.
Sometimes it is named tree, sometimes sun,
Sometimes lake, and sometimes cloud.
'Tis one, though it has thousands of manifestations;
Its least manifestation is eternal life!
Though 'tis one, it has a thousand manifestations,
The names that fit that one are countless.
That one is to thy personality a father,
In regard to another person He may be a son.
In relation to another He may be wrath and vengeance,
In relation to another, mercy and goodness.
He has thousands of names, yet is One,—
Answering to all of His descriptions, yet indescribable.
Every one who seeks names, if he is a man of credulity,
Like thee, remains hopeless and frustrated of his aim.
Why cleavest thou to this mere name of tree,
So that thou art utterly balked and disappointed?
Pass over names and look to qualities,
So that qualities may lead thee to essence!
The differences of sects arise from His names;
When they pierce to His essence they find His peace!"

This story is followed by another anecdote illustrative of the same thesis that attending merely to names and outward forms, rather than to the spirit and essence of religion, leads men into error and delusion. Four persons, a Persian, an Arab, a Turk, and a Greek, were travelling together, and received a present of a dirhem. The Persian said he would buy "*angúr*" with it, the Arab said he would buy "*ináb*," while the Turk and the Greek were for buying "*úzum*" and "*astaphíl*" (*staphyle*), respectively. Now all these words mean one and the same thing, viz., "grapes;" but, owing to their ignorance of each other's languages, they fancied they each wanted to buy something different, and accordingly a violent quarrel arose beween them. At last a wise man who knew all their languages came up and explained to them that they were all wishing for one and the same thing.

Story XVIII. *The Young Ducks who were brought up under a Hen* (p. 184).

Although a domestic fowl may have taken thee,
Who art a duckling, under her wing and nurtured thee,
Thy mother was a duck of *that* ocean,
Thy nurse was earthy, and her wing dry land.
The longing for the ocean which fills thy heart,—
That natural longing of thy soul comes from thy mother.
Thy longing for dry land comes to thee from thy nurse;
Quit thy nurse, for she will lead thee astray.
Leave thy nurse on the dry land and push on,
Enter the ocean of real Being, like the ducks!
Though thy nurse may frighten thee away from water,
Do thou fear not, but haste on into the ocean!
Thou art a duck, and flourishest on land and water,
And dost not, like a domestic fowl, dig up the house.

Thou art a king of "the sons of Adam honoured by God,"[1]
And settest foot alike on sea and land;—
For impress on thy mind, "We have carried them *by sea*,"
Before the words, "We have caried them *by land*."
The angels go not on dry land,
And the animals know nothing of the sea;
Thou in body art an animal, in thy soul an angel;
Hence thou goest both upon earth and on heaven."
Hence to outward view "He is a man like you,"[2]
While to his sharp-seeing heart "it hath been revealed."
His earthy form has fallen on earth,
His spirit revolving above highest heaven.
O boy, we are all of us waterfowl,
The sea knows full well our language.
Solomon[3] is, as it were, that sea, and we as the birds;
In Solomon we hold our course to eternity.
Along with Solomon plunge into the ocean,[4]
Then, like David, the water will make us coats-of-mail.
That Solomon is present to every one,
But negligence closes their eyes and bewitches them.
Hence, through ignorance, sloth, and folly,
Though he stands hard by us, we are shut off from him.
The noise of thunder makes the head of the thirsty ache;
When he knows not that it unlocks the blessed showers,
His eyes are fixed on the running stream,
Unwitting of the sweetness of the rain from heaven.
He urges the steed of his desire towards the *caused*,
And perforce remains shut off from the *Causer*.
Whoso beholds the *Causer* face to face,
How can he set his heart on things *caused* on earth?

[1] Koran xvi. 72: "And now have we honoured the sons of Adam, by sea and by land have we carried them."

[2] Koran xviii. 110: "Say, In sooth I am only a man like you. It hath been revealed unto me that your God is one only God."

[3] Koran xxvii. 16: "Solomon said, O men, we have been taught the speech of birds."

[4] Koran xxvii. 44 and xxi. 80.

Book III.

Story I. *The Travellers who ate the Young Elephant* (p. 190).

A party of travellers lost their way in a wilderness, and were well nigh famished with hunger. While they were considering what to do, a sage came up and condoled with them on their unfortunate plight. He told them that there were many young elephants in the adjacent woods, one of which would furnish them an ample meal, but at the same time he warned them that if they killed one, its parents would in all probability track them out and be revenged on them for killing their offspring. Shortly after the travellers saw a plump young elephant, and could not resist killing and eating it. One alone refrained. Then they lay down to rest; but no sooner were they fast asleep than a huge elephant made his appearance and proceeded to smell the breath of each one of the sleepers in turn. Those whom he perceived to have eaten of the young elephant's flesh he slew without mercy, sparing only the one who had been prudent enough to abstain.

God's care for His children (p. 190).

O son, the pious are God's children,
Absent or present He is informed of their state.
Deem Him not absent when they are endangered,
For He is jealous for their lives.
He saith, "These saints are my children,
Though remote and alone and away from their Lord.
For their trial they are orphans and wretched,

Yet in love I am ever holding communion with them.
Thou art backed by all my protection,
My children are, as it were, parts of me.
Verily these Darveshes of mine
Are thousands on thousands, and yet no more than One;
For if not, how did Moses with one magic staff
Turn the realm of Pharaoh upside down?
And if it were not so, how did Noah with one curse
Make East and West alike drowned in his flood?
Nor could one prayer of eloquent Lot
Have razed their strong city against their will,—
Their mighty city, like to Paradise,
Became as a Tigris of black water; go, see its vestige!
Towards Syria is this vestige and memorial,
Thou seest it in passing on the way to Jerusalem.
Thousands of God-fearing prophets
In every age hold divine chastisements in hand.
Should I tell of them my limits would be exceeded,
And not hearts only but very hills would bleed."

Evil deeds give men's prayers an ill savour in God's nostrils (p. 192).

Thou art asleep, and the smell of that forbidden fruit
Ascends to the azure skies,—
Ascends along with thy foul breath,
Till it overpowers heaven with stench;—
Stench of pride, stench of lust, stench of greed.
All these stink like onions when a man speaks.
Though thou swearest, saying, "When have I eaten?
Have I not abstained from onions and garlic?"
The very breath of that oath tells tales,
As it strikes the nostrils of them that sit with thee.
So too prayers are made invalid by such stenches,[1]
That crooked heart is betrayed by its speech.
The answer to that prayer is, "Be ye driven into hell,"[1]
The staff of repulsion is the reward of all deceit.
But, if thy speech be crooked and thy meaning straight,
Thy crookedness of words will be accepted of God.
That faithful Bilál, when he called to prayer,
Would devoutly cry, "Come hither, come hither!"
At last men said, "O Prophet, this call is not right,
This is wrong; now, what is thy intention?
O Prophet, and O ambassador of the Almighty,
Provide another Mu'azzin of better talent,
'Tis an error at the beginning of our divine worship
To utter the words, 'Come to the asylum!'"[2]
The wrath of the Prophet boiled up, and he said
(Uttering one or two secrets from the fount of grace),
"O base ones, in God's sight the 'Ho!' of Bilál
Is better than a hundred 'Come hithers' and ejaculations.
Ah! excite not a tumult, lest I tell forth openly
Your secret thoughts from first to last.
If ye keep not your breath sweet in prayer,
Go, desire a prayer from the Brethren of Purity!"
For this cause spake God to Moses,
At the time he was asking aid in prayer,
"O Moses! desire protection of me
With a mouth that thou hast not sinned withal."
Moses answered, "I possess not such a mouth."
God said, "Call upon me with another mouth!
Act so that all thy mouths
By night and by day may be raising prayers.
When thou hast sinned with one mouth,
With thy other mouth cry, 'O Allah!'
Or else cleanse thy own mouth,
And make thy spirit alert and quick.
Calling on God is pure, and when purity approaches,
Impurity arises and takes its departure.
Contraries flee away from contraries;

[1] "Whoever eats garlic or onions must keep away from me or from the *Masjid*" (Mishkát ul Masábih, ii. 321).

[1] Koran xxiii. 110: "He will say, 'Be ye driven down into it, and address me not.'

[2] Rules for the call to prayer are given in Mishkát ul Masábih, i. 141."

When day dawns night takes flight.
When the pure name (of God) enters the mouth,
Neither does impurity nor that impure mouth remain!"

The man whose calling "O Allah" was equivalent to God's answering him, "Here am I"[1] (p. 192).

That person one night was crying, "O Allah!"
That his mouth might be sweetened thereby,
And Satan said to him, "Be quiet, O austere one!
How long wilt thou babble, O man of many words?
No answer comes to thee from nigh the throne,
How long wilt thou cry 'Allah' with harsh face?"
That person was sad at heart and hung his head,
And then beheld Khizr present before him in a vision,
Who said to him, "Ah! thou hast ceased to call on God,
Wherefore repentest thou of calling upon Him?"
The man said, "The answer 'Here am I' came not,
Wherefore I fear that I am repulsed from the door."
Khizr replied to him, "God has given me this command;
Go to him and say, 'O much-tried one,
Did not I engage thee to do my service?
Did not I engage thee to call upon me?
That calling 'Allah' of thine *was* my 'Here am I,'
And that pain and longing and ardour of thine my messenger;
Thy struggles and strivings for assistance
Were my attractions, and originated thy prayer.
Thy fear and thy love are the covert of my mercy,
Each 'O Lord!' of thine contains many 'Here am I's.''
The soul of fools is alien from this calling on God,
Because it is not their wont to cry, 'O Lord!'
On their mouths and hearts are locks and bonds,[2]
That they may not cry to God in time of distress.
God gave Pharaoh abundance of riches and wealth,
So that he boasted that he was 'Lord Supreme.'
In the whole of his life he suffered no headache,
So that he never cried to God, wretch that he was.
God granted him the absolute dominion of the world,
But withheld from him pain and sorrow and cares;
Because pain and sorrow and loads of cares
Are the lot of God's friends in the world.
Pain is better than the dominion of the world,
So that thou mayest call on God in secret.
The cries of those free from pain are dull and cold,
The cries of the sorrowful come from the burning hearts."

[1] Or, "What dost thou require of me?"

[2] Koran ii. 6.

STORY II. *The Villager who invited the Townsman to visit him* (p. 193).

A certain villager paid a visit to the town, and there received hospitality from one of the townsmen. At his departure the villager was profuse of thanks, and pressed the townsman to come and see him in his village, and bring his family with him. The townsman hesitated long before accepting his invitation, having doubts as to his sincerity, and remembering the *Hadis*, "Caution consists in suspecting others."[1] But after ten years' solicitation he at length yielded, and set off with his family to the village. On his arrival the villager shut the door in his face, saying that he did not know him, and the townsman had to pass five nights in the cold and rain. At last, exhausted with suffering, he implored the villager to give him shelter, promising to render service in return. The villager granted it on condition that he would protect his garden from the wolves. The townsman accepted this condition, and taking bow and arrows, proceeded to patrol the garden, but, owing to the rain and the darkness, and his own fears, ended by shooting the villager's pet ass in mistake for a wolf. The villager abused him roundly, saying that he

[1] Freytag, Arabum Proverbia, i. p. 370, ascribes this saying to the poet, Aqzam bin Zaid.

himself would not have taken an ass for a wolf, even on the darkest night. The townsman replied, "If that be so, you are self-convicted of inhumanity, for you must have recognised me, your friend of ten years' standing, the moment I knocked at your door. As for me, I am ignorant of all but Allah, and, moreover, was unable to see in the darkness; and God has said, 'No criminality is imputed to the blind.'[1] But your blindness in refusing to recognise me was wilful, and your claims to humanity are thus proved to be false by the test to which you have been submitted."

Jesus healing the sick (p. 195).

The house of 'Isa was the banquet of men of heart,
Ho! afflicted one, quit not this door!
From all sides the people ever thronged,
Many blind and lame, and halt and afflicted,
To the door of the house of 'Isa at dawn,
That with his breath he might heal their ailments.
As soon as he had finished his orisons,
That holy one would come forth at the third hour;
He viewed those impotent folk, troop by troop,
Sitting at his door in hope and expectation;
He spoke to them, saying, "O stricken ones!
The desires of all of you have been granted by God;
Arise, walk without pain or affliction,
Acknowledge the mercy and beneficence of God!"
Then all, as camels whose feet are shackled,
When you loose their feet in the road,
Straightway rush in joy and delight to the halting-place,
So did they run upon their feet at his command.
How many afflictions caused by thyself to thyself
Hast thou escaped through these princes of the faith?
How long that lameness of thine was thy steed!
How seldom was thy soul void of sorrow and grief!

[1] Koran xxiv. 60.

O careless straggler, bind a rope upon thy feet,
Lest thou lose even thine own self!
But thy ingratitude and unthankfulness
Forget the honey draught thou hast sipped.
That road was perforce closed to thee
When thou didst wound the hearts of the men of heart.
Quick! clasp them and ask pardon of them;
Like the clouds, shed tears of lamentation,
So that their rose-garden may bloom for thee,
And their ripe fruits burst open of themselves.
Press around that door, be not viler than a dog,
If thou wouldest rival the Seven Sleepers' dog.

God's claims to our gratitude (p. 195).

Whereas want of fidelity is shameful even in dogs,
How can it be right in men?
God Almighty Himself makes boast of fidelity,
Saying, "Who more faithful to his promise than We?"[1]
Know, infidelity is fidelity to God's adversary,
No one has pre-eminence over the rights of God.
The claims of a mother are less than God's, for He,
That bounteous One, made her debtor for thy embryo.
He gave thee a form whilst thou wast in her womb,
In her womb He gave thee needful rest and nurture.
He viewed her as a part united to thee,
Then His wisdom separated that united part.
God devised a thousand plans and arts,
To make thy mother lavish affection upon thee.
Wherefore the claims of God predominate over the mother's,
Whoso acknowledges not God's claims is a fool.
He who made mother and breast and milk
United mother to father also,—despise Him not!
O Lord, O Ancient of days, Thy mercies,
Whether known to us or unknown, are all from Thee!
Thou hast commanded, saying, "Remember thy God,"
Because God's claims are never exhausted!

[1] Koran. ix. 112.

Since thou hast been led astray by faithless men,
Turn now from thy evil doubts to the opposite mind.
I am free from error and all faithlessness;
Thou must come to me and rescind evil doubts.
Cut off these evil doubts and cast them away,
For in the presence of such thou becomest double.
Therefore thou hast chosen harsh friends and companions;
If I ask where they are thou sayest they are gone.
The good friend goes up to highest heaven,
Evil friends sink beneath the bottom of the earth,
Whilst thou art left alone in the midst, forlorn,
Even as the fires left by the departed caravan."
O brave friend, grasp His skirt,
Who is removed alike from the world above and below;
Who neither, like Jesus, ascends to heaven,
Nor, like Korah, sinks into the earth;
Who will abide with thee in the house and abroad
When thou lackest house and home.
He will bring forth peace out of perturbations,
And when thou art afflicted will keep His promise.

How false pretensions to sanctity are distinguished from true sanctity (p. 203).

O son, a hundred thousand tests await thee,
Whoever thou art who sayest "I am a prince of the gate,"
If the vulgar detect not such an one by tests,
Yet the skilled wayfarers seek of him a sign.
When a man makes pretension to be a tailor,
The master places before him a piece of silk,
Saying, "Cut out a large head-dress,"
And failure in the test leads him to the pillory.
If all the evil men were not tested,
Every catamite would through fraud pass for a Rustam.
Suppose he wears the semblance of one clad in mail,
Yet when wounded he is at once taken captive.
The God-intoxicated are not sobered by old age,
They remain beside themselves till the last trump.
The wine of God is true, and not false,
But thou hast drunk only sour whey.
Thou makest thyself out to be a Junaid or a Bayazid;
Go! for do I not know a hatchet from a ploughshare?
O plotter, how canst thou conceal by fraud
Baseness, sloth, covetousness, and lust?

. . . . . .

Thou holdest thyself out as a lover of God,
But thou hast coquetted with the evil demon.
The lover and the beloved on the last day
Will be joined together and raised in sight of all.
How foolish and silly thou hast made thyself!
Thou hast drunk blood of grapes, nay, my blood!
Go! for I know thee not. Get away!
I am a lover beside himself, whose words are wild.
Thou fanciest thyself near to God,
Saying, "The maker of the dish is not far from the dish."
Knowest thou not that the nearness of saints to God
Involves the power to do mighty works and signs?
Iron was as wax in the hands of David,
Wax in thy hands is as iron.
God's nearness and His beneficence are common to all,
But only eminent saints enjoy inspired love.
Nearness is of various kinds, O son,
The sun shines alike on rocks and on gold.
Yet the sun possesses a nearness to gold,
Whereof the common willow has no cognisance.
The dry branch and the green are alike near the sun,
Does the sun veil himself from either?
Yet what is the nearness of that green branch,
Wherefrom thou eatest ripe fruits?
But as for the dry branch, from its nearness to the sun,
What does it but more quickly grow dry and sapless?
Be not intoxicated after the manner of this branch,
Which, when it becomes sober, has cause for repentance,
But, like those drunkards who, when they drink wine,
Bear ripe fruits of wisdom of penitence.

STORY III. *The Jackal who pretended to be a Peacock* (p. 204).

A jackal fell into a dye-pit, and his skin was dyed of various colours. Proud of his splendid appearance, he returned to his companions, and desired them to address him as a peacock. But they proceeded to test his pretensions, saying, "Dost thou scream like a peacock, or strut about gardens as peacocks are wont to do?" And he was forced to admit that he did not, whereupon they rejected his pretensions. Another story, also on the subject of false pretenders, follows. A proud man who lacked food procured a skin full of fat, greased his beard and lips with it, and called on his friends to observe how luxuriously he had dined. But his belly was vexed at this, because it was hungry, and he was destroying his chance of being invited to dinner by his friends. So the belly cried to God, and a cat came and carried off the skin of fat, and so the man's false pretences were exposed. The poet takes occasion to point out that Pharaoh's pretensions to divinity exactly resembled the pretensions of this jackal, and adds that all such false pretenders may be detected by the mark noted in the Koran, "Ye shall know them by the strangeness of their speech."[1] This recalls the story of Harut and Marut, two angels who were very severe on the frailties of mankind, and whom God sent down upon the earth to be tempted, with the result that they both succumbed to the charms of the daughters of men.[2]

STORY IV. *Moses and Pharaoh* (p. 207).

Then follows a long account of the birth of Moses, of Pharaoh's devices to kill him in his infancy, of his education in Pharaoh's house, of his desiring Pharaoh to let the children of Israel go, and of his contest with the magicians of Egypt, and his victory over them. In the course of the story the following anecdote is narrated:—

A snake-catcher, who was following his occupation in the mountains, discovered a large snake frozen by the cold, and, imagining it to be dead, he tied it up and took it to Baghdad. There all the idlers of the city flocked together to see it, and the snake, thawed by the warmth of the sun, recovered life, and immediately destroyed the spectators.

Comparison of fleshly lust to the snake (p. 213).

Lust is that snake; How say you it is dead?
It is only frozen by the pangs of hunger.
If it obtains the state of Pharaoh,
So as to command the (frozen) rivers to flow,
Straightway it is led to pride like Pharaoh's,
And it plunders the goods of many a Moses and Aaron.
Through pressure of want this snake is as a fly,
It becomes a gnat through wealth and rank and luxury.
Beware, keep that snake in the frost of humiliation,
Draw it not forth into the sunshine of 'Iraq!
So long as that snake is frozen, it is well;
When it finds release from frost you become its prey.
Conquer it and save yourself from being conquered,
Pity it not, it is not one who bears affection.
For that warmth of the sun kindles its lust,
And that bat of vileness flaps its wings.
Slay it in sacred war and combat,
Like a valiant man will God requite you with union.
When that man cherished that snake,
That stubborn brute was happy in the luxury of warmth;
And of necessity worked destruction, O friend;
Yea, many more mischiefs than I have told.
If you wish to keep that snake tied up
Without trouble, be faithful, be faithful!
But how can base men attain this wish?

[1] Koran xlvii. 32.
[2] Koran ii. 96.

It requires a Moses to slay serpents;
And a hundred thousand men were slain by his serpent,
In dire confusion, according to his purpose.

Story V. *The Elephant in a Dark Room* (p. 217).

Some Hindoos were exhibiting an elephant in a dark room, and many people collected to see it. But as the place was too dark to permit them to see the elephant, they all felt it with their hands, to gain an idea of what it was like. One felt its trunk, and declared that the beast resembled a water-pipe; another felt its ear, and said it must be a large fan; another its leg, and thought it must be a pillar; another felt its back, and declared the beast must be like a great throne. According to the part which each felt, he gave a different description of the animal. One, as it were, called it "*Dal*," and another "*Alif*."

Comparison of the sensual eye to the hand of one that felt the elephant (p. 217).

The eye of outward sense is as the palm of a hand,
The whole of the object is not grasped in the palm.
The sea itself is one thing, the foam another;
Neglect the foam, and regard the sea with your eyes.
Waves of foam rise from the sea night and day,
You look at the foam ripples and not the mighty sea.
We, like boats, are tossed hither and thither,
We are blind though we are on the bright ocean.
Ah! you who are asleep in the boat of the body,
You see the water; behold the Water of waters!
Under the water you see there is another Water moving it,
Within the spirit is a Spirit that calls it.
Where were Moses and Jesus when that Sun
Showered down water on the fields sown with corn?
Where were Adam and Eve what time
God Almighty fitted the string to His bow?

The one form of speech is evil and defective;
The other form, which is not defective, is perfect.
If I speak thereof your feet stumble,
Yet if I speak not of it, woe be to you!
And if I speak in terms of outward form,
You stick fast in that same form, O son.
You are footbound like the grass in the ground,
And your head is shaken by the wind uncertainly.
Your foot stands not firmly till you move it,
Nay, till you pluck it not up from the mire.
When you pluck up your foot you escape from the mire,
The way to this salvation is very difficult.
When you obtain salvation at God's hands, O wanderer,
You are free from the mire, and go your way.
When the suckling is weaned from its nurse,
It eats strong meats and leaves the nurse.
You are bound to the bosom of earth like seeds,
Strive to be weaned through nutriment of the heart.
Eat the words of wisdom, for veiled light
Is not accepted in preference to unveiled light.
When you have accepted the light, O beloved,
When you behold what is veiled without a veil,
Like a star you will walk upon the heavens;
Nay, though not in heaven, you will walk on high.

. . . . . .

Keep silence, that you may hear Him speaking
Words unutterable by tongue in speech.
Keep silence, that you may hear from that Sun
Things inexpressible in books and discourses.
Keep silence, that the Spirit may speak to you;
Give up swimming and enter the ark of Noah;
Not like Canaan when he was swimming,
Who said, "I desire not to enter the ark of Noah passing by."

Noah and his unbelieving son Canaan (p. 218).

Noah cried, "Ho! child, come into the ark and rest,
That you be not drowned in the flood, O weak one."[1]
Canaan said, "Nay! I have learned to swim,
I have lit a torch of my own apart from thy torch."
Noah replied, "Make not light of it, for 'tis the flood of destruction,
Swimming with hands and feet avails naught to-day.
The wind of wrath and the storm blow out torches;
Except the torch of God, all are extinguished."
He answered, "Nay! I am going to that high mountain,
For that will save me from all harm."
Noah cried, "Beware, do not so, mountains are now as grass;
Except the Friend none can save thee."
He answered, "Why should I listen to thy advice?
For thou desirest to make me one of thy flock.
Thy speech is by no means pleasing to me,
I am free from thee in this world and the next."

. . . . . .

Thus the more good advice Noah gave him,
The more stubborn refusals he returned.
Neither was his father tired of advising Canaan,
Nor did his advice make any impression on Canaan;
While they were yet talking a violent wave
Smote Canaan's head, and he was overwhelmed.

Reconciliation of the two traditions, "Acquiescence in infidelity is infidelity," and "Whoso acquiesces not in God's ordinance desires another Lord besides me" (p. 219).

Yesterday an inquirer questioned me,
Since he was interested in the foregoing narrative,
Saying, "The Prophet, whose words are as a seal,

[1] Koran xi. 44.

Said, 'Acquiescence in infidelity is infidelity.'
And again, 'Acquiescence in God's ordinance
Is incumbent on all true believers.'
Infidelity and hypocrisy are not ordained of God;
If I acquiesce in them I am at variance with God.
And yet, if I acquiesce not, that again is wrong;
What way of escape is there from this delemma?"
I said to him, "This infidelity is ordained, not ordinance,[1]
Though this infidelity is the work of the ordinance.
Therefore distinguish the ordinance from the ordained,
That thy difficulty may be at once removed.
I acquiesce in infidelity so far as it is God's ordinance,
Not so far as it is our evil and foul passions.
Infidelity *quâ* ordinance is not infidelity,
Call not God an infidel. Set not foot in this place.
Infidelity is folly, ordained infidelity wisdom,
How can mercy and vengeance be the same?
Ugliness of the picture is not ugliness of the painter,
Not so, for he erases ugly pictures.
The ability of the painter is shown in this,
That he can paint both ugly and beautiful pictures.
If I should pursue this argument properly,
So that questions and answers should be prolonged,
The unction of the mystery of love would escape me,
The picture of obedience would become another picture."

Bewilderment from intense love of God puts an end to all thinking and argument[2] (p. 219).

A certain man whose hair was half grey came in haste
To a barber who was a friend of his,
Saying, "Pluck out the white hairs from my beard,
For I have selected a young bride, O my son.
The barber cut off his beard and laid it before him,
Saying, "Do you part them, the task is beyond me."

[1] Or "decreed, not decree" (*maqzi nai qaza*). I confess I do not understand the distinction.

[2] See Gulshan i Raz, l. 287.

Questions are white and answers black; do you choose,
For the man of faith knows not how to choose.
Thus, one smote Zaid a blow,
And Zaid attacked him for his treachery.
The striker said, "Let me first ask you a question,
Give me an answer to it and then strike me;
I struck your back and a bruise appeared,
Now I ask you a question in all kindliness,
Did this bruise proceed from my hand,
Or from the smitten part of your back, O complainer?"
Zaid replied, "Through pain I am not in a condition
To enter upon thought and consideration of this.
You, who are free from pain, think this out;
Such trifling thoughts occur not to a man in pain."
[Men in pain have no time for other thoughts,
Whether you enter mosque or Christian church.
Your carelessness and injustice suggest thoughts
And unprecedented difficulties to your imagination.
The man in pain cares only for the faith,
He is aware only of man and his work.
He set's God's command upon his head and face,
And for thinking, he puts it aside.[1]]

Story VI. *The Lover who read Sonnets to his Mistress* (p. 220).

A lover was once admitted to the presence of his mistress, but, instead of embracing her, he pulled out a paper of sonnets and read them to her, describing her perfections and charms and his own love towards her at length. His mistress said to him, "You are now in my presence, and these lover's sighs and invocations are a waste of time. It is not the part of a true lover to waste his time in this way. It shows that I am not the real object of your affection, but that what you really love is your own effusions and ecstatic raptures. I see, as it were, the water which I have longed for before me, and yet you withhold it. I am, as it were, in Bulgaria, and the object of your love is in Cathay. One who is really loved is the single object of her lover, the Alpha and Omega of his desires. As for you, you are wrapped up in your own amorous raptures, depending on the varying states of your own feelings, instead of being wrapped up in me."

[1] The four last couplets are omitted in the Bulaq edition.

The true mystic must not stop at mere subjective religious emotions, but seek absolute union with God (p. 220).[1]

Whoso is restricted to religious raptures is but a man;
Sometimes his rapture is excessive, sometimes deficient.
The Sufi is, as it were, the "son of the season,"
But the pure (*Sáfi*) is exalted above season and state.
Religious raptures depend on feelings and will,
But the pure one is regenerated by the breath of Jesus.
You are a lover of your own raptures, not of me;
You turn to me only in hope of experiencing raptures.
Whoso is now defective, now perfect,
Is not adored by Abraham; he is "one that sets."
Because the stars set, and are now up, now down,
He loved them not; "I love not them that set."[2]
Whoso is now pleasing and now unpleasing
Is at one time water, at another fire.
He may be the house of the moon, but not the true moon;
Or as the picture of a mistress, but not the living one.
The mere Sufi is the "child of the season;"
He clings to seasons as to a father,
But the pure one is drowned in overwhelming love.
A child of any one is never free from season and state.
The pure one is drowned in the light "that is not begotten,"
"What begets not and is not begotten" is God.[3]
Go! seek such love as this, if you are alive;

[1] See Gulshan i Raz, l. 850.
[2] Koran vi. 77.
[3] Koran cxii. 3.

He was on his way, when he saw the famous Sheikh Pass by, riding on the back of a lion

If not, you are enslaved by varying seasons.
Gaze not on your own pictures, fair or ugly,
Gaze on your love and the object of your desire.
Gaze not at the sight of your own weakness or vileness,
Gaze at object of your desire, O exalted one.

STORY VII. *The Man who prayed earnestly to be fed without work* (p. 221).

In the time of the prophet David there was a man who used to pray day and night, saying, "Thou hast created me weak and helpless; give me my daily bread without obliging me to work for it." The people derided him for making such a foolish petition, but he still persisted, and at last a cow ran into his house of its own accord, and he killed and ate it. This illustrates the saying of the Prophet that God loves earnest petitioners, because He regards the sincerity of the prayer more than the nature of the thing prayed for. All things praise God, but the praises of inanimate things are different from the praises of men, and those of a Sunni different from those of a Compulsionist (*Jabri*). Each says the other is in the way of error, but none but the truly spiritual man knows the truth.

Knowledge or conviction opposed to opinion (p. 223).

Little is known by any one but the spiritual man,
Who has in his heart a touchstone of vital truth.
The others, hovering between two opinions,
Fly towards their nest on a single wing.
Knowledge has two wings, opinion only one wing;
Opinion is weak and lopsided in its flight.
The bird having but one wing quickly drops down,
And again flies on two steps or more.
This bird of opinion goes on rising and falling
On one wing, in hope to reach his nest.
When he escapes from opinion and knowledge is seen,
This bird gains two wings and spreads both of them.
Afterwards he "goes upright on a straight path,
Not grovelling on his face or creeping." [1]
He flies up on two wings even as the angel Gabriel,
Free of opinion, of duplicity, and of vain talk.
Though the whole world say to him,
"Thou art firm in the road of God's faith,"
He is not made more ardent by their saying this,
Nor is his lofty soul inclined from its course.
And though all say to him, "Thou art in the wrong way,
Thou thinkest thyself a rock who art but a blade of grass,"
He relapses not into opinion at their rebukes,
Nor is he vexed at their malevolence.
Nay, even if sea and mountains should cry out,
Saying, "Thou art mated with error,"
He would not relapse one jot into vain imaginations,
Nor would he be grieved by the reproaches of his foes.

STORY VIII. *The Boys and their Teacher* (p. 223).

To illustrate the force of imagination or opinion, a story is told of a trick played by boys upon their master. The boys wished to obtain a holiday, and the sharpest of them suggested that when the master came into the school each boy should condole with him on his alleged sickly appearance. Accordingly, when he entered, one said, "O master, how pale you are looking!" and another said, "You are looking very ill to-day," and so on. The master at first answered that there was nothing the matter with him, but as one boy after another continued assuring him that he looked very ill, he was at length deluded into imagining that he must really be ill. So he returned to his house, making the boys follow him there, and told his wife that he was not well, bidding her mark how pale he was. His wife assured him he was not looking pale, and offered to

[1] Koran lxvii. 22.

convince him by bringing a mirror; but he refused to look at it, and took to his bed. He then ordered the boys to begin their lessons; but they assured him that the noise made his head ache, and he believed them, and dismissed them to their homes, to the annoyance of their mothers. *Apropos* of the sharpness of the boy who devised this trick, the poet takes occasion to controvert the opinion of the *Mu'tazalites*, that all men are born with equal ability, and to express his agreement with the doctrine of the *Sunnis,* that the innate capacities of men vary very greatly.

STORY IX. *The Darvesh who Broke his Vow* (p. 225).

There was once a Darvesh who took up his abode in the mountains, in order to enjoy perfect solitude. In that place were many fruit-trees, and the Darvesh made a vow that he would never pluck any of the fruit, but eat only what was shaken down by the wind. For a long time he kept his vow; but a time came when there was no wind, and consequently no fruit was shaken down. The Darvesh was true to his vow for five days, but he could then endure the pangs of hunger no longer, and he stretched out his hand and plucked some of the fruit from the branches. The reason of this lapse on his part was that he had omitted to say "If God will" when making his vow; and as nothing can be accomplished without God's aid, he could not possibly keep his vow. Shortly afterwards the chief of the police visited the mountains in pursuit of a band of robbers, and arrested the Darvesh along with them, and cut off his hand. When he discovered his mistake he apologised very earnestly; but the Darvesh reassured him, saying that men were not to blame, as God had evidently designed to punish him for breaking his vow by depriving him of the hand which had sinned in plucking the fruit.[1]

[1] Cp. Cranmer.

All things dependent upon the will of God (p. 226).

Therefore hath God commanded, "Make an exception,
Couple the words 'If God will' with your vows.[1]
Because the governance of actions is in my hands,
The wills of all are subject to my will.
Every moment I impart a fresh bias to the heart,
Every instant I set a fresh mark on the heart;
Each day I am engaged in a fresh work,[2]
There is naught that swerves from my purpose."
There is a tradition, "The heart is like a feather
In the desert, which is borne captive by the winds;[3]
The wind drives it everywhere at random,
Now to right and now to left in opposite directions."
According to another tradition, know the heart is like
To water in a kettle boiling on the fire.
So every moment a fresh purpose occurs to the heart,
Not proceeding from itself, but from its situation.
Why, then, are you confident about the heart's purposes?
Why make you vows only to be covered with shame?
All these changes proceed from the effect of God's will;
Although you see the pit, you cannot avoid it.
The strange thing is, not that winged fowl
Fall into the deadly snare without seeing it,
But that they see the snare and the limed twig,
And yet fall into it, whether they will or no;
Their eyes and ears are open and the snare is in front,
Yet they fly into the snare with their own wings!

Comparison of the divine decrees to something that is hidden, yet whose effects are seen (p. 226).

Behold that king's son clad in rags,
With bare head and fallen into distress;
Consumed by lusts and riotous living,

[1] Koran xviii. 23.
[2] Koran lv. 29; cp. John v. 17.
[3] Freytag, Arabum Proverbia, vol. iii. p. 490.

Having sold all his clothes and substance;
Having lost house and home, utterly disgraced,
Fulfilling the desire of his enemies by his disgrace.
If he sees a pious man he cries, " O sir,
Aid me, for the love of God;
For I have fallen into this dire disgrace;
I have squandered goods and gold and wealth.
Aid me so that perchance I may escape hence,
And extricate myself from this deep slough."
He repeats this prayer to high and low,
" Release me, release me, release me!"
His eyes and ears are open, and he is free from bonds,
No jailer watches him, no chain binds him;
What, then, is the bond from which he asks release?
What is the prison from which he seeks an exit?
'Tis the bond of God's purpose and hidden decrees;
Ah! none but the pure in sight can see that bond;
Though not visible, that bond exists in concealment;
'Tis more stringent than prison or chains of iron,
For the mason can pull down prison walls,
And blacksmiths can break asunder iron chains;
But, strange to say, this ponderous hidden bond,—
Blacksmiths are impotent to break this asunder!
Ahmad alone could see that bond on Omm Jahil's back,[1]
And the rope of palm fibre bound upon her neck;
Yea, he saw wood on the back of the wife of Bu Lahab,
And she, the bearer of the firewood, said it was heavy.
No eye but his saw that rope and that firewood,
For to him things unseen were visible.
The others explained it, saying
That Ahmad was beside himself, and they in their senses.
Nevertheless from the weight of the load her back bent,
And she complained of its weight before him,
Saying, " Aid me to escape from this load,
And to shake off this grievous burden."
He who sees clearly these indications,
Does he not know also the doomed from the elect?
Yea, he knows them, yet conceals it by command of God,
Since God permits him not to reveal it.

[1] See Koran cxi.: Abu Lahab, at the instigation of his wife, Omm Jahil, rejected Muhammad's claim to the prophetic office, and Muhammad declared that they should be "burned in the fiery flame," and the wife "laden with firewood, and on her neck a rope of palm fibre."

STORY X. *The Old Man who made no Lamentation at the Death of his Sons* (p. 229).

After short anecdotes of Pharaoh's magicians, of the mule who complained to the camel that he was always stumbling, and of the prophet Ezra, comes the story of the old man who wept not for the death of his sons.

An old man who was noted for sanctity, and who realised the saying of the Prophet, " The *'ulama* of the faith are as the prophets of Israel," lost all his sons, but showed no grief or regret. His wife therefore rebuked him for his want of feeling, whereupon he replied to her as follows:—

He turned to his wife and said, " O dame,
The harvest of December is not as that of July;
Though they be dead or though they be living,
Are they not equally visible to the eyes of the heart?
I behold them clearly before me,
Wherefore should I disfigure my countenance like you?
Though they have gone forth by revolution of fortune,
They are with me still, playing round me.
The cause of lamentation is separation or parting,
But I am still with my dear ones, and embrace them.
Ordinary people may see them in dreams,
But I see them clearly, though wide awake.
I conceal myself a while from this world,
I shake down the leaves of outward sense from the tree.
Know, O wife, outward sense is captive to reason,
And reason, again, is captive to spirit.

Spirit unlooses the chained hands of reason;
Yea, it opens all things that are closed.
Sensations and thoughts resemble weeds
Which occupy the surface of pure water.
The hand of reason puts these weeds aside,
And the pure water is then visible to the wise.
Weeds in plenty cover the stream like bubbles;
When they are swept aside, the water is seen;
But when God unlooses not the hands of reason,
The weeds on our water grow thick through carnal lust;
Yea, they cover up your water more and more,
While your lust is smiling and your reason weeping.
When fear of God binds the hands of lust,
Then God unlooses the two hands of reason.
Then the powerful senses are subdued by you,
When you submit to reason as your commander.
Then your sleepless sense is lulled into sleep,
That mysteries may appear to the soul.
You behold visions when broad awake,
And the gates of heaven are open before you."

STORY XI. *Bahlol and the Darvesh* (p. 232.)

The foregoing story is followed by anecdotes of a blind saint who was miraculously enabled to read the Koran, of Luqman and David, and a description of the saints who, mindful of the saying, "Patience is the key of happiness," resign themselves to the dispensations of Providence, and never pray to have them altered. The story of Bahlol and the Darvesh is then given as an example of this resignation to the will of God. Bahlol once paid a visit to a saintly Darvesh, and asked him how he fared. The Darvesh replied, "I fare like a man who directs the course of the world as he wills, to whom death and life are subservient, and whom the stars themselves obey." Bahlol then pressed him to explain his meaning more clearly, and the Darvesh replied as follows:—

He said, "This at least is notorious to all men,
That the world obeys the command of God.
Not a leaf falls from a tree
Without the decree and command of that Lord of lords;
Not a morsel goes from the mouth down the throat
Till God says to it, 'Go down.'
Desire and appetite, which are the reins of mankind,
Are themselves subservient to the rule of God.

. . . . . .

Hear this much, that, whereas the totality of actions
Is not effected without God's direction,
When the decree of God becomes the pleasure of man,
Then man desires the fulfilment of God's decrees;
And this too spontaneously, not in hope of reward,
But because his very nature is congruous therewith.
He desires not even his own life for himself,
Nor is he relying on the hope of sweets of life to come.
Whatever path is taken by the eternal decree,
Whether it be life or death, 'tis all one to him.
He lives for the sake of God, not for wealth;
He dies for the sake of God, not in fear and grief.
His faith is based on his desire to do God's will,
Not on hope to gain paradise with its groves and founts.
His avoidance of infidelity is also for God's sake,
It proceeds not from fear of falling into the fire.
Thus this temper of his arises from his very nature,
Not from any discipline and endeavour of his own.
At times he laughs when he contemplates God's pleasure,
God's decrees are to him as sweetmeats of sugar.
I ask, does not the world march agreeably to the will
And commands of a man rejoicing in this disposition?
Why, then, should such an one make prayers and petitions,
Saying, 'O God, change such and such a decree?'
His own death and his children's deaths
For God's sake seem to him as sweets in the mouth.
In the view of that faithful one his children's deaths
Are as sweetmeats to a starving beggar.

Why, therefore, should he make prayers
Unless he pray for what is pleasing to God?
These prayers and petitions, not those of self-pity
Make that man to be endued with salvation.
He utterly burned up all his self-pity,
At the time when he lit the lamp of love to God.
His love was the hell that burned up his inclinations;
Yea, he burned up his own inclinations one by one."

STORY XII. *The Visions seen by the Saint Daqúqi* (p. 232).

To illustrate the exalted state of identification of the will with the Divine will just described, the poet tells the story of the visions and mighty works of the holy Daqúqi. Daqúqi was journeying in pious fervour, and in hope to see the splendour of "The Friend" in human shape, the Ocean in a drop of water, and the Sun in an atom, when late one evening he arrived at the sea-shore. Turning his eyes to heaven, he saw seven great lights never before seen of men, for "God directs whom He will."[1] Overwhelmed with awe, he watched these lights, and while he still watched them they united into one light. Still more amazed, he watched on, and the single light shortly assumed the likeness of seven men. Afterwards these seven men changed into seven trees; but, strange to say, although crowds of people were passing by, none of them could see these trees, so that Daqúqi shared the feelings of the apostles "who lost all hope" (of convincing the world), "and deemed that they were reckoned as liars."[2] Possessing his soul in patience, Daqúqi still watched on, and saw the seven trees bowing down in prayer, and was reminded of the text, "Plants and trees bend in adoration."[3] Presently the seven trees again changed into seven men, and Daqúqi was appointed to conduct their devotions. While he was yet acting as Imam in front of them, and they were following the prayers he recited, a ship was seen in great distress and all but lost. At Daqúqi's earnest prayer the crew were saved, but straightway vanished from sight; and this led his followers to doubt the reality of the miracle which had just been performed before their eyes.

[1] Koran ii. 136. [2] Koran xii. 110. [3] Koran lv. 5.

Description of a saint whose will was identified with God's will (p. 232).

That Daqúqi possessed a sweet aspect,
As a lover of God and a worker of miracles.
He resembled the moon of heaven come down on earth,
He was as a light to them that walked in darkness.
He rarely tarried in one place,
And seldom stayed two days in one village.
He said, "If I tarry in one house two days,
Attachment to that house becomes a passion with me.
I guard myself from being deceived into loving a home;
Up! Soul, and travel in search of eternal wealth.
My heart's inclination is not satisfied by houses,
So that they should be places of temptation for me."
Thus by day he travelled, and by night prayed,
His eyes were always gazing on the King as a falcon's;
Cut off from mankind, though not for any fault,
Severed from men and women, though not for baseness;
Having compassion on mankind, and wholesome as water,
A kind intercessor, and one whose prayers were heard.
Benevolent to the good and the bad, and a firm ally,
Better than a mother, and kinder than a father.
The Prophet said, "To you, O blessed ones,
I am as a father, affectionate and indulgent;
For this cause, that you are all portions of me."
Wherefore should you tear away the parts from the whole?
If the part be severed from its whole it is useless;
If a limb be rent from the body it dies.
Till it is again joined to its whole,
'Tis a dead thing, and a stranger to life.
. . . .

Thus Daqúqi, in devotions and praises and prayers,
Was ever seeking the particular favourites of God.
Throughout his long journeyings his object was this,
To interchange a word with the favourites of God.
He cried continually as he went his way,
"O Lord, let me draw near to Thy chosen ones!"

. . . . . .

So Daqúqi (the mercy of God be upon him!)
Said, "I journeyed long time to East and to West,
I journeyed years and months for love of that Moon,
Heedless of the way, absorbed in God.
With bare feet I trod upon thorns and flints,
Seeing I was bewildered, and beside myself, and senseless.
Think not my feet touched the earth,
For the lover verily travels with the heart.
What knows the heart of road and stages?
What of distant and near, while it is drunk with love?
Distance and nearness are attributes of bodies,
The journeyings of spirits are after another sort.
You journeyed from the embryo state to rationality
Without footsteps or stages or change of place,
The journey of the soul involves not time and place.
And my body learnt from the soul its mode of journeying,
Now my body has renounced the bodily mode of journeying;
It journeys secretly and without form, though under a form."
He added, "One day I was thus filled with longing
To behold in human form the splendours of 'The Friend,'
To witness the Ocean gathered up into a drop,
The Sun compressed into a single atom;
And when I drew near to the shore of the sea
The day was drawing to a close."

All religions are in substance one and the same (p. 237).

In the adorations and benedictions of righteous men
The praises of all the prophets are kneaded together.
All their praises are mingled into one stream,
All the vessels are emptied into one ewer.
Because He that is praised is, in fact, only One,
In this respect all religions are only one religion.
Because all praises are directed towards God's light,
Their various forms and figures are borrowed from it.
Men never address praises but to One deemed worthy,
They err only through mistaken opinions of Him.
So, when a light falls upon a wall,
That wall is a connecting-link between all its beams;
Yet when it casts that reflection back to its source,
It wrongly shows great as small, and halts in its praises.
Or if the moon be reflected in a well,
And one looks down the well, and mistakenly praises it,
In reality he is intending to praise the moon,
Although, through ignorance, he is looking down the well.
The object of his praises is the moon, not its reflection;
His infidelity arises from mistake of the circumstances.
That well-meaning man goes wrong through his mistake;
The moon is in heaven, and he fancies it in the well.
By these false idols mankind are perplexed,
And driven by vain lusts to their sorrow.

STORY VII. (*continued*). *The Man in the time of the Prophet David who prayed to be fed without having to work for his food* (p. 241).

After the petitioner had slain and eaten the cow, the owner of the cow came up and accused him of theft, and seizing him by the collar, dragged him before the judgment-seat of the prophet David. When he had stated his case, David ordered the accused to make restitution, telling him that he must not break the law. At this order the accused redoubled his cries, telling David that he was siding with an oppressor. David was staggered at the man's assurance, and finally resolved to take further time for consideration before deciding the case. After private meditation he reversed his former sentence, and directed the plaintiff to relinquish his claim. On the plaintiff refusing to do this, and stoutly protesting against David's injustice, David further ordered that all the plaintiff's goods should be given to the accused. The reason for this decision was, that David discovered the plaintiff had formerly slain the grandfather of the accused, and stolen all his goods. David then led all the Musulmans to a tree in the desert where the murder had been perpetrated, and there put the murderer to death.

The hands and feet of criminals betray their crimes even in this world (p. 244).

He of himself lifted the veil that hid his crime;
Had he not done so, God would have kept it hidden.
Criminals and sinners, even in the course of sinning,
Themselves rend the coverings of their crimes.
Their sins are veiled among the heart's secrets,
Yet the criminal himself exposes them to view,
Saying, "Behold me wearing a pair of horns,
A cow of hell in sight of all men."
Thus, even here, in the midst of thy sin, thy hand and foot
Bear witness of the secrets of thy heart.
Thy secret thought is as a governor who says to thee,
"Tell forth thy convictions, withhold them not;"
Especially in seasons of passion and angry talk
It betrays thy secrets one by one.
Thy secret sins and crimes govern hand and foot,
Saying, "Disclose us to men, O hand and foot!"
And since these witnesses take the bit in their mouths,
Especially in times of passion and wrath and revenge,
Therefore the same God who appointed this governor
To blazen forth thy secret sins to the world
Is also able to create many more governors
To divulge thy secret sins on the day of judgment.[1]
O man whose only handiwork is crime and sin,
Thy secret sins are manifest; no divulging is needed.
There is no need to proclaim thy sins,
All men are cognisant of thy sin-burnt heart.
Thy soul every moment casts up sparks of fire,
Which say, "See me a man destined to the fire;
I am a part of the fire, and go to join my whole;
Not a light, so that I should join the Source of light."

Comparison of lust to the murderer in the story (p. 245).

Kill thine own lust and give life to the world;
It has killed its lord, reduce it to servitude.
That claimant of the cow is thy lust; Beware!
It has made itself lord and master.
That slayer of the cow is thy reason; Go!
Be not obdurate to the prayers of him that kills the cow.
Reason is a poor captive, and ever cries to God
For meat on its dish without labouring and toiling.
On what depends its getting meat without toiling?
On its killing the cow of the body, the source of evil.
Lust says, "Why hast thou killed my cow?"
It says, "Because lust's cow is the form of the body."[2]
Reason, the Lord's child, has become a pauper,
Lust, the murderer, has become a lord and chief.
Know'st thou what is meat untoiled for?
'Tis the food of spirits and the aliment of the Prophet.
But it is attainable only by slaying the cow;
Treasure is gained by digging, O digger of treasure!

[1] "On that day shall their hands speak unto us, and their feet shall bear witness of that which they have done" (Koran xxxvi. 65).

[2] Baháu-'d-Din Amili, in his Nán wa Halwa, chap. iv., compares lust to a cow, referring to Koran ii. 63.

Story XIII. *The People of Saba* (p. 247).

After an anecdote of 'Isa being obliged to ascend a mountain to get away from the fools comes the story of the men of Saba. "A sign there was to Saba in their dwelling-places—two gardens, the one on the right hand and the other on the left;—'Eat ye of your Lord's supplies, and give thanks to Him; goodly is the country and gracious is the Lord.' But they turned aside, so we sent upon them the flood of Iram. Such was our retribution on them for their ingratitude."[1] The men of Saba were all fools, and brought destruction on themselves by their ingratitude to God. One was far-sighted, and yet blind; another sharp of hearing, and yet deaf; and a third naked, and yet wearing a long robe. Avarice is blind to its own faults, but sees those of others; the sharp-eared deaf man hears death approaching others, but not himself, and the long-robed naked man is he who fears robbers, though he has nothing to lose. In fact, all these men of Saba were afflicted with follies and self-delusions of this kind, and gave no thanks to God for the blessings which they enjoyed. Accordingly thirteen prophets were sent to admonish them, but their admonitions were not listened to, the men of Saba questioning their divine mission and demanding a miracle as a sign. They also told the prophets a parable of a clever hare, who, wishing to frighten an elephant away from a fountain, went to the elephant, pretending to be an ambassador from the moon.[2] The prophets were naturally indignant at the effrontery of the men of Saba in misapplying parables to discredit their divine mission, and reminded them that wicked men had flouted the prophet Noah in the same way when he was warning them of the flood. And they demonstrated at length how the men of Saba had misapplied the parable of the hare and the elephant, and again adjured them to believe. But the men of Saba continued refractory, and would not accept the Prophets' counsels. They plied the prophets with the arguments of the Compulsionists (*Jabriyán*), and refused to be convinced of the fallacy of their reasoning. So at last the prophets despaired of them, and left them to their doom.

[1] Koran xxxiv. 14.
[2] Anvar i Suhaili, chap. iv. Story IV.

Not every one can properly use similitudes and parables in divine matters (p. 252).

The faculty of using similitudes is peculiar to a saint
Who is signally marked by knowledge of hidden mysteries.
What know you of the mystery hid in aught, that you
In your folly should use similitudes of curl and cheek?
Moses took his staff to be a stick, though it was not;
It was a serpent, and its mystery was revealed.
If a saint such as he knew not the mystery of a stick,
What know you of the mystery of the snare and grains?
When the eye of a Moses erred as to a similitude,
How can a presumptuous mouse understand one?
Those similitudes of yours are changed into serpents
To tear you into pieces with their jaws.
Such a parable did cursed Iblis use,
So that he became cursed of God till the day of doom.
Such a parable did Korah use in his argument,
So that he was swallowed up in the earth with his wealth.
Such parables know to be as crows and owls,
Whereby a hundred households are annihilated.
When Noah was building the ark in the desert,
A hundred parable-mongers attacked him with irony,
Saying, "In the desert, where is no water or well,
He builds a boat! What ignorant folly is this!"

The arguments of the Jabriyán, i.e., the Fatalists or Compulsionists (p. 255).

The men of Saba said, "O preachers, enough!
What you say is enough, if there are any wise here.
God has placed a 'lock upon our hearts,'[1]
And no man can overcome the Creator.
That great Painter has painted us thus;
His painting cannot be altered by argument.
Keep telling for ever a stone to become a ruby,
Keep telling for ever the old to become young!
Tell earth to assume the quality of water,
Bid water to become honey or milk!
God is the creator of heaven and them that dwell therein;
Also of water and of earth, and them that dwell therein;
To heaven He gave its revolutions and its purity,
To the earth its dark look and appearance.
Can the heaven will to become as dregs?
Can earth will to assume the clearness of pure wine?
That Person has assigned to each its lot,
Can mountain by endeavour become as grass?"
The prophets answered, "Verily God has created
Some qualities in you which you cannot alter;
But He has created other accidental qualities,
Which, being objectionable, may be made good.
Bid stone become gold—that is impossible;
Bid copper become gold—that is possible.
Bid sand bloom as a rose—it cannot;
Bid dust turn to mud—that is within its capacity.
God has sent some pains for which there is no cure,
Such, for instance, as lameness, loss of nose, and blindness.
God has sent other pains for which there are cures,
To wit, crooked mouth and headache.
God has ordained these remedies of His mercy;
The use of these in pain and anguish is not in vain.

[1] Koran xxxvi. 6.

Nay, the majority of pains may be cured;
When you seek those cures earnestly you find them."
The men of Saba replied, "O men, these pains of ours
Are not of the sort that admit of cure.
Long time ye utter these presages and warnings,
But our bonds are made thereby heavier every moment.
If our sickness admitted of a cure,
It would certainly have been lessened by your spells.
When the body is obstructed water reaches not the liver,
Though one drinks the ocean, it passes elsewhere.
Then of course the hands and feet become dropsical,
And yet that draught does not quench his thirst."
The prophets replied, "To despair is wrong,
The mercy and grace of God are boundless.
One must not despair of the grace of such a Benefactor,
One must cling to the stirrup-straps of God.
Ah! many are the conditions which at first are hard,
But are afterwards relieved and lose their harshness.
Oftentimes hope succeeds to hopelessness,
Many times does sunlight succeed to darkness.
We admit that ye are weighted as with stones,
And that ye have locks upon your ears and your hearts.[1]
No condition of ours is altogether as we wish,
Our business is to be resigned and to obey.
God has enjoined this servitude upon us;
We say not this merely on our own authority.
We enjoy life on condition of doing His will;
If He bids us, we sow our seed upon the sand.
The soul of the prophet cares for naught but God,
It has naught to do with approving or disapproving His works."

. . . .

The men of Saba replied, "If ye yourselves are happy,
Ye make us miserable and annoy and disturb us.
Our souls were void of all anxieties,
And ye have plunged us into cares and anxieties.

[1] Koran lxi. 5: "God led their hearts astray."

The comfort and harmony which we enjoyed heretofore
Have been rent in pieces by your evil presages.
We used to be as parrots munching sugar,
Ye have made us as fowls brooding on death.
On every side stories inspiring anxiety,
On every side sounds exciting fears:
On every side in the world an evil presage,
On every side evil portents threatening punishment:—
This is the burden of your parables and presages,
This the purport of your awe-inspiring stories."
The prophets replied, "Our evil presages
Are corroborated by the state of your souls.
Suppose you are sleeping in a place of danger,
And serpents are drawing near to bite your heads,
A kind friend will inform you of your danger,
Saying, 'Jump up, lest the serpent devour you.'
You reply, 'Why do you utter evil presages?'
He answers, 'What presage? Up, and see for yourself!
By means of this evil presage I rouse you,
And release you from danger and lead you to your home.'
Like a prophet he warns you of hidden danger,
For a prophet sees what worldlings cannot see."

Mercy inclines the good to devotion, but vengeance the bad (p. 257).

If you do a kindness to a generous man, 'tis fitting,
For each kindness he will return seven hundredfold.
When you treat a base man with scorn and contumely,
He will become your slave in all sincerity.
Infidels when enjoying prosperity do wrong,
When they are in hell they cry, "O our Lord!"
For base men are purified when they suffer evil,
And when they enjoy prosperity they do evil.
Wherefore the mosque of their devotion is hell,
As the snare is the fetter of wild fowl.
The prison is the hermitage of the wicked thief,
For when he is there he is ever crying to God.
Whereas the object of man's being is to worship God,
Hell is ordained as a place of worship for the proud.[1]
Man has the power to engage in any actions soever,
But worship of God is the main object of his existence.
Read the text,[2] "I have not created Jinns and men but to worship me."
The only object of the world is to worship God.
Though the object of a book is to teach an art,
If you make a pillow of it, it serves that purpose too.
Yet its main object is not to serve as a pillow,
But to impart knowledge and useful instruction.
If you use a sword for a tent-peg,
You prefer the worse use of it to the better.
Though the object of all men's being is wisdom,
Yet each man has a different place of worship.
The place of worship of the noble is nobility,
The place of worship of the base is degradation.
Smite the base to make them bow the head,
Give to the noble to make them repay liberally.
Inasmuch as the base are evil and arrogant,
Hell and humbling are the "small gate" for them.
Verily God has created two places of adoration,
Hell for the base and increased bliss for the noble.
Even so Moses made a small gate in Jerusalem,[3]
To make the Israelites bow the head in entering it.

The discussion is continued and illustrated by anecdotes of the Sufi who preferred a table with no food upon it, because he ever sought "not-being," of Jacob's vision of Joseph, and of a devout slave who obtained leave of his master to say his prayers in a mosque, but tarried there so long that the doors were shut, and he could not get out, nor his master in. The prophets at last despaired of making any impression upon the unbelievers, but called to

[1] God said, "Come ye either in obedience, or in spite of your wishes" (Koran xli. 10).

[2] Koran li. 56.

[3] See Koran ii. 55, with Sale's note.

mind the text "When at last the Apostles lost all hope, and deemed that they were reckoned as liars, our aid reached them, and we delivered whom we would, but our vengeance was not averted from the wicked."[1]

The despair of the prophets (p. 259).

The prophets said, "How long, in our benevolence,
Shall we give to this and that one good advice?
How long shall we hammer cold iron in vain?
How long waste breath in blowing into a lattice?
Men are moved by God's decree and fixed ordinance,[2]
As sharp-set teeth are caused by heat of belly.
'Tis Primal Soul that dominates the Second Soul,[3]
Fish begins to stink at the head, not the tail.
Yet be advised and keep your steed straight as an arrow,
When God says 'Proclaim' we must obey.[4]
O men, ye know not to which party ye belong,[5]
Exert yourselves then, till ye see which ye are.
When you place goods upon a ship,
You do it in trust that the voyage will be prosperous;
You know not which of the two events will befall you,
Whether you will be drowned or come safe to land.
If you say, 'Till I know which will be my fate
I will not set foot upon the ship;
Shall I be drowned on the voyage or a survivor?
Reveal to me in which class I shall be.
I shall not undertake the voyage on the chance—
On the bare hope of reaching land, as the rest do.'
In that case no trade at all will be undertaken by you,
As the secret of these two events is always hidden.
The lamp of the heart, that is a timid trader,

[1] Koran xii. 11.
[2] "All things have we created after a fixed decree,
Every action great and small is written."
—Koran liv. 49.
[3] The Logos or first Emanation produced the second or "Universal Soul."
[4] "O Apostle! proclaim all that hath been sent down" (Koran v. 71).
[5] "Which party," *i.e.*, those doomed to be saved or those doomed to destruction.

Acquires neither loss nor gain by its ventures.[1]
Nay, it acquires loss, for it is precluded from gain;
'Tis the lamp that takes fire that acquires light.
Since all things are dependent on probability,
Religion is so first of all, for thereby you find release.
In this world no knocking at the door is possible
Save hope, and God knows what is best."

Probability the guide of life in religion as well as in common matters. "Religion dependent on hope and fear"[2] (p. 259).

The final cause of trading is hope or probability,
When traders work themselves lean as spindles.[3]
When the merchant goes to his shop in the morning,
He does so in hope and probability of gaining bread.
If you have no hope of getting bread, why go?
There is the fear of loss, since you are not strong.
But does not this fear of utter loss in your trade
Become weakened in the course of your exertions?
You say, "Although the fear of loss is before me,
Yet I feel greater fear in remaining idle.
I have a better hope through exerting myself;
My fear is increased by remaining idle."
Why then, O faint-hearted one, in the matter of religion
Are you paralysed by the fear of loss?
See you not how the traders in this market of ours
Make large profits, both apostles and saints?
What a mine of wealth awaits them on leaving it,
Seeing they make such profits while still here!
Fire is soft to them as cotton raiment,
The ocean bears them gently like a porter;
Iron in their hands is soft as wax,
The winds are their obedient slaves.

[1] "Nothing shall be reckoned to a man save that for which he hath made effort" (Koran liii. 40).
[2] So Sa'di Bostan, Book I. Cp. Butler's Analogy, Conclusion.
[3] *I.e.*, exert themselves much.

STORY XIV. *Miracles performed by the Prophet Muhammad* (p. 260).

It is related that the Prophet was once present at a banquet, and after he had eaten and drunk, his servant Anas threw the napkin which he had used into the fire, and the napkin was not burnt, but only purified by the fire. On another occasion a caravan of Arabs was travelling in the desert, and was in sore distress through lack of water, whereupon the Prophet miraculously increased the water in a single water-skin, so that it sufficed to supply the needs of all the travellers. Moreover, the negro who carried the water-skin was rendered as white and fair as Joseph. Again, a heathen woman came to the Prophet carrying her infant, aged only two months, and the infant saluted the Prophet as the veritable apostle of God. Again, when the prophet was about to put on his sandals, an eagle swooped down upon one of them and carried it off, when a viper was seen to drop from the sandal. The Prophet was at first inclined to grumble at this stroke of ill-luck; but when he saw the viper his discontent was turned into thankfulness to God, who had thus miraculously saved him from being bitten by the viper.

In difficulties there is provided a way of salvation [1] (p. 263).

In this tale there is a warning for thee, O Soul,
That thou mayest acquiesce in God's ordinances,
And be wary and not doubt God's benevolence,
When sudden misfortunes befall thee.
Let others grow pale from fear of ill fortune,
Do thou smile like the rose at loss and gain;
For the rose, though its petals be torn asunder,
Still smiles on, and it is never cast down.
It says, "Why should I fall into grief in disgrace?
I gather beauty even from the thorn of disgrace."
Whatsoever is lost to thee through God's decree
Know of a surety is so much gained from misfortune.
What is Sufiism? 'Tis to find joy in the heart
Whensoever distress and care assail it.
Know troubles to be that eagle of the Prophet's
Which carried off the sandal of that holy one,
In order to save his foot from the bite of the viper—
O excellent device!—to preserve him from harm.
'Tis said, "Mourn not for your slaughtered cattle
If a wolf has harried your flocks;"
For that calamity may avert a greater calamity,
And that loss may ward off a more grievous loss.

[1] Freytag, Arabum Proverbia, vol. iii. p. 334.

STORY XV. *The Man who asked Moses to teach him the language of animals* (p. 264).

A certain man came to Moses and desired to be taught the language of animals, for, he said, men used their language only to get food and for purposes of deception, and possibly a knowledge of animals' languages might stimulate his faith. Moses was very unwilling to comply with his request, as he knew such knowledge would prove destructive to him, but, on his persisting, took counsel of God, and finally taught him the language of fowls and dogs. Next morning the man went amongst the fowls, and heard a discussion between the cock and the dog. The dog was abusing the cock for picking up the morsels of bread which fell from their master's table, because the cock could find plenty of grains of corn to eat, whereas the dog could only eat bread. The cock, to appease him, said that on the morrow the master's horse would die, and then the dog would have enough and to spare. The master, hearing this, at once sold his horse, and the dog, being disappointed of his meal, again attacked the cock. The cock then told him the mule would die, whereupon the master sold the mule. Then the cock foretold the

Digging a grave when burial was not practised
Required good thinking and wiliness.

death of a slave, and the master again sold the slave. At this the dog, losing patience, upbraided the cock as the chief of deceivers, and the cock excused himself by showing that all three deaths had taken place just as he had predicted, but the master had sold the horse, mule, and slave, and had thrown the loss on others. He added that, to punish him for his fraudulent dealing, the master would himself die on the morrow, and there would be plenty for the dog to eat at the funeral feast. Hearing this, the master went to Moses in great distress, and prayed to be saved. Moses besought the Lord for him, and gained permission that he should die in the peace of God.

Why freewill is good for man (p. 264).

God said, "Do thou grant his earnest request,
Enlarge his faculty according to his freewill.
Freewill is as the salt to piety,
Otherwise heaven itself were matter of compulsion.
In its revolutions reward and punishment were needless,
For 'tis freewill that has merit at the great reckoning.
If the whole world were framed to praise God,
There would be no merit in praising God.
Place a sword in his hand and remove his impotence,
To see if he turns out a warrior or a robber.
Because freewill is that wherewith 'we honour Adam,'[1]
Half the swarm become bees and half wasps.
The faithful yield honeycombs like bees,
The infidels yield store of poison like wasps.
For the faithful feed on choice herbs,
So that, like bees, their chyle yields life-giving food,
Whilst infidels feed on filth and garbage,
And generate poison according to their food."
Men inspired of God are the fountain of life;
Men of delusions are a synonym for death.
In the world the praise "Well done, faithful servant!"
Is given to freewill which is used with prudence.
If all dissolute men were shut up in prison,
They would all be temperate and devout and pious.
When power of choice is absent actions are worthless;
But beware lest death snatch away your capital!
Your power of choice is a capital yielding profit,
Remember well the day of final account!

[1] Koran xvii. 72.

Story XVI. *The Woman who lost all her infants* (p. 267).

A woman bore many children in succession, but none of them lived beyond the age of three or four months. In great distress she cried to God, and then beheld in a vision the beautiful gardens of Paradise, and many fair mansions therein, and upon one of these mansions she read her own name inscribed. And a voice from heaven informed her that God would accept the sorrows she had endured in lieu of her blood shed in holy war, as, owing to her sex, she was unable to go out to battle like the men. On looking again, the woman beheld in Paradise all the children she had lost, and she cried, "O Lord! they were lost to me, but were safe with Thee!"

This story is followed by anecdotes of Hamza going out to battle without his coat-of-mail, of the Prophet advising a man who complained of being cheated in his bargains to take time before completing them, and of the death of Bilal, Muhammad's crier, and by illustrations of the illusive nature of the world, of the difference between things self-evident and mere matters of inference, and between knowing a thing through illustrations and on the authority of others and knowing it as it really is in its essence.

The difference between knowing a thing merely by similitudes and on the authority of others, and knowing the very essence thereof (p. 272).

God's mercy is known through the fruits thereof,
But who save God knows His essence? [1]
No one knows the very essence of God's attributes
But only in their effects and by similitudes.
A child knows naught of the nature of sexual intercourse,
Except what you tell him, that it is like sweetmeats.
Yet how far does the pleasure of sexual intercourse
Really resemble that derived from sweetmeats?
Nevertheless the fiction produces a relation
Between you, with your perfect knowledge, and the child;
So that the child knows the matter by a similitude,
Though he knows not its essence or actual nature.
Hence if he says, "I know it," 'tis not far wrong,
And if he says, "I know it not," 'tis not wrong.
Should one say, "Do you know Noah,
That prophet of God and luminary of the Spirit?"
If you say, "Do I not know him, for that moon
Is more famed than the sun and moon of heaven?
Little children in their schools,
And elders in their mosques,
All read his name prominently in the Koran,
And preachers tell his story from times of yore;"—
You say true, for you know him by report,
Though the real nature of Noah is not revealed to you.
On the other hand, if you say, "What know I of Noah
As his contemporaries knew him?
I am a poor ant—what can I know of the elephant?
What knows a fly of the motions of the elephant?"—
This statement also is true, O brother,
Seeing that you know not his real nature.
But this impotence to perceive real essence,
Though common to ordinary men, is not universal;
Because essence and its deepest secrets
Are open and manifest to the eyes of the perfect.

. . . .

Negation and affirmation of one proposition are lawful;
When the aspects differ the relation is double.
"Thou castest not when thou castest" [1] shows such relation,
Here negation and affirmation are both correct.
Thou castest it, since it is in thy hand,
Thou castest not, since 'tis God who affords the strength.
The might of the sons of Adam is limited,
How can a handful of sand shatter an army?
The sand was in man's hands, the casting was God's.
Owing to the two relations negation and affirmation are both true.
The infidels know the prophets,
As well as they doubtless know their own children;
Yea, the infidels know them as well as their own sons,
By a hundred tokens and a hundred evidences,
But from envy and malice conceal their knowledge,
And incline themselves to say, "We know them not."
So when God says in one place "knows them,"
In another He says, "None knows them beside me."
For in truth they are hid under God's overshadowing, [2]
And none but God knows them by actual experience.
Therefore take this declaration with its context,
Remembering how you know and do not know Noah.

STORY XVII. *The Vakil of the Prince of Bokhara* (p. 272).

The Prince of Bokhara had a Vakil who, through fear of punishment for an offence he had committed, ran away and remained concealed in Kuhistan and the desert for the

[1] There is a *Hadis*, "Think on God's mercies, and not on His essence."

[1] Koran viii. 17. Said of the sand cast into the eyes of the men of Mecca at Beder.

[2] See Gulshan i Raz, l. 354, where the commentator says the allusion is to Moses at Mount Sinai. Koran vii. 139.

space of ten years. At the end of that time, being unable to endure absence from his lord and his home any longer, he determined to return to Bokhara and throw himself at his lord's feet, and endure whatever punishment his lord might be pleased to inflict upon him. His friends did all they could to dissuade him, assuring him that the Prince's wrath was still hot against him, and that if he appeared at Bokhara he would be put to death, or at least imprisoned for the rest of his life. He replied, "O advisers, be silent, for the force of the love which is drawing me to Bokhara is stronger than the force of prudent counsels. When love pulls one way all the wisdom of Abu Hanifa and Ash-Shafi'i is impotent to withstand it. If it shall please my lord to slay me, I will yield up my life without reluctance, for this life of estrangement from him which I am now leading is the same as death, and release from it will be eternal happiness. I will return to Bokhara and throw myself at my lord's feet, and say to him, 'Deal with me as thou wilt, for I can no longer bear absence from thee, and life or death at thy hands is all the same to me!'" Accordingly, he journeyed back to Bokhara, counting the very toils and discomforts of the road sweet and delightful, because they were steps in his homeward course. When he reached Bokhara his friends and relations all warned him not to show himself, as the Prince was still mindful of his offence and bent on punishing him; but he replied to them as to his other advisers, that he was utterly regardless of his life, and was resolved to commit himself to his lord's good pleasure. He then went to the court and threw himself at his lord's feet and swooned away. The Prince, seeing the strong affection borne to him by his repentant servant, conceived a similar affection towards him, and descended from his throne and graciously raised him from the ground, and pardoned his offence. Thus it is that eternal life is gained by utter abandonment of one's own life. When God appears to His ardent lover the lover is absorbed in Him, and not so much as a hair of the lover remains. True lovers are as shadows, and when the sun shines in glory the shadows vanish away. He is a true lover of God to whom God says, "I am thine, and thou art mine!"

In the course of this story, which is narrated at great length, are introduced anecdotes of a lover and his mistress, of the Virgin Mary being visited by the "Blessed Spirit" or Angel Gabriel,[1] of the fatal mosque, of Galen's devotion to carnal learning, of Satan's treachery to the men of Mecca at the battle of Bedr,[2] and of Solomon and the gnat. There also occur comments on various texts, and a curious comparison of the trials and wholesome afflictions of the righteous to the boiling of potherbs in a saucepan by the cook.

The reply of the lover when asked by his mistress which city of all those he had seen was most pleasing in his sight (p. 276).

A damsel said to her lover, "O fond youth,
You have visited many cities in your travels;
Which of those cities seems most delightful to you?"
He made answer, "The city wherein my love dwells.
In whatever nook my queen alights,
Though it be as the eye of a needle, 'tis a wide plain;
Wherever her Yusuf-like face shines as a moon,
Though it be the bottom of a well, 'tis Paradise.
With thee, my love, hell itself were heaven,
With thee a prison would be a rose-garden.
With thee hell would be a mansion of delight,
Without thee lilies and roses would be as flames of fire!"

[1] Koran xix. 18. [2] Koran viii. 10.

The answer of the Vakil to those who advised him not to court death by yielding himself up to his lord (p. 277).

He said, "I am a drawer of water; water attracts me,
Even though I know water may be my death.
No drawer of water flees from water,
Even though it may cause him a hundred deaths.
Though it may make my hand and belly dropsical,
My love for water will never be lessened.
I should say, when they asked me about my belly,
'Would that the ocean might flow into it!'
Though the bottle of my belly were burst with water,
And though I should die, my death would be acceptable.
Wheresoever I see one seeking water, I envy him,
And cry, 'Would I were in his place!'
My hand is a tabor and my belly a drum,
Like the rose I beat the drum of love of water.
Like the earth or like a fœtus I devour blood,
Since I became a lover this is my occupation.
If that 'Faithful Spirit' should shed my blood,
I would drink it up drop by drop like the earth.
At night I boil on the fire like a cooking-pot,
From morn till eve I drink blood like the sand.
It repents me that I planned a stratagem,
And that I fled from before his wrath.
Tell him to sate his wrath on my poor life,
He is the 'Feast of Sacrifice,' and I his loving cow.[1]
The cow, whether it eats or sleeps,
Thinks of naught but sacrificing itself.
Know me to be that cow of Moses which gave its life,
Each part of me gives life to the righteous.
That cow of Moses was made a sacrifice,
And its least part became a source of life.
That murdered man leapt up from his deadness
At the words, 'Strike the corpse with part of her.'[1]
O pious ones, slay the cow (of lust),
If ye desire true life of soul and spirit!
I died as inanimate matter and arose a plant,
I died as a plant and rose again an animal.[2]
I died as an animal and arose a man.
Why then should I fear to become less by dying?
I shall die once again as a man
To rise an angel perfect from head to foot!
Again when I suffer dissolution as an angel,
I shall become what passes the conception of man!
Let me then become non-existent, for non-existence
Sings to me in organ tones, 'To him shall we return.'[3]
Know death to be the gathering together of the people,
The water of life is hidden in the land of darkness.
Like a water-lily seek life there!
Yea, like that drawer of water, at the risk of life,
Water will be his death, yet he still seeks water,
And still drinks on,—and God knows what is right.
O lover, cold-hearted and void of loyalty,
Who from fear for your life shun the beloved!
O base one, behold a hundred thousand souls
Dancing towards the deadly sword of his love:
Behold water in a pitcher; pour it out;
Will that water run away from the stream?
When that water joins the water of the stream
It is lost therein, and becomes itself the stream.
Its individuality is lost, but its essence remains,
And hereby it becomes not less nor inferior.
I will hang myself upon my lord's palm-tree
In excuse for having fled away from him!"
Even as a ball rolling along on head and face,

[1] The Id ul Azha, or the Feast of Sacrifices, held on the tenth day of the month Zul Hijja. It is also called "The Cow Festival."

[1] This refers to Koran ii. 63. The cow was to be sacrificed in order that a murderer might be discovered by striking the corpse with a piece of her flesh.

[2] *I.e.*, Earth losing its own form becomes vegetable, vegetable again perishes to feed and be transmuted into animal, and in like manner animal becomes man. See the passage of Milton quoted below, and Gulshan i Raz, l. 490 and note.

[3] Koran ii. 153: "Verily we are God's, and to Him shall we return."

He fell at the feet of the Prince with streaming eyes.
The people were all on the alert, expecting
That the Prince would burn him or hang him,
Saying, "Moth-like he has seen the blaze of the light,
And fool-like has plunged therein and lost his life."
But the torch of love is not like that torch,
'Tis light, light in the midst of light,
'Tis the reverse of torches of fire,
It appears to be fire, but is all sweetness.

Love generates love. "If ye love God, God will love you"[1] (p. 289).

That Bokharian then cast himself into the flame,
But his love made the pain endurable;
And as his burning sighs ascended to heaven,
The love of the Prince was kindled towards him.

. . . . . .

The heart of man is like the root of a tree,
Therefrom grow the leaves on firm branches.[2]
Corresponding to that root grow up branches
As well on the tree as on souls and intellects.
The tops of the perfect trees reach the heavens,
The roots firm, and the branches in the sky.
Since then the tree of love has grown up to heaven,
How shall it not also grow in the heart of the Prince?
A wave washes away the remembrance of the sin from his heart,
For from each heart is a window to other hearts.
Since in each heart there is a window to other hearts,
They are not separated and shut off like two bodies.
Thus, even though two lamp-dishes be not joined,
Yet their light is united in a single ray.
No lover ever seeks union with his beloved,
But his beloved is also seeking union with him.

[1] Koran iii. 29.
[2] "Seest thou not to what God likeneth a good word? To a good tree, its root firmly fixed, and its branches in the heaven" (Koran xiv. 29).

But the lover's love makes his body lean,
While the beloved's love makes hers fair and lusty.
When in *this* heart the lightning spark of love arises,
Be sure this love is reciprocated in *that* heart.
When the love of God arises in thy heart,
Without doubt God also feels love for thee.
The noise of clapping of hands is never heard
From one of thy hands unaided by the other hand.
The man athirst cries, "Where is delicious water?"
Water too cries, "Where is the water-drinker?"
This thirst in my soul is the attraction of the water;
I am the water's and the water is mine.
God's wisdom in His eternal foreknowledge and decree
Made us to be lovers one of the other.
Nay more, all the parts of the world by this decree
Are arranged in pairs, and each loves its mate.
Every part of the world desires its mate,
Just as amber attracts blades of straw.
Heaven says to earth, "All hail to thee!
We are related to one another as iron and magnet."
Heaven is man and earth woman in character;
Whatever heaven sends it, earth cherishes.
When earth lacks heat, heaven sends heat;
When it lacks moisture and dew, heaven sends them.
The earthy sign[1] succours the terrestrial earth,
The watery sign (Aquarius) sends moisture to it;
The windy sign sends the clouds to it,
To draw off unwholesome exhalations.
The fiery sign (Leo) sends forth the heat of the sun,
Like a dish heated red-hot in front and behind.
The heaven is busily toiling through ages,
Just as men labour to provide food for women.
And the earth does the woman's work, and toils
In bearing offspring and suckling them.
Know then earth and heaven are endued with sense,
Since they act like persons endued with sense.

[1] *I.e.*, of the Zodiac.

If these two lovers did not suck nutriment from each other,
Why should they creep together like man and wife?
Without the earth how could roses and saffron grow?
For naught can grow from the sole heat and rain of heaven.
This is the cause of the female seeking the male,
That the work of each may be accomplished.
God has instilled mutual love into man and woman,
That the world may be perpetuated by their union.

. . . .

Earth says to the earth of the body, "Come away,
Quit the soul and come to me as dust.
Thou art of my *genus*, and wilt be better with me,
Thou had'st better quit the soul and fly to me!"
Body replies, "True, but my feet are fast bound,
Though like thee I suffer from separation."
Water calls out to the moisture of the body,
"O moisture, return to me from your foreign abode!"
Fire also calls out to the heat of the body,
"Thou art of fire; return to thy root!"
In the body there are seventy-and-two diseases;
It is ill compacted owing to the struggle of its elements.
Disease comes to rend the body asunder,
And to drag apart its constituent elements.
The four elements are as birds tied together by the feet;
Death, sickness and disease loose their feet asunder.
The moment their feet are loosed from the others,
The bird of each element flies off by itself.
The repulsion of each of these principles and causes
Inflicts every moment a fresh pang on our bodies.
That it may dissolve these composite bodies of ours,
The bird of each part tries to fly away to its origin;
But the wisdom of God prevents this speedy end,
And preserves their union till the appointed day.
He says, "O parts, the appointed time is not yet;
It is useless for you to take wing before that day."
But as each part desires reunion with its original,
How is it with the soul who is a stranger in exile?
It says, "O parts of my habitation here below,
My absence is sadder than yours, as I am heaven-born.
The body loves green pastures and running water,
For this cause that its origin is from them.
The love of the soul is for life and the living one,
Because its origin is the Soul not bound to place.
The love of the soul is for wisdom and knowledge,
That of the body for houses, gardens, and vineyards;
The love of the soul is for things exalted on high,
That of the body for acquisition of goods and food.
The love too of Him on high is directed to the soul:
Know this for 'He loves them that love Him.'"[1]
The sum is this, that whoso seeks another,
The soul of that other who is sought inclines to him.

. . . .

Let us quit the subject.—Love for that soul athirst
Was kindled in the breast of the Prince of Bokhara.
The smoke of that love and the grief of that burning heart
Ascended to his master and excited his compassion.

The praises addressed to the Prince by the Vakil (p. 296).

He said, "O phœnix of God and goal of the spirit
I thank thee that thou hast come back from Mount Qaf!
O Israfil of the resurrection-day of love,
O love, love, and heart's desire of love!
Let thy first boon to me be this,
To lend thine ear to my orisons.
Though thou knowest my condition clearly,
O protector of slaves, listen to my speech.
A thousand times, O prince incomparable,
Has my reason taken flight in desire to see thee,
And to hear thee and to listen to thy words,

[1] Koran v. 59.

And to behold thy life-giving smiles.
Thy inclining thine ear to my supplications
Is as a caress to my misguided soul.
The baseness of my heart's coin is known to thee,
But thou hast accepted it as genuine coin.
Thou art proud towards the arrogant and proud;
All clemencies are as naught to thy clemency.
First hear this, that while I remained in absence,
First and last alike escaped me.
Secondly, hear this, O prince beloved,
That I searched much, but found no second to thee.
Thirdly, that when I had departed outside thee,
I said it was like the Christian Trinity.[1]
Fourthly, when my harvest was burned up,
I knew not the fourth from the fifth.
Wheresoever thou findest blood on the roads,
Trace it, and 'tis tears of blood from my eyes.
My words are thunder, and these sighs and tears
Are drawn by it as rain from the clouds.
I am distracted between speaking and weeping.
Shall I weep, or shall I speak, or what shall I do?
If I speak, my weeping ceases;
If I weep, I cease to praise and magnify thee."
He spoke thus, and then fell to weeping,
So that high and low wept with him.
So many "Ahs" and "Alases" proceeded from his heart,
That the people of Bokhara formed a circle round him.
Talking sadly, weeping sadly, smiling sadly,
Men and women, small and great, were all assembled.
The whole city wept in concert with him;
Men and women mingled together as on the last day.
Then Heaven said to Earth,
"If you never saw a resurrection-day, see it here!"
Reason was amazed, saying, "What love, what ecstasy!
Is his separation more wondrous, or his reunion?"

[1] "They surely are infidels who say, 'God is the third of three,' for there is no God but one God" (Koran v. 77).

Story XVIII. *The Deadly Mosque* (p. 278).

In the suburbs of a certain city there was a mosque in which none could sleep a night and live. Some said it was haunted by malevolent fairies; others, that it was under the baneful influence of a magic spell; some proposed to put up a notice warning people not to sleep there, and others advised that the door should be kept locked. At last a stranger came to that city and desired to sleep in the mosque, saying that he did not fear to risk his life, as the life of the body was naught, and God has said, "Wish for death if you are sincere."[1] The men of the city warned him again and again of the danger, and rebuked him for his foolhardiness, reminding him that not improbably Satan was tempting him to his own destruction, as he tempted the men of Mecca at the battle of Bedr.[2] The stranger, however, would not be dissuaded, but persisted in his purpose of sleeping in the mosque. He said that he was as one of the devoted agents of the Ismailians, who were always ready to sacrifice their lives at the bidding of their chiefs, and that the terrors of death did not appal him any more than the noise of a little drum beaten by a boy to scare away birds could appal the great drum-bearing camel that used to march at the head of King Mahmud's army. Accordingly, he slept in the mosque, and at midnight he was awakened by a terrible voice, as of one about to attack him. But instead of being dismayed, he bethought himself of the text "Assault them with thy horsemen and thy footmen,"[3] and confronted his unseen foe, challenging him to show himself and stand to his arms. At these words the spell was dissipated, and showers of gold fell on all sides, which the brave hero proceeded to appropriate.

[1] Koran ii. 88. [2] Koran viii. 50. [3] Koran xvii. 66.

The " knowledge of certainty" and the "eye of certainty" (p. 283).

Our body and substance are snow, doomed to perish,
God is He who buys them, for " God hath bought them."[1]
You prefer this perishing snow to God's price
Because you are in doubt and have not certainty;
And, strange to say, opinion abides in you, O weak one,
And never flies away to the garden of certainty.
Every opinion is aiming at certainty, O son,
And more and more moves its wings towards certainty.
When it reaches knowledge it stands erect,
And its knowledge again hastes on towards certainty,
Because in the approved road of the faith
Knowledge is lower than certainty, but above opinion.
Know knowledge aspires to certainty,
And certainty again to sight and ocular evidence.
In the chapter, "Desire of riches occupieth you,"[2]
After " Nay," read " Would that ye knew!"
Knowledge conducts you to sight, O knower!
" If ye are certain, ye shall *see* hell-fire."
Sight follows on certainty with no interval,
Just as reasoned knowledge is born of opinion.
See the account of this in the chapter cited,
How knowledge of certainty becomes the eye of certainty.
As for me, I am above both opinion and certainty;
My head is not affected by your cavils.
Since my mouth has eaten of *His* sweetmeats,
I am become clear-sighted, and see *Him* face to face!

[1] "Verily of the faithful hath God bought their persons and their substance, on condition of Paradise for them in return" (Koran ix. 112).
[2] "The desire of riches occupieth you till ye come to the grave. Nay! but in the end ye shall know. Nay! would that ye knew it with *knowledge of certainty*. Surely ye shall see hell-fire. Ye shall surely see it with the *eye of certainty*" (Koran cii.)

The righteous are exposed to trials for their improvement, as potherbs are boiled to make them fit for food (p. 284).

Behold these potherbs boiling in the pot,
How they jump and toss about in the heat of the fire.
Whilst they are boiling, they keep leaping up,
Even to the top of the pot, and utter cries,
Saying to the housewife, " Why do you set us on the fire?
Now you have bought us, why should you afflict us?"
The housewife pushes them down with her spoon, saying,
" Be still, and boil well, and leap not off the fire.
I do not boil you because I dislike you,
But that you may acquire a good savour and taste.
When you become food you will be mingled with life;
This trial is not imposed on you to distress you.
In the garden you drank water soft and fresh;
That water-fed one was reserved for this fire.
Mercy was first shown to it before vengeance,
That mercy might train it to be proof against trial;
Mercy was shown to it previously to vengeance,
That it might acquire its substance of being.
Because flesh and skin grow not without tender care,
How should they not grow when warmed by the Friend's love.
If vengeance follows as a necessary consequence,
That you may make an offering of that substance,
Mercy follows again to compensate for it,
That you may be purified and raised above your nature.

. . . .

I am Abraham, and you his son under the knife.
Lay down your head! 'I have seen I must sacrifice you.'[1]
Yield your head to vengeance, your heart to constancy,
That I may cut your throat like an Ismailian's.
I cut off your head, but that head is such
That it is restored to life by being cut off!"

[1] Koran xxxvii. 101.

My main object herein is to inculcate resignation,
O Musulman! it behoves you to seek resignation.[1]
O potherbs, you boil in trials and sufferings
That neither existence nor self may remain in you.
Though you once smiled in that earthly garden,
You are really roses of the garden of life and sight.
If you are torn away from the garden of earth,
You become sweet food to revive man's life;
Yea, become his food and strength and thought![2]
You were only milk, you become a lion of the forest!
You issue from God's attributes at first;
Return again back to those attributes with all speed!
You come from the clouds and sunshine and sky,
Then assume moral qualities and ascend the sky.
You come in the form of rain and sunshine,
You depart endued with excellent attributes.
You begin as a part of the sun, clouds, and stars,
You rise to be breath, act, word, and thought!
The life of animals comes from the death of plants.
True is the saying, 'Kill me, O faithful ones!'
Since such exaltation awaits us after death.
True it is that 'In our death is life.'
Acts, words, and faith are the food of the King,
So that in this ascent one attains to heaven.
Thus, as potherbs become the food of men,
They rise above the grade of minerals to that of animals.

Objections of fools to the Masnavi (p. 285).

A certain goose pops his head out of his coop,
And displays himself as a critic of the Masnavi,
Saying, "This poem, the Masnavi, is childish;
'Tis but a story of the prophets, and so on.
'Tis not an account of the arguments and deep mysteries,
Whereto holy men direct their attention;—
Concerning asceticism, and so on to self-annihilation,
Step by step, up to communion with God;—
An explanation and definition of each several state,
Whereto the men of heart ascend in their flight."
Whereas the Book of God resembles the Masnavi in this,
The infidels abused it in the same manner,
Saying, 'It contains old tales and stories;[1]'
There is no deep analysis or lofty investigation therein.
Little boys can understand it;
It only contains commands and prohibitions,
Accounts of Yusuf and his curled locks,
Accounts of Jacob, of Zulaikha and her love,
Accounts of Adam, of the wheat, and of the serpent Iblis,
Accounts of Hud, of Noah, of Abraham, and the fire."

. . . .

Know the words of the Koran are simple,
But within the outward sense is an inner secret one.[2]
Beneath that secret meaning is a third,
Whereat the highest wit is dumbfoundered.
The fourth meaning has been seen by none
Save God, the Incomparable and All-sufficient.
Thus they go on, even to seven meanings, one by one,
According to the saying of the Prophet, without doubt.
Do thou, O son, confine not thy view to the outward meaning,
Even as the demons saw in Adam only clay.[3]
The outward meaning of the Koran is like Adam's body,
For its semblance is visible, but its soul is hidden.

. . . .

O reviling dog! thou makest a clamour,

[1] According to its etymology, Islam means self-surrender to God, as well as safety, peace, and obedience to divine laws.
[2] Cp. Milton, Paradise Lost, v. 482—

"Flow'rs and their fruit,
Man's nourishment, by gradual scale sublim'd
To vital spirits aspire, to animal,
To intellectual."

[1] Koran xxvii. 7.
[2] There is a Hadis to the effect that each word of the Koran has seven meanings. See Koran iii. 5.
[3] Koran xvii. 63.

Thou makest thy abuse of the Koran thy destruction.[1]
This is not a lion, wherefrom thou canst save thy life,
Or canst secure thyself from his talons!
The Koran cries out even to the last day,
"O people, given up as a prey to ignorance,
If ye have imagined me to be only empty fables,
Ye have sown the seed of reviling and infidelity.
Ye yourselves who abuse me will see yourselves
Annihilated, and made like a tale that is told!"

Solomon and the gnat (p. 295).

A gnat came in from the garden and fields,
And called on Solomon for justice,
Saying, "O Solomon, you extend your equity
Over demons and the sons of Adam and fairies.
Fish and fowl dwell under the shelter of your justice;
Where is the oppressed one whom your mercy has not sought?
Grant me redress, for I am much afflicted,
Being cut off from my garden and meadow haunts."

. . . .

Then Solomon replied, "O seeker of redress,
Tell me from whom do you desire redress?
Who is the oppressor, who, puffed up with arrogance,
Has oppressed you and smitten your face?"

. . . .

The gnat replied, "He from whom I seek redress is the Wind,
'Tis he who has emitted the smoke of oppression at me;
Through his oppression I am in a grievous strait,
Through him I drink blood with parched lips!"

. . . .

Solomon replied to him, "O sweet-voiced one,
You must hear the command of God with all your heart.
God has commanded me saying, 'O dispenser of justice,
Never hear one party without the other!'
Till both parties come into the presence,
The truth is never made plain to the judge."

. . . .

When the Wind heard the summons, it came swiftly,
And the gnat instantly took flight.
In like manner the seekers of God's presence-seat,—
When God appears, those seekers vanish.
Though that union is life eternal,
Yet at first that life is annihilation.

The book ends with the beginning of a story which is finished in the fourth book.

[1] The Lucknow commentator says that Faizi (brother of Abul Fazl, Akbar's minister) once spoke disrespectfully of the Koran and the Masnavi, and on the leaves being turned over, this passage presented itself.

Book IV.

STORY I. *The Lover and his Mistress* (p. 303).

THE fourth book begins with an address to Husamu-'d-Din, and this is followed by the story of the lover and his mistress, already commenced in the third book. A certain lover had been separated from his mistress for the space of seven years, during which he never relaxed his efforts to find her. At last his constancy and perseverance were rewarded, in accordance with the promises "The seeker shall find," and "Whoso shall have wrought an atom's weight of good shall behold it."[1] One night, as he was wandering through the city, he was pursued by the patrol, and, in order to escape them, took refuge in a garden, where he found his long-sought mistress. This occasioned him to reflect how often men "hate the things that are good for them,"[2] and led him to bless the rough patrol who had procured him the bliss of meeting with his mistress. *Apropos* of this, an anecdote is told of a preacher who was in the habit of blessing robbers and oppressors, because their evil example had turned him to righteousness. The moment the lover found himself alone with his mistress, he attempted to embrace her, but his mistress repulsed him, saying, that though no men were present, yet the wind was blowing and that showed that God, the mover of the wind, was also present. The lover replied, "It may be I am lacking in good manners, but I am not lacking in constancy and fidelity towards you." His mistress replied, "One must judge of the hidden by the manifest; I see for myself that your outward behaviour is bad, and thence I cannot but infer that your boast of hidden virtues is not warranted by actual facts. You are ashamed to misconduct yourself in the sight of men, but have no scruple to do so in the presence of the All-seeing God, and hence I doubt the existence of the virtuous sentiments which you claim to possess, but which can only be known to yourself." To illustrate this, she told the story of a Sufi and his faithless wife. This wife was one day entertaining a paramour, when she was surprised by the sudden return of her husband. On the spur of the moment she threw a woman's dress over her paramour and presented him to her husband as a rich lady who had come to propose a marriage between her son and the Sufi's daughter, saying she did not care for wealth, but only regarded modesty and rectitude of conduct. To this the Sufi replied, that as from her coming unattended it was plain that the lady had not the wealth she pretended to have, it was more than probable that her pretensions to extraordinary modesty and humility were also fictitious. The lover then proceeded to excuse himself by the plea that he had wished to test his mistress, and ascertain for himself whether she was a modest woman or not. He said he of course knew beforehand that she would prove to be a modest woman, but still he wished to have ocular demonstration of the fact. His mistress reproved him for trying to deceive her with false pretences, assuring him that after he had been detected in a fault, his only proper course was to confess it, as Adam had done. Moreover, she added that an attempt to put her to the test would have been an extremely unworthy proceeding, only to be paralleled by Abu Jahl's attempt to prove the truth of the Prophet's claims by calling on him to perform a miracle.

[1] Koran xcix. 7.

[2] Koran ii. 213.

The soul of good in things evil. Evil only relative
(p. 303).

The lover invoked blessings on that rough patrol,
Because their harshness had wrought bliss for him.
They were poison to most men, but sweets to him,
Because those harsh ones had united him with his love.
In the world there is nothing absolutely bad;
Know, moreover, evil is only relative.
In the world there is neither poison nor antidote,
Which is not a foot to one and a fetter to another;
To one the power of moving, to another a clog;
To one a poison, to another an antidote.
Serpents' poison is life to serpents,
In relation to mankind it is death.
To the creatures of the sea the sea is a garden,
To the creatures of the land it is fatal.
In the same way, O man, reckon up with intelligence
The relations of these things in endless variety.
In relation to this man Zaid is as Satan,
In relation to another he is as a Sultan.
The latter calls Zaid a sincere Mussulman,
The former calls him a Gueber deserving to be killed.
Zaid, one and the same person, is life to the one,
And to the other an annoyance and a pest.
If you desire that God may be pleasing to you,
Then look at Him with the eyes of them that love Him.
Look not at that Beauty with your own eyes,
Look at that Object of desire with His votaries' eyes;
Shut your own eyes from beholding that sweet Object,
And borrow from His admirers their eyes;
Nay, borrow from Him both eyes and sight,
And with those eyes of His look upon His face,
In order that you may not be disappointed with the sight.
God says, "Whoso is God's, God also is his."
God says, "I am his eye, his hand, his heart,"[1]
That his good fortune may emerge from adversity.
Whatsoever is hateful to you, if it should lead you
To your beloved, at once becomes agreeable to you.

Why God is named "Hearing," "Seeing," and "Knowing"
(p. 307).

God calls himself "Seeing," to the end that
His eye may every moment scare you from sinning.
God calls himself "Hearing," to the end that
You may close your lips against foul discourse.
God calls himself "Knowing," to the end that
You may be afraid to plot evil.
These names are not mere accidental names of God,
As a negro may be called *Kafúr* (white);
They are names derived from God's essential attributes,
Not mere vain titles of the First Cause.
For if so, they would be only empty pleasantries,
Like calling the deaf a hearer and the blind a seer,
Or a name like "impudent" for a modest man,
Or "beautiful" for an ugly negro,
Or such a title as "*Háji*" for a new-born boy,
Or that of "*Ghází*" applied to a noble idler.
If such titles as these are used in praising persons
Who do not possess the qualities implied, 'tis wrong;
'Twould be jesting or mockery or madness.
"God is exalted above" what is said by evil men.[2]
I knew you before I met you face to face,
That you had a fair face but an evil heart;
Yea, I knew you before I saw you,
That you were rooted in iniquity through guile.
When my eye is red owing to inflammation,
I know 'tis so from the pain, though I see it not.

[1] "My servant draws nigh to me by pious deeds till I love him, and, when I love him, I am his eye, his ear, his tongue, his foot, his hand, and by me he sees, hears, talks, walks, and feels."—*Hadis.*

[2] Cp. Koran xvi. 3.

One day I wrecked a ship on the high seas, said Death
Breaking it up at Your behest into small bits

You regarded me as a lamb without a shepherd;
You fancied that I had no guardian.
Lovers have suffered chastisement for this cause,
That they have cast ill-timed looks at fair ones.
They have supposed the fawn to have no shepherd,
They have supposed the captive to be going a begging;
Till in the twinkling of an eye an arrow pierces them,
Saying, "I am her guardian; look not at her rashly!"
What! am I less than a lamb or a fallow deer,
That I should have none to shepherd me?
Nay, I have a Guardian worthy of dominion,
Who knows every wind that blows upon me.
He is aware whether that wind is chill or mild,
He is not ignorant nor absent, O mean one.
The carnal soul is made by God blind and deaf;
I saw with the heart's eye your blindness afar off.
For this cause I never inquired about you for eight years
Because I saw you filled with ignorance and duplicity.
Why indeed should I inquire about one in the furnace,
Who is bowed down with reproach, like yourself?

Comparison of the world to a bath stove, and of piety to the hot bath (p. 307).

The lust of the world is like a bath stove,
Whereby the bath of piety is heated;
But the lot of the pious is purity from the stove's filth,
Because they dwell in the bath and in cleanliness.
The rich are as those that carry dung
To heat the furnace of the bath withal.
God has instilled into them cupidity,
That the bath may be warmed and pleasant.
Quit this stove and push on into the bath;
Know quitting the stove to be the bath itself.
Whoso is in the stove-room is as a servant
To him who is temperate and prudent.

. . . . . .

Your lust is as fire in the world,
With a hundred greedy mouths wide open.
In the judgment of reason this gold is foul dung,
Although, like dung, it serves to kindle the fire.

. . . . . .

Whoso was born in the stove-room and never saw purity,
The smell of sweet musk is disagreeable to him.

In illustration of this, a story follows of a tanner who was accustomed to bad smells in the course of his trade, and who was half killed by the smell of musk in the bazaar of the perfumers, but was cured by the accustomed smell of dung.

STORY II. *The Building of the "Most Remote Temple" at Jerusalem* (p. 311).

King David purposed to build a temple at Jerusalem, but was forbidden to do so by a divine voice, because he had been a man of blood. But, it was added, the work should be accomplished by his son Solomon, and Solomon's work would be reckoned the same as David's, in accordance with the texts, "The faithful are brethren," and "Sages are as a single soul," and "We make no distinction between any of the apostles."[1] Accordingly, when Solomon came to the throne, he set about the building, which was attended with many miraculous circumstances, *e.g.*, the stones in the quarry crying out and moving of themselves to the site of the temple. Bilqis, Queen of Saba, sent Solomon a present of forty camels laden with ingots of gold; but Solomon would not receive them, and sent her messengers back with a letter commanding her to abandon the worship of the sun and embrace Islam.[2] At the same time he charged the messengers to report fully to the Queen all they had seen in his kingdom, and to urge her to comply with his commands to renounce her sovereignty and present herself in all humility at his

[1] Koran xlix. 10; xxxi. 27; ii. 285.

[2] The letter is given in Koran xxvii. 30.

court. As she delayed to come, Solomon again sent to assure her that he had no sinister views regarding her, and desired her attendance at his court solely for her own spiritual benefit. At last Bilqis renounced her royal state and cast away all care for worldly things, and, impelled by earnest desire to learn the true faith, presented herself at the court of King Solomon. Then Solomon commanded that the throne of Bilqis should be brought from Saba, and an 'Afrit offered to fetch it, but Asaf, the vizier, anticipated him.[1] Afterwards Solomon proceeded with the building of the temple, wherein he was assisted by devils and fairies. Then God tried Solomon by placing on his throne a false counterpart of him. His miracle-working signet was stolen by a devil named Sakhar, who thereupon assumed his shape and personated him for forty days, during which Solomon had to wander about and beg his bread. After this he regained his throne, and having completed the temple, began to worship therein. One day he observed that a tuft of coarse grass had sprung up in a corner of the temple, and he was greatly distressed because he thought it portended the ruin of the building, but he took comfort from the thought that while he himself lived the temple would not be allowed to fall into ruin; so long as he lived, at least, he would root up all evil weeds that threatened the safety of the temple, as well the temple built with hands as the spiritual temple in his heart.

In the course of this story, which is told at great length, there occur anecdotes of the beginning of the reign of 'Othman, of the miracles of 'Abd Ullah Moghrabi, and others, of which abstracts are given below.

[1] All these legends are derived from Koran xxi., xxvii., and xxxviii. See Sale's notes.

Though philosophers call man the microcosm, divines call him the macrocosm (p. 314).

In outward form thou art the microcosm,
But in reality the macrocosm.[1]
Seemingly the bough is the cause of the fruit,[2]
But really the bough exists because of the fruit.
Were he not impelled by desire of fruit,
The gardener would never have planted the tree.
Therefore in reality the tree is born from the fruit,
Though seemingly the fruit is born from the tree.
For this cause Mustafa said, "Adam and all prophets
Are my followers and gather under my standard.
Though to outward view I am a son of Adam,
In reality I am his first forefather,
Because the angels worshipped him for my sake,
And 'twas in my footsteps that he ascended to heaven.
Hence in reality our first parent was my offspring,
As in reality the tree is born of its own fruit."

What is first in thought is last in act.
Thought is the special attribute of the Eternal.
This product goes forth from heaven very swiftly,
And comes to us like a caravan.[3]
'Tis not a long road that this caravan travels;
Can the desert stop the deliverer?
The heart travels to the Ka'ba every moment,
And by divine grace the body acquires the same power.
Distance and nearness affect only the body,
What do they matter in the place where God is?
When God changes the body,
It regards not parasangs or miles.
Even on earth there is hope of approaching God.
Press on like a lover, and cease vain words, O son!

[1] This refers to Muhammad, who is at once the "First reason" (Logos) and the "Perfect man," who is "the sum of all the worlds" and the "Great world." See Notices et Extraits des MSS., x. p. 86.

[2] He was also the final cause of creation. "If it had not been for thee, the worlds had not been created."

[3] Muhammad as the Logos is the channel by which divine grace is conveyed to man. The "change of the body" is an allusion to the ascension of Muhammad (*Mi raj*).

In the course of his rebuke to the messengers of Bilqis for bringing him mere gold instead of a humble heart, Solomon tells the story of the druggist who used soapstone or Persian earth for a weight. A man came to him to buy sugar-candy, and as he had no weight at hand, he used a lump of soapstone instead; but, while his back was turned, the purchaser stole a bit of the soapstone. The druggist, though he saw what he was doing, would not interrupt him, for he knew that the more soapstone the purchaser stole, the less sugar-candy he would get. In like manner the more men grasp at the transitory wealth of this world, the less they will obtain of the stable wealth of the world to come.

Part of Solomon's message to Bilqis (p. 317).

Report to Bilqis what marvels ye have seen,
And what plains of gold belong to Solomon;
How ye beheld forty mansions faced with gold,
And how ye were ashamed of your presents;
That she may know Solomon is not covetous of gold;
He has received gold from the Creator of gold.
The moment he wills it, every grain of earth's dust
Is changed into gold and precious pearls.
For this cause, O thou that lovest gold,
On the last day God will make earth all silver (white).[1]

. . . .

Quit thy wealth, even if it be the realm of Saba;
Thou wilt find many realms not of this earth.
What thou callest a throne is only a prison;
Thou thinkest thyself enthroned, but art outside the door.
Thou hast no sovereignty over thine own passions,
How canst thou sway good and evil?
Thy hair turns white without thy concurrence,
Take shame to thyself for thy evil passions.
Whoso bows his head to the King of kings
Will receive a hundred kingdoms not of this world;

[1] A *Hadis*.

But the delight of bowing down before God
Will seem sweeter to thee than countless glories."

An anecdote follows of a darvesh who saw in a dream some saints, and prayed them to provide him with his daily bread without obliging him to mix in worldly affairs. The saints ordered him to go to the forest, and there he found that all the wild fruits were rendered fit for his food. Having a few grains of gold by him, which he had gained by worldly labour before this miracle had been wrought for him, he was about to give them to a poor woodcutter who was passing that way. But this woodcutter was a saint, and at once read his thoughts, and to show, like Solomon, that he had no need of worldly wealth, he offered up a short prayer to God, and straightway his bundle of firewood was changed into gold, and immediately after, at another prayer, was changed back again into firewood.

Ibrahim bin Adham and his fondness for music[1] (p. 318).

Haste to renounce thy kingdom, like Ibrahim bin Adham,
To obtain, like him, the kingdom of eternity.
At night that king would sleep on his throne,
With his guards of state surrounding his palace,
Though he needed no guards for the purpose
Of warding off robbers and vagabonds;
For he who is a just king knows everything,
And is safe from harm and his mind is at peace.
Justice is the guardian of his steps,
Not guards with drums round his palace.
His purpose in having this band of music was this,
To recall to his longing heart that call of God.[2]
The wailing of horn and the thunder of drum

[1] Music is much used in the religious services of the "Maulavi" order of Darveshes, founded by Jalalu-d-Din Rumi. See "The Dervishes," by J. P. Brown, p. 197.

[2] "Am not I your lord?" (Koran vii. 171).

Resemble in some sort that dread "trumpet blast."[1]
Wherefore philosophers say that we have learned
Our melodies from those of the revolving spheres.
The song of the spheres in their revolutions
Is what men sing with lute and voice.
The faithful hold that the sweet influences of heaven
Can make even harsh voices melodious.
As we are all members of Adam,
We have heard these melodies in Paradise;
Though earth and water have cast their veil upon us,
We retain faint reminiscences of those heavenly songs.
But while we are thus shrouded by gross earthly veils,
How can the tones of the dancing spheres reach us?[2]

. . . .

Hence it is that listening to music is lovers' food,
Because it recalls to them their primal union with God.
The inward feelings of the mind acquire strength,
Nay, are shown outwardly, under influence of music.
The fire of love burns hotter under stimulus of music,
Even as occurred in the case of the nut-gatherer.

Ibrahim's abdication (p. 318).

Once that noble Ibrahim, as he sat on his throne,
Heard a clamour and noise of cries on the roof,
Also heavy footsteps on the roof of his palace.
He said to himself, "Whose heavy feet are those?"
He shouted from his window, "Who goes there?
'Tis no man's step; surely 'tis a fairy."
His guards, filled with confusion, bowed their heads,
Saying, "It is we who are going the rounds in search."
He said, "What seek ye?" They said, "Our camels."[3]
He said, "Who ever searched for camels on a housetop?"

[1] "When there shall be a trumpet blast, that shall be a dreadful day" (Koran lxxiv. 7).

[2] The so-called Pythagorean doctrine of the "Harmony of the spheres" was as well known to Persian poets as to Shakespeare.

[3] This is an allusion to the story of the "Believer's lost camel." Book ii., Story xi.

They said, "We follow thy example,
Who seekest union with God while sitting on a throne."
This was all, and no man ever saw him again,
Just as fairies are invisible to men.
His *substance* was hid from men, though he was with them,
For what can men see save the outward aspect and dress?
As he was removed from the sight of friends and strangers,
His fame was noised abroad like that of the 'Anka.
For the soul of every bird that reaches Mount Qaf
Confers glory on the whole family of birds.[1]

The anecdote of the nut-gatherer, introduced in the above story, is only another version of the story of the thirsty man who threw bricks into the water in order to hear the sound of the splash.[2] This is followed by an address to Husamu-'d-Din, in which the poet says that his object in writing the Masnavi was to elicit words from Husam, as his words were the same as the words of God.

Solomon's preaching to the people of Bilqis. The art of preaching (p. 321).

I tell the tale of Saba in lovers' style.
When the breeze bore Solomon's words to that garden,
'Twas as when bodies meet souls at the resurrection,
Or as when boys return to their loved homes.
The people of love are hidden amongst the peoples,
As a liberal man encompassed by the contumely of the base.
Souls are disgraced by union with bodies,
Bodies are ennobled by union with souls.
Arise, O lovers; this sweet draught is yours;
Ye are they that endure; eternal life is yours.
Ho! ye that seek, arise and take your fill of love,
Snuff up that perfume of Yusuf!

[1] This alludes to the well-known poem of Faridu-d-Din 'Attar, the "Mantiqu-t-Tair."

[2] Book ii., Story v.

Approach, O Solomon, thou that knowest birds' language,
Sound the note of every bird that draws near.[1]
When God sent thee to the birds,
He taught thee first the notes of all the birds.
To the predestinarian bird talk predestination,
To the bird with broken wings preach patience,
To the patient well-doer preach comfort and pardon,
To the spiritual 'Anka relate the glories of Mount Qaf,
To the pigeon preach avoidance of the hawk,
To the lordly hawk mercy and self-control;
As for the bat, who lingers helpless in the dark,
Acquaint him with the society of the light;
To the fighting partridge teach peace,
To the cock the signs of dawning day.
In this way deal with all from the hoopoo to the eagle.

Then follows a long account of various miraculous incidents that occurred during the childhood of the Prophet,—how he was suckled by Halima, a woman of the Bani Sa'ad,—how the idols bowed down before him,—how he strayed from home,—how his grandfather, Abd ul Muttalib, prayed to God that he might be found,—and how he was at last found in the Ka'ba and restored to his grandfather. Next a story is told of a cur who attacked a blind man (*Kur*) in the street, rather than hunt the wild ass (*Gor*) on the mountains in company with well-bred dogs. This is an illustration of the thesis that mankind is prone to run after mean earthly objects, and to neglect aspiring to the spiritual world.

Solomon's admonitions to Bilqis (p. 327).

Ah! Bilqis, bestir thyself now the market is thronged,
Flee away from them whose traffic is unprofitable![2]
Arise, Bilqis, now that thou hast the choice,
Before that death lays his heavy hand upon thee.
Soon will death pull thy ears, as if thou wert
A thief dragged before the officer in deadly fear.
How long wilt thou steal shoes from asses of the world?
If thou must steal, steal pearls of the world above.
Thy sisters have found the kingdom that lasts for ever,
Thou cleavest to the kingdom of darkness.
Happy is he who quits this earthly kingdom,
Which sooner or later death will destroy.
Arise! O Bilqis, at least behold
The kingdom of the royal kings of the faith!
In reality they are seated in the garden of the spirit,
Though to outward view they are guiding their friends.
That spiritual garden accompanies them everywhere,
Yet it is never revealed to the eyes of the people,—
Its fruits ever asking to be gathered,
Its fount of life welling up to be drunk!
Go round about the heavens without aid of wings,
Like sun or full moon or new moon!
Thou wilt move as a spirit without aid of feet,
Thou wilt eat sweet viands without mouth or palate.
No crocodile of sorrow will attack thy bark,
Nor will sad thoughts of death assail thee.
Thou wilt be at once queen, army, and throne,
Endued with good fortune and fortune itself.[1]
Thou sayest thou art a great queen of good fortune;
But thy fortune is apart from thee and will soon fade,
Thou wilt be left like a beggar without sustenance;
Therefore, O chosen one, become thy own fortune.
When, O spiritual one, thou hast become thy own fortune,
Then, being thyself thy fortune, thou wilt never lose it.
How, O fortunate one, canst thou ever lose thyself,
When thy real self is thy treasure and thy kingdom?

[1] Koran xxvii. 16. There is a *Hadis*, "Speak to men according to the amount of their intelligence."

[2] "These are they who have bought error at the price of guidance, but their traffic hath not been gainful" (Koran ii. 15).

[1] Union attained, all duality and separate phenomenal existence are swallowed up in the One (Noumenon). (See Gulshan i Raz, l. 835 and 845).

How men and demons helped Solomon in building the temple (p. 327).

When Solomon laid the foundations of the temple,
Men and Jinns came and lent their aid to the work,
Some of them with good-will, and others on compulsion,
Even as worshippers follow the road of devotion.
Men are as demons, and lust of wealth their chain,
Which drags them forth to toil in shop and field.
This chain is made of their fears and anxieties.
Deem not that these men have no chain upon them.
It causes them to engage in labour and the chase,
It forces them to toil in mines and on the sea,
It urges them towards good and towards evil.
God saith, "On their necks is a rope of palm fibre,"[1]
And "Verily on their necks have we placed ropes,"[2]
"We make this rope out of their own dispositions;
There is none either impure or intelligent,
But we have fastened his work about his neck."[3]
Thy lust is even as fire burning in thy evil deeds;
The black coal of these deeds is lighted by the fire;
The blackness of the coal is first hidden by the fire,
But, when it is burnt, the blackness is made visible.

. . . .

The building of the prophets was without lust,
And accordingly its splendour ever increased.
Yea, many are the noble temples they have raised,
Though all were not named "The Most Remote Temple."
The Ka'ba, whose renown waxes greater every moment,
Owed its foundation to the piety of Abraham.
Its glory is not derived from stones and mortar,
But from being built without lust or strife.
Neither are the prophets' writings like other writings;
Nor their temples, nor their works, nor their families;
Nor their manners, nor their wrath, nor their chastisements;
Nor their dreams, nor their reason, nor their words.
Each one of them is endued with a different glory,
Each soul's bird winged with different feathers.

. . . .

Ho! pious ones, build the lively temple of the heart,
That the Divine Solomon may be seen, and peace be upon you!
And if your demons and fairies be recalcitrant,
Your good angels must place collars on their necks.
If your demons go astray through guile and fraud,
Chastisement must overtake them swift as lightning.
Be like Solomon, so that your demons
May dig stones for your spiritual edifice.
Be like Solomon, free from evil thoughts and guile,
So that carnal demons and Jinns may be submissive to you.
Your heart is as Solomon's signet; take good care
That it falls not a prey to demons,
For then demons will rule over you as over Solomon.
Guard then your signet from the demons, and be at peace.

Then follows a story of a poet who recited a panegyric in honour of a liberal king. The king commanded that he should receive one thousand pieces of gold, but the vazir, named Abu-'l-Hasan, gave him ten thousand. The poet went to his home well contented, but after some years fell into poverty, and naturally bethought him of the generous king and his vazir, who had before assisted him. Sibawayh, the grammarian of Shiraz, says "Allah" is derived from "*Alah*" (fleeing for refuge), and thus we see all creatures, and even the elements themselves, ever looking to Allah to sustain them in existence. The poet, therefore, again presented himself to the king with a new panegyric, and the king, on hearing it, commanded as before that a thousand pieces of gold should be given him. But the new vazir, who was also named Abu-'l-Hasan,

[1] Koran iii. 5.
[2] Koran xxxvi. 7.
[3] "And every man's work have we fastened about his neck, and on he last day will we bring forth to him a book, which shall be shown to him wide open. Read thy book; there needeth none but thyself to make out an account against thee that day" (Koran xvii. 14).

persuaded the king that the exchequer could not afford this large outlay, and kept the poet waiting so long for his money, that at last he was glad to get away with only one hundred pieces of gold. These two vazirs recall Asaf, the good vazir of King Solomon, who deserves the title "Light upon light,"[1] and Haman, the evil vazir of Pharaoh, who turned his heart against Moses, and brought many plagues upon the kingdom of Egypt.

How all creatures cry to God for sustenance (p. 329).

Yea, all the fish in the seas,
And all feathered fowl in the air above,
All elephants, wolves, and lions of the forest,
All dragons and snakes, and even little ants,
Yea, even air, water, earth, and fire,
Draw their sustenance from Him, both winter and summer.
Every moment this heaven cries to Him, saying,
"O Lord, quit not Thy hold of me for a moment!
The pillar of my being is Thy aid and protection;
The whole is folded up in that right hand of Thine."[2]
And earth cries, "O keep me fixed and steadfast,
Thou who hast placed me on the top of waters!"
All of them are waiting and expecting His aid,
All have learned of Him to represent their needs.
Every prophet extols this prescription,
"Seek ye help with patience and with prayer."[3]
Ho! seek aid of Him, not of another than Him
Seek water in the ocean, not in a dried-up channel.

The next anecdote is that of the raven who taught Cain the art of digging graves and burying corpses, as told in Koran v. 34. This is designed to illustrate the thesis that unaided human reason can discover no new truth, unless inspired by Divine wisdom, of which the prophets, and especially "Universal Reason," or the Prophet Muhammed, are the channels. Thus physicians and herbalists have derived their knowledge of the virtues of plants from the instructions originally given by King Solomon when he classified the plants that grew in the court of the temple. The inner eye sees more than is visible to the sight of the vulgar. To illustrate this, an anecdote is told of a Sufi who had accompanied his friends to a beautiful garden, but instead of looking about and enjoying the fragrance of the flowers and fruits, sat with his head sunk on his breast in Sufi fashion. His friends said to him, in the words of the Koran, "Look at the signs of God's mercy, how after its death He quickeneth the earth!"[1] He answered them that these signs were far more plainly visible to him in his heart than in the outward creation, which was merely as it were a blurred reflection from the spiritual creation enshrined in his heart. For God says, "The life of the world is naught but a cheating fruition."[2] In other words, "Nature conceals God, but the supernatural in man reveals Him."[3]

[1] Koran xxiv. 35. [2] Koran xxxix. 67. [3] Koran ii. 148.

On cleansing the inward temple of the heart from self-conceit and reliance on carnal reason (p. 333).

When the body bows in worship, the heart is a temple,
And where there is a temple, there bad friends are weeds.
When a liking for bad friends grows up in you,
Flee from them, and avoid converse with them.
Root up those weeds, for, if they attain full growth,
They will subvert you and your temple together.
O beloved, this weed is deviation from the "right way,"
You crawl crookedly, like infants unable to walk.
Fear not to acknowledge your ignorance and guilt,
That the Heavenly Master may not withhold instruction.

[1] Koran xxx. 49.
[2] Koran iii. 182.
[3] "But is it unreasonable to confess that we believe in God, not by reason of the nature which conceals him, but by reason of the supernatural in man, which alone reveals him and proves him to exist?" (Jacobi, quoted in Sir W. Hamilton's Lectures on Metaphysics, vol. i. p. 40).

When you say, "I am ignorant; O teach me,"
Such open confession is better than false pride.
O ingenuous one, learn of our father Adam,
Who said of yore, "O Lord, we have dealt unjustly."[1]
He made no vain excuses and prevaricated not,
Nor did he raise the standard of guile and craft.
On the other hand, Iblis raised arguments, saying,
"I used to be honourable; Thou hast disgraced me.
My stain is owing to Thee; Thou art my dyer;
Thou hast caused my sin and transgression."
Read the text, "Lord, Thou hast caused me to err,"[2]
That you plead not compulsion, and so err (like Iblis).
How long will you climb into that tree of compulsion?
How long cast out of sight your own freewill?
How long, like Iblis and his evil crew,
Throw the blame of your own sins upon God?
How were you compelled to sin when you took such pleasure
And pride in engaging in those sins?
Does a man feel such pleasure in acting on compulsion
As he exhibits when committing wrong actions?
You battle like twenty men against those
Who give you good advice not to do that act;
Saying to them, "This is right and quite proper;
Who dissuades me from it but men of no account?"
Does a man acting on compulsion talk like this?
Or rather one who is erring of his own freewill?
Whatever your lust wills you deem freewill,
What reason demands you deem compulsion.
Whoso is wise and prudent knows this,
That cleverness comes from Iblis, but love from Adam.
Cleverness is like Canaan's swimming in the ocean;[3]
'Tis no river or small stream; 'tis the mighty ocean.
Away with this attempt to swim; quit self-conceit.

[1] Koran vii. 22.
[2] He said, "That thou hast caused me to err" (Koran vii. 15). This is the burden of many of 'Omar Khayyam's poems.
[3] Koran xi. 43. See Book iii., Story v.

'Twill not save you; Canaan was drowned at last.
Love is as the ark appointed for the righteous,
Which annuls the danger and provides a way of escape.
Sell your cleverness and buy bewilderment;
Cleverness is mere opinion, bewilderment intuition.
Make sacrifice of your reason at the feet of Mustafa,
Say, "God sufficeth me, for He is sufficient for me."[1]
Do not, like Canaan, hang back from entering the ark,
Being puffed up with vain conceit of cleverness.
He said, "I will escape to the top of high mountains,
Why need I put myself under obligation to Noah?"

. . . .

Ah! better for him had he never learnt swimming!
Then he would have based his hopes on Noah's ark.
Would he had been ignorant of craft as a babe!
Then like a babe he would have clung to his mother.
Would he had been less full of borrowed knowledge!
Then he would have accepted inspired knowledge from his father.
When, with inspiration at hand, you seek book-learning,
Your heart, as if inspired, loads you with reproach.[2]
Traditional knowledge, when inspiration is available,
Is like making ablutions with sand when water is near.
Make yourself ignorant, be submissive, and then
You will obtain release from your ignorance.
For this cause, O son, the Prince of men declared,
"The majority of those in Paradise are the foolish."[3]
Cleverness is as a wind raising storms of pride;
Be foolish, so that your heart may be at peace;
Not with the folly that doubles itself by vain babble,
But with that arising from bewilderment at "The Truth."
Those Egyptian women who cut their hands were fools[4]—

[1] Koran ix. 130.
[2] Knowledge of "The Truth" is to be attained not by exercise of the reason, but by illumination from above. When the light of "The Truth" is revealed, reason is drowned in bewilderment. Gulshan i Raz, Answer ii.
[3] Freytag, Arabum Proverbia, vol. ii. p. 898; 1 Cor. iv. 10.
[4] "They were amazed at Yusuf, and cut their hands, and said, 'God keep us, this is no man!'" (Koran xii. 31).

Fools as to their hands, being amazed at Yusuf's face.
Make sacrifice of reason to love of "The Friend,"
True reason is to be found where He is.
Men of wisdom direct their reason heavenwards,
Vain babblers halt on earth where no "Friend" is.
If through bewilderment your reason quits your head,
Every hair of your head becomes true reason and a head.

Then follow commentaries on the text, "O thou enfolded in thy mantle;"[1] on the proverb, "Silence is the proper answer to a fool;" on the *Hadis*, "God created the angels with reason and the brutes with lust, but man he created with both reason and lust; the man who follows reason is higher than the angels, and the man who follows lust is lower than the brutes;" on the text, "As to those in whose heart is a disease, it will add doubt to their doubt, and they shall die infidels,"[2] and a comparison of the struggle between reason and lust to that between Majnun and his she-camel, he trying to get to his mistress Laila, and the she-camel trying to run home to her foal.

STORY III. *The Youth who wrote a letter of complaint about his rations to the King* (p. 337).

A certain youth in the service of a great king was dissatisfied with his rations, so he went to the cook and reproached him with dishonouring his master by his stinginess. The youth would not listen to his excuses, but wrote off an angry letter of complaint to the king, in terms of outward compliment and respect, but betraying an angry spirit. On receiving this letter, the king observed that it contained only complaints about meat and drink, and evinced no aspirations after spiritual food, and therefore needed no answer, as "the proper answer to a fool is silence."[3] When the youth received no answer to his letter, he was much surprised, and threw the blame on the cook and on the messenger, ignoring the fact that the folly of his own letter was the real reason of its being left unanswered. He wrote in all five letters, but the king persisted in his refusal to reply, saying that fools are enemies to God and man, and that he who has any dealings with a fool fouls his own nest. Fools only regard material meat and drink, whereas the food of the wise is the light of God, as it is said by the Prophet, "I pass the night in the presence of my Lord, who giveth me meat and drink,"[1] and again, "Fasting is the food of God," *i.e.*, the means by which spiritual food is obtained.[2]

[1] Koran lxxiii. 1.
[2] Koran ix. 126.
[3] See Freytag, Arabum Proverbia, i. 551, for a parallel.

Explanation of the text, "And Moses conceived a secret fear within him. We said 'Fear not, for thou shalt be uppermost (over Pharaoh's magicians)'"[3] (p. 340).

Moses said, "Their sorcery confuses them;
What can I do? These people have no discernment."
God said, "I will generate in them discernment;
I will make their undiscerning reason to see clearly.
Although like a sea their waves cast up foam,
O Moses, thou shalt prevail over them; fear not!"
The magicians gloried in their own achievements,
But when Moses' rod became a snake, they were confounded.
Whoso boasts of his beauty and wit,
The stone of death is a touchstone of his boasts.
Sorcery fades away, but the miracles of Moses advance.
Both resemble a dish falling from a roof:
The noise of the dish of sorcery leaves only cursing;
The noise of the dish of faith leaves edification.
When the touchstone is hidden from the sight of all,
Then come forth to battle and boast, O base coin!
Your time for boasting is when the touchstone is away;

[1] Koran xxvi. 79.
[2] See Mishkat ul Masabih, vol. i. p. 463.
[3] Koran xx. 70.

The hand of power will soon crush your exaltation.
The base coin says to me with pride every moment,
"O pure gold, how am I inferior to you?"
The gold replies, "Even so, O comrade;
But the touchstone is at hand; be ready to meet it!"
Death of the body is a benefaction to the spiritual;
What damage has pure gold to dread from the shears?
If the base coin were of itself far-sighted,
It would reveal at first the blackness it shows at last.
If it had showed its blackness at first on its face,
'Twould have avoided hypocrisy now and misery at last.
'Twould have sought the alchemy of grace in due time;
Its reason would have prevailed over its hypocrisy.
If it became broken-hearted through its own bad state,
'Twould look onward to Him that heals the broken;
'Twould look to the result and be broken-hearted,
And be made whole at once by the Healer of broken hearts.
Divine grace places base copper in the alembic,
Adulterated gold is excluded from that favour.
O adulterated gold, boast not, but see clearly
That thy Purchaser is not blind to thy defects.
The light of the judgment-day will enlighten his eyes
And destroy the glamour of thy fascinations.
Behold them that have regard to the ultimate result,
And also the regrets of foolish souls and their envy.
Behold them that regard only the present,
And cast away thoughts of evil to come from their minds.

STORY IV. *Bayazid and his impious sayings when beside himself* (p. 343).

The holy saint Bayazid before his death predicted the birth of the saint Abu-'l-Hasan Khirqani, and specified all the peculiar qualities which would be seen in him. And after his death it came to pass as he had predicted, and Abu-'l-Hasan, hearing what Bayazid had said, used to frequent his tomb. One day he visited the tomb as usual, and found it covered with snow, and a voice was heard saying, "The world is fleeting as snow. I am calling thee! Follow me and forsake the world!"

How Bayazid cried out, when beside himself, "Glory be to me!" and how his disciples were scandalised at this saying, and how Bayazid answered them (p. 349).

Once that famous saint Bayazid came to his disciples,
Saying, "Lo, I myself am God Almighty."
That man of spiritual gifts being visibly beside himself,
Said, "There is no God beside me; worship me!"
Next morning, when his ecstatic state had passed,
They said, "You said so and so, which was impious."
He answered, "If I do so again,
Straightway slay me with your knives!
God is independent of me; I am in the body.
If I say that again you must kill me!"
When that holy person had given this injunction,
Each of his disciples made ready his knife.
Again that overflowing cup became beside himself,
And his recent injunctions passed from his mind.
Alienation came upon him, reason went astray,
The dawn shone forth and his lamp paled at its light.
Reason is like an officer when the king appears;
The officer then loses his power and hides himself.
Reason is God's shadow; God is the sun.
What power has the shadow before the sun?
When a man is possessed by an evil spirit
The qualities of humanity are lost in him.
Whatever he says is really said by that spirit,
Though it seems to proceed from the man's mouth.
When the spirit has this rule and dominance over him,
The agent is the property of the spirit, and not himself;
His self is departed, and he has become the spirit.
The Turk without instruction speaks Arabic; [1]

[1] Alluding to the story of the Kurd, Syad Abu-'l-Wafa, Book i Story xiv. note.

When he returns to himself he knows not a word of it.
Seeing God is lord of spirits and of man,
How can He be inferior in power to a spirit?

. . . . . .

When the eagle of alienation from self took wing,
Bayazid began to utter similar speeches;
The torrent of madness bore away his reason,
And he spoke more impiously than before.
"Within my vesture is naught but God,
Whether you seek Him on earth or in heaven."
His disciples all became mad with horror,
And struck with their knives at his holy body.
Each one, like the assassins of Kardkoh,[1]
Without fear aimed at the body of his chief.
Each who aimed at the body of the Shaikh,—
His stroke was reversed and wounded the striker.
No stroke took effect on that man of spiritual gifts,
But the disciples were wounded and drowned in blood.
Each who had aimed a blow at his neck,
Saw his own throat cut, and gave up the ghost;
He who had struck at his breast
Had cleft his own breast and killed himself.
They who knew better that lord of felicity,
Who had not courage enough to strike a deadly blow,
Their half-knowledge held their hands back;
They saved their lives but slightly wounded themselves.
On the morrow those disciples, diminished in number,
Raised lamentations in their houses.
They went to Bayazid, thousands of men and women,
Saying, "The two worlds are hidden in thy vesture;
If this body of thine were that of a man,
It would have perished of sword-wounds, like a man's."
The man in his senses fought with him beside himself,
And thrust the thorn into his own eyes."
Ah! you who smite with your sword him beside himself,
You smite yourself therewith; Beware!

[1] A hill in Mazandaran.

For he that is beside himself is annihilated and safe;
Yea, he dwells in security for ever.
His form is vanished, he is a mere mirror;
Nothing is seen in him but the reflection of another.
If you spit at it, you spit at your own face,
And if you hit that mirror, you hit yourself;
And if you see an ugly face in it, 'tis your own,
And if you see an 'Isa there, you are its mother Mary.
He is neither this nor that—he is void of form;
'Tis your own form which is reflected back to you.
But when the discourse reaches this point, lip is closed;
When pen reaches this point, it is split in twain.
Close then your lips, though eloquence be possible.
Keep silence; God knows the right way!

This is followed by an anecdote of the Prophet appointing an Hudhaili youth to be captain of a band of warriors amongst whom were many older and more experienced soldiers, and of the objections made to this appointment, and of the Prophet's answer to the objectors.

Why the Prophet promoted the youth to command his seniors (p. 351).

The Prophet said, "O ye who regard only the outside,
Regard him not as a youth void of talents.
Many are they whose beards are black yet are old,
Many too have white beards and hearts like pitch.
I have made trial of his wisdom often and often,
And that youth has shown himself old in his actions.
Age consists in maturity of wisdom, O son,
Not in whiteness of the beard and hair.
How can any one be older than Iblis?
Yet, if he has no wisdom, he is naught.
Suppose him an infant, if he has 'Isa's soul,
He is pure from pride and from carnal lust.
That whiteness of the hair is a sign of maturity

Only to purblind eyes whose vision is limited.
Since that shortsighted one judges by outward signs,
He seeks the right course by outward tokens.
For his sake I said that if ye desire counsel
Ye ought to make choice of an old man.
He who has emerged from the veil of blind belief
Beholds by the light of God all things that exist.
His pure light, without signs or tokens,
Cleaves for him the rind and brings him to the kernel.
To the regarder of externals, genuine and base coin are alike.
How can he know what is inside the basket?
Many are the gold coins made black with smoke,
So that they elude the clutches of greedy thieves;
Many are the copper coins gilded with gold,
And sold as gold to men of slender wits.
We who regard the inside of the world,
We look at the heart and disregard the outside.
The judges who confine their view to externals
And base their decisions on outward appearances,
As they testify and make outward show of faith,[1]
Are straightway dubbed faithful by men of externals.
Therefore these heretics, who regard only externals,
Have secretly shed the blood of many true believers.
Strive then to be old in wisdom and in faith,
That, like Universal Reason, you may see within."[2]

STORY V. *The Three Fishes* (p. 352).

This story, which is taken from the book of Kalila and Damnah,[3] is as follows. There was in a secluded place a lake, which was fed by a running stream, and in this lake were three fishes, one very wise, the second half wise, and the third foolish. One day some fishermen passed by that lake, and having espied the fish, hastened home to fetch their nets. The fish also saw the fishermen and were sorely disquieted. The very wise fish, without a minute's delay, quitted the lake and took refuge in the running stream which communicated with it, and thus escaped the impending danger. The half wise fish delayed doing anything till the fishermen actually made their appearance with their nets. He then floated upon the surface of the water, pretending to be dead, and the fisherman took him up and threw him into the stream, and by this device he saved his life. But the foolish fish did nothing but swim wildly about, and was taken and killed by the fishermen.

The marks of the wise man, of the half wise, and of the fool (p. 351).

The wise man is he who possesses a torch of his own;
He is the guide and leader of the caravan.
That leader is his own director and light;
That illuminated one follows his own lead.
He is his own protector; do ye also seek protection
From that light whereon his soul is nurtured.
The second, he, namely, who is half wise,
Knows the wise man to be the light of his eyes.
He clings to the wise man like a blind man to his guide,
So as to become possessed of the wise man's sight.
But the fool, who has no particle of wisdom,
Has no wisdom of his own, and quits the wise man.
He knows nothing of the way, great or small,
And is ashamed to follow the footsteps of the guide.
He wanders into the boundless desert,
Sometimes halting and despairing, sometimes running.
He has no lamp wherewith to light himself on his way,
Nor half a lamp which might recognise and seek light.
He lacks wisdom, so as to boast of being alive,
And also half wisdom, so as to assume to be dead?

[1] "And some there are who say, 'We believe in God and in the last day,' yet they are not believers" (Koran ii. 7).

[2] Universal Reason, here applied to Muhammad. "The first thing which God created was ('aql) Reason or Intelligence," *i.e.*, the Logos.

[3] Anvar i Suhaili, Book i. Story 15.

Rise and shine, for today the world is at our feet

That half wise one became as one utterly dead
In order to rise up out of his degradation.
If you lack perfect wisdom, make yourself as dead
Under the shadow of the wise, whose words give life.
The fool is neither alive so as to companion with 'Isa,
Nor yet dead so as to feel the power of 'Isa's breath.
His blind soul wanders in every direction,
And at last makes a spring, but springs not upwards.

The counsels of the bird (p. 253).

A man captured a bird by wiles and snares;
The bird said to him, "O noble sir,
In your time you have eaten many oxen and sheep,
And likewise sacrificed many camels;
You have never become satisfied with their meat,
So you will not be satisfied with my flesh.
Let me go, that I may give you three counsels,
Whence you will see whether I am wise or foolish.
The first of my counsels shall be given on your wrist,
The second on your well-plastered roof,
And the third I will give you from the top of a tree.
On hearing all three you will deem yourself happy.
As regards the counsel on your wrist, 'tis this,—
'Believe not foolish assertions of any one!'"
When he had spoken this counsel on his wrist, he flew
Up to the top of the roof, entirely free.
Then he said, "Do not grieve for what is past;
When a thing is done, vex not yourself about it."
He continued, "Hidden inside this body of mine
Is a precious pearl, ten drachms in weight.
That jewel of right belonged to you,
Wealth for yourself and prosperity for your children.
You have lost it, as it was not fated you should get it,
That pearl whose like can nowhere be found."
Thereupon the man, like a woman in her travail,
Gave vent to lamentations and weeping.
The bird said to him, "Did I not counsel you, saying,
'Beware of grieving over what is past and gone?'
When 'tis past and gone, why sorrow for it?
Either you understood not my counsel or are deaf.
The second counsel I gave you was this, namely,
'Be not misguided enough to believe foolish assertions.'
O fool, altogether I do not weigh three drachms,
How can a pearl of ten drachms be within me?"
The man recovered himself and said, "Well then,
Tell me now your third good counsel!"
The bird replied, "You have made a fine use of the others,
That I should waste my third counsel upon you!
To give counsel to a sleepy ignoramus
Is to sow seeds upon salt land.
Torn garments of folly and ignorance cannot be patched.
O counsellors, waste not the seed of counsel on them!"

STORY VI. *Moses and Pharaoh* (p. 354).[1]

Then follows a very long account of the dealings of Moses, an incarnation of true reason, with Pharaoh, the exponent of mere opinion or illusion. It begins with a long discussion between Moses and Pharaoh. Moses tells Pharaoh that both of them alike owe their bodies to earth and their souls to God, and that God is their only lord. Pharaoh replies that he is lord of Moses, and chides Moses for his want of gratitude to himself for nurturing him in his childhood. Moses replies that he recognises no lord but God, and reminds Pharaoh how he had tried to kill him in his infancy. Pharaoh complains that he is made of no account by Moses, and Moses retorts that in order to cultivate a waste field it is necessary to break up the soil; and in order to make a good garment, the stuff must first be cut up; and in order to make bread, the wheat must first be ground in the mill, and so on. The best

[1] This story is an expansion of Koran xliii. 50 and following verses, and of Koran xi.

return he can make to Pharaoh for his hospitality to him in his infancy is to set him free from his lust-engendered illusions, like a fish from the fish-hook which has caught him. Pharaoh then twits Moses with his sorceries in changing his staff into a serpent, and thereby beguiling the people. Moses replies that all this was accomplished not by sorcery, like that of Pharaoh's own magicians, but by the power of God, though Pharaoh could not see it, owing to his want of perception of divine things. The ear and the nose cannot see beautiful objects, but only the eye, and similarly the sensual eye, blinded by lust, is impotent to behold spiritual truth. On the other hand, men of spiritual insight, whose vision is purged from lust, become as it were all eyes, and no longer see double, but only the One sole real Being. Man's body, it is true, is formed of earth, but by discipline and contrition it may be made to reflect spiritual verities, even as coarse and hard iron may be polished into a steel mirror. Pharaoh ought to cleanse the rust of evil-doing from his soul, and then he would be able to see the spiritual truths which Moses was displaying before him. The door of repentance is always open. Moses then promised that if Pharaoh would obey one admonition he should receive in return four advantages. Pharaoh was tempted by this promise, and asked what the admonition was. Moses answered that it was this, that Pharaoh should confess that there is no God except the One Creator of all things in heaven and on earth. Pharaoh then prayed him to expound the four advantages he had promised, saying that possibly they might cure him of infidelity, and cause him to become a vessel of mercy, instead of one of wrath. Moses then explained that they were as follows:—(1.) Health. (2.) Long life, ending in the conviction that death is gain. Even as one who knows of a treasure hid in a ruined house pulls down the house to find that treasure, so does the wise man, full of years and experience, pull down the house of the body to gain the treasure of eternal life. The tradition "I was a hidden treasure," &c., bears on this matter. (3.) A better kingdom than that of Egypt, one of peace in place of one of enmity and contention. (4.) Perpetual youth. Pharaoh then proceeded to take counsel with his wife, Asiya, whether it would be advisable to quit his infidelity and believe in the promises of Moses. Asiya, being a pious woman and well inclined to Moses, whom she had nurtured in his infancy, urged him to do so, but Pharaoh said he would first consult his vazir Haman. Asiya had a bad opinion of Haman, whom she knew to be as blind to spiritual truths as Pharaoh himself, and she did her best to dissuade Pharaoh from consulting him. To illustrate Haman's spiritual blindness, she told the story of a royal falcon who fell into the hands of an ignorant old woman. This old woman knew nothing of the virtues of a falcon, and was displeased at the falcon's appearance, and said to it, "What was your mother about to leave your claws and beak so long?" She then proceeded to trim them short, according to her fancy, and of course spoiled the falcon for all purposes of falconry. Pharaoh, however, would not be diverted from his purpose of consulting Haman, and Asiya was fain to console herself with the reflection that like always herds with like, and so Pharaoh must needs consort with Haman, who was in so many respects a duplicate of himself. To illustrate this she recalled the story of a woman whose infant had crawled to the brink of a canal, where it persisted in remaining, at the imminent peril of its life, despite all her calls and entreaties. In her distress she asked aid of 'Ali, who told her to place another infant on the top of the bank. She did so, and her own infant, seeing its playfellow, left the brink of its own accord and came to join its fellow. The spirit of man is of like *genus* with the holy prophets, but man's animal lust with the demons. And as things of like nature attract one another, so unlike things repel one another. Thus it is said that when holy men pray to be delivered from hell, hell also prays that they may be kept away from it. Pharaoh then proceeded to consult Haman, and Haman, on hearing that Moses had proposed to Pharaoh to humble himself and confess the supreme lordship of Allah, was indignant and rent his clothes, saying, "Is not the kingdom of Egypt thine? Art thou not mightier than this despicable fellow?[1] Who is he to degrade Pharaoh from his 'supreme lordship?'" So Pharaoh listened to Haman and refused to be converted to the true faith. Then Moses was much discouraged, but he was consoled by a voice from heaven assuring him that he was well-beloved of God, because in spite of disappointments and through good and evil he clung to God.

On the tradition, "I was a hidden treasure and I desired to be known, and I created the world in order to be known" (p. 360).

Destroy your house, and with the treasure hidden in it[2]
You will be able to build thousands of houses.
The treasure lies under it; there is no help for it;
Hesitate not to pull it down; do not tarry!
For with the coin of that treasure
A thousand houses can be built without labour.
At last of a surety that house will be destroyed,
And the divine treasure will be seen beneath it.
But 'twill not belong to you, because in truth[3]
That prize is the wages for destroying the house.
When one has not done the work he gets no wages;
"Man gets nothing he has not worked for."[4]
Then you will bite your finger, saying, "Alas!
That bright moon was hidden under a cloud.
I did not do what they told me for my good;
Now house and treasure are lost and my hand is empty."
You have taken your house on lease or hired it;
'Tis not your own property to buy and sell.
As to the term of the lease, it is till your death;
In that term you have to turn it to use.

. . . . . .

If before the end of the term of the lease
You omit to derive profit from the house,
Then the owner puts you out of it,
And pulls it down himself to find the gold-mine.
While you are now smiting your head in deep regret,
And now tearing your beard to think of your folly,
Saying, "Alas! that house belonged to me;
I was blind and did not derive profit from it.
Alas! the wind has carried off my dwelling
For ever! 'O misery that rests on slaves!'[1]
In that house of mine I saw but forms and pictures;
I was enchanted with that house so fleeting!
I was ignorant of the treasure hidden beneath it,
Otherwise I would have grasped an axe as a perfume.
Ah! if I had administered the justice of the axe,
I should now have been quit of sorrow.
But I fixed my gaze on outward forms,
Like an infant I sported with playthings.
Well said the famous Hakim Sanai,
'Thou art a child; thy house is full of pictures.'
In his divine poem he gives this advice,
'Sweep away the dust from thy house!'"

They who recognise the almighty power of God do not ask where heaven is or where hell is (p. 366).

"O Pharaoh, if you are wise, I show you mercy;
But if you are an ass, I give you the stick as an ass.
So I will drive you out of your stable,

[1] See Koran xliii. 50.
[2] Compare the *Hadis*, "Die before you die," *i.e.*, mortify your carnal desires, and you will find spiritual treasure.
[3] The Turkish commentator translates *ruh* by *Haqq Yoluna*, "for the sake of truth," "in the way of truth." The Lucknow commentator, as usual, shirks the difficulty.
[4] Koran liii. 40.

[1] Koran xxxvi. 29.

Even as I make your head and ears bleed with my stick.
In this stable asses and men alike
Are deprived of peace by your oppressions.
See! I have brought a staff for the purpose of correcting
Every ass who does not prove tractable.
It turns into a serpent in vengeance against you,
Because you have become a serpent in deed and character.
You are an evil serpent, swelled to the size of a hill.
Yet look at the Serpent (constellation) in heaven.
This staff is a foretaste to you of hell,
Saying, 'Ho, take refuge in the light!
Otherwise you will fall into my jaws,
And will find no escape from my clutches!'
This staff even now became a serpent,
So that you need not ask, 'Where is God's hell?'
God makes a hell wheresover He wills;
He makes the very sky a snare and trap for birds.
He produces pains and aches in your teeth,
So that you say, ''Tis a hell and serpent's bite.'
Or again He makes your spittle as honey,
So that you say, ''Tis heaven and wine of Paradise.'
He makes sugar to grow in your mouth,
That you may know the might of the divine decrees.
Therefore, bite not the innocent with your teeth;
Bear in mind the divine stroke that tarries not."
God made the Nile blood to the Egyptians,
He preserved the Israelites from the peril,
That you might know how God discerns
Between the wise and the foolish wayfarers.
The Nile learned of God discernment
When it let the ones through and engulphed the others.
God's mercy made the Nile wise,
His wrath made Cain foolish.
Of His mercy He created wisdom in inanimate things,
And of His wrath He deprived the wise of wisdom.
Of His mercy wisdom accrued to inanimate things,
As a chastisement He took wisdom from the wise.
Here at His command wisdom was shed down like rain,
Whilst there wisdom saw His wrath and fled away.
Clouds and sun, and moon and lofty stars,
All come and go in obedience to His ordinance;
No one of them comes save at His appointed time;
It lingers not behind nor anticipates that time.
Whereas you understood not this secret, the prophets
Have instilled this knowledge into stone and staff;
So that you may infer that other inanimate things
Without doubt resemble in this stones and staves.
The obedience of stone and staff is shown to you,
And informs you of that of other inanimate things.
They cry, "We are all aware of God and obey Him;
We are not destructive by mere fortuitous chance."
Thus you know the water of the Nile when in flood
Made distinction between the Egyptians and the Israelites.
You know the others are wise as earth, who, when cleft,
Knew Qarun and swallowed him up in vengeance.
Or like the moon, who heard the command and hasted
To sever itself into two halves in the sky.[1]
Or like the trees and stones, which in all places
Were seen to bow down at the feet of Mustafa.

The arguments between a Sunni and a Materialist[2] (*Dahri*) *decided by the arbitrament of fire* (p. 367).

Last night a Sunni said, "The world is transitory;
The heavens will pass away; 'God will be the heir.'"[3]
A philosopher replied, "How know you they are transitory?
How knows the rain the transitory nature of the cloud?
Are you not a mere mote floating in the sunbeams?
How know you that the sun is transitory?
A mere worm buried in a dung-heap,

[1] Koran liv. 1.
[2] Ghazzali divides the ancient Greek philosophers into three classes—Dahriyun, Tabayi'un, and Ilahiyun. Schmölders, Écoles Philosophiques, p. 29.
[3] Koran xv. 23.

How can it know the origin and end of the earth?
In blind belief you have accepted this from your father,
And through folly have clung to it ever since.
Tell me what is the proof of its transitoriness,
Or else be silent and indulge not in idle talk."
The Sunni said, "One day I saw two persons
Engaged in argument on this deep question,—
Yea, in dispute and controversy and argument.
At last a crowd was gathered round them.
I proceeded towards that company
To inform myself of the subject of their discourse.
One said, 'This sky will pass away;
Doubtless this building had a builder.'
The other said, 'It is eternal and without period;
It had no builder, or it was its own builder.'
The first said, 'Do you then deny the Creator,
The Bringer of day and night, the Sustainer of men?'
He answered, 'Without proof I will not listen
To what you say; 'tis only based on blind belief.
Go! bring proof and evidence, for never
Will I accept this statement without proof.'
He answered, 'The proof is within my heart,
Yea, my proofs are hidden in my heart.
From weakness of vision you see not the new moon;
If I see it, be not angry with me!'
Much talk followed, and the people were perplexed
About the origin and end of the revolving heavens.
Then the first said, 'O friend, within me is a proof
Which assures me of the transitoriness of the heavens.
I hold it for certain, and the sign of certainty
In him who possesses it is entering into fire.
Know this proof is not to be expressed in speech,
Any more than the feeling of love felt by lovers.
The secret I labour to express is not revealed
Save by the pallor and emaciation of my face.
When the tears course down my cheeks,
They are a proof of the beauty and grace of my beloved.'
The other said, "I take not these for a proof,
Though they may be a proof to common people."
The Sunni said, "When genuine and base coin boast,
Saying, 'Thou art false, I am good and genuine,'
Fire is the test ultimately,
When the two rivals are cast into the furnace."

. . . . . .

Accordingly both of them entered the furnace,
Both leapt into the fiery flame;
And the philosopher was burnt to ashes,
But the God-fearing Sunni was made fairer than before.

Story VII. *The Courtier who quarrelled with his Friend for saving his Life* (p. 369).

A king was enraged against one of his courtiers, and drew his sword to slay him. The bystanders were all afraid to interfere, with the exception of one who boldly threw himself at the king's feet and begged him to spare the offender. The king at once stayed his hand, and laid down his sword, saying, "As you have interceded for him, I would gladly pardon him, even if he had acted as a very demon. I cannot refuse your entreaties, because they are the same as my own. In reality, it is not you who make these entreaties for him, but I who make them through your mouth. I am the real actor in this matter, you are only my agent. Remember the text, 'You shot not when you shot;'[1] you are, as it were, the foam, and I the mighty ocean beneath it. The mercy you show to this offender is really shown by me, the king." The offender was accordingly released and went his way; but, strange to say, he showed no gratitude to his protector, but, on the contrary, omitted to greet him when he met him, and in other ways refused to recognise the favour he had received from him. This behaviour excited remark, and people questioned him as to the cause of his ingratitude to his benefactor. He

[1] Koran viii. 17.

replied, "I had offered up my life to the king when this man intervened. It was a moment when, according to the tradition, 'I was with God in such a manner that neither prophet nor angel found entrance along with me,[1]' and this man intruded between us. I desired no mercy save the king's blows; I sought no shelter save the king. If the king had cut off my head he would have given me eternal life in return for it. My duty is to sacrifice my life; it is the king's prerogative to give life. The night which is made dark as pitch by the king scorns the brightness of the brightest festal day. He who beholds the king is exalted above all thoughts of mercy and vengeance. Of a man raised to this exalted state no description is possible in this world, for he is hidden in God, and words like 'mercy' and 'vengeance' only express men's partial and weak views of the matter. It is true 'God taught Adam the names of all things,'[2] but that means the real qualities of things, and not such names as ordinary men use, clad in the dress of human speech. The words and expressions we use have merely a relative truth, and do not unfold absolute truth."

He illustrates this by the reply made to the angel Gabriel by Abraham when he was cast into the fire by Nimrod.[3] Gabriel asked him if he could assist him, and Abraham answered, "No! I have no need of your help." When one has attained union with God he has no need of intermediaries. Prophets and apostles are needed as links to connect ordinary men with God, but he who hears the "inner voice" within him has no need to listen to outward words, even of apostles. Although that intercessor is himself dwelling in God, yet my state is higher and more lovely than his. Though he is God's agent, yet I desire not his intercession to save me from evil sent me by God, for evil at God's hand seems to me good. What seems mercy and kindness to the vulgar seems wrath and vengeance to God-intoxicated saints. God's severity and chastisements serve to exalt his saints, though they make the vulgar more ungodly than before, even as the water of the Nile was pure water to the Israelites, but blood to the Egyptians.

[1] See Gulshan i Raz, l. 120.
[2] Koran ii. 29.
[3] See Koran xxi. 68, and the Commentators thereon.

Moses asks the Almighty, "Why hast Thou made men to destroy them?"[1] (p. 371).

Moses said, "O Lord of the day of account,
Thou makest forms; wherefore, then, destroyest Thou them?
Thou makest charming forms, both men and women;
Wherefore, then, dost Thou lay them waste?"
God answered, "I know that this query of thine
Proceeds not from negation or vain curiosity.
Otherwise I should chastise and punish thee;
Yea, I should rebuke thee for this question.
But thou seekest to discover in my actions
The ruling principle and the eternal mystery,
In order to inform the people thereof,
And to make 'ripe' every 'raw' person.
Yea, O messenger, thou questionest me that I may reveal
My ways to the people, though thou knowest them.

. . . .

O Moses, go and sow seed in the ground
In order to do justice to this question."
When Moses had sowed and his seed had grown up,
He took a sickle and reaped the corn,
And then a divine voice reached his ears:—
"Why hast thou sown and nurtured the corn,
And then cut it down directly it was ripe?"
Moses replied, "Lord, I cut it and lay it low
Because here I have grain and straw.
Grain is out of place in the straw-yard,
And straw is useless in the wheat-barn.

[1] So Job x. 8: "Thy hands have made me, yet Thou dost destroy me."

'Tis wrong to mix these two,
It is needful to sift them one from the other."
God said, "From whom learnest thou this knowledge
Whereby thou hast constructed a threshing-floor?"
Moses said, "O Lord, Thou hast given me discernment."
God said, "Then have not I also discernment?
Amongst my creatures there are pure spirits,
And also dark and befouled spirits.
The oyster-shells are not all of the same value;
Some contain pearls, and others black stones.
It is needful to discern the bad from the good,
Just as much as to sift wheat from straw.
The people of this world exist in order to manifest
And to disclose the 'hidden treasure.'
Read, 'I was a hidden treasure, and desired to be known;'
Hide not the hidden treasure, but disclose it.
Your true treasure is hidden under a false one,
Just as butter is hidden within the substance of milk.
The false one is this transitory body of yours,
The true one your divine soul.
Long time this milk is exposed to view,
And the soul's butter is hidden and of no account.

. . . . . .

Stir up your milk assiduously with knowledge,
So that what is hidden in it may be disclosed;
Because this mortal is the guide to immortality,
As the cries of revellers indicate the cup-bearer."

STORY VIII. *The Prince who, after having been beguiled by a Courtesan, returned to his True Love* (p. 373).

A certain king dreamed that his dearly beloved son, a youth of great promise, had come to an untimely end. On awaking he was rejoiced to find that his son was still alive; but he reflected that an accident might carry him off at any moment, and therefore decided to marry him without delay, in order that the succession might be secured. Accordingly he chose the daughter of a pious Darvesh as a bride for his son, and made preparations for the wedding. But his wife and the other ladies of his harem did not approve of the match, considering it below the dignity of the prince to marry the daughter of a beggar. The king rebuked them, saying that a Darvesh who had renounced worldly wealth for the sake of God was not to be confounded with an ordinary beggar, and insisted on the consummation of the marriage. After the marriage the prince refused to have anything to do with his bride, though she was very fair to look on, and he carried on an intrigue with an ugly old woman who had bewitched him by sorcery. After a year, however, the king found some physicians who succeeded in breaking the spell, and the prince returned to his senses, and his eyes were opened to the superior attractions of his wife, and he renounced his ugly paramour and fell in love with his wife. This is a parable, the true wife being the Deity, the old paramour the world, and the physicians the prophets and saints. Another illustration is a child who played at besieging a mimic fort with his fellows, and succeeded in capturing it and keeping the others out. At this moment God "bestowed on him wisdom, though a child,"[1] and it became to him a day "when a man flees from his brethren,"[2] and he recognised the emptiness of this idle sport, and engaged in the pursuit of holiness and piety. This is followed by an anecdote of a devotee who had so concentrated his thoughts on things above that he was utterly careless of all earthly troubles, and was cheerful and rejoicing even in the midst of a severe famine.

[1] Koran xix. 13. [2] Koran lxxx. 34.

The world is the outward form of "Universal Reason" (Muhammad), and he who grieves him must expect trouble in the world [1] (p. 377).

The whole world is the outward form of Universal Reason,
For it is the father of all creatures of reason.
When a man acts basely towards Universal Reason,
Its form, the world, shows its teeth at him.
Be loyal to this father and renounce disobedience,
That this earthy house may furnish you golden carpets.
Then the judgment-day will be the "cash of your state,"
Earth and heavens will be transfigured before you.[2]
I am ever in concord with this father of ours,
And earth ever appears to me as a Paradise.
Each moment a fresh form, a new beauty,
So that weariness vanishes at these ever-fresh sights.
I see the world filled with blessings,—
Fresh waters ever welling up from new fountains.
The sound of those waters reaches my ears,
My brain and senses are intoxicated therewith.
Branches of trees dancing like fair damsels,
Leaves clapping hands like singers.
These glories are a mirror shining through a veil;
If the mirror were unveiled, how would it be?
I tell not one in a thousand of them,
Because every ear is stopped with doubt.
To men of illusions these tales are mere good tidings,
But men of knowledge deem them not tidings, but ready cash.

This is illustrated by an anecdote of Ezra or 'Uzair and his sons.[3] On his return from Babylon, whither he had been carried captive by Nebuchadnezzar, Ezra beheld the ruins of Jerusalem, and he said, "How shall God give life to this city after it hath been dead?" And God caused him to die for a hundred years, and then raised him again to life, and said to him, "How long hast thou waited?" He said, "I have waited a day." God said, "Nay, thou hast waited a hundred years. Look at the dead bones of thine ass; we will raise them and clothe them with flesh." Ezra was raised from the dead as a young man, whereas his sons were then, of course, very old men. They met him, and asked if he had seen their father. He replied, "I have seen him; he is coming." Some of them rejoiced, considering this good news; but others, who had loved him more dearly, knew him and fainted with joy. What was mere good tidings to the men of opinion was the "ready money of their state" to men of real knowledge.

[1] "*Aql i Kull*, Universal Reason, or the Logos, was identified with the prophet Muhammad."

[2] Koran xiv. 49.

[3] This story comes from Koran ii. 261.

STORY IX. *The Mule and the Camel* (p. 379).

A mule said to a camel, "How is it that I am always stumbling and falling down, whilst you never make a false step?" The camel replied, "My eyes are always directed upwards, and I see a long way before me, while your eyes look down, and you only see what is immediately under your feet." The mule admitted the truth of the camel's statement, and besought him to act as his guide in future, and the camel consented to do so. Just so partial reason cannot see beyond the grave, but real reason looks onward to the day of judgment, and, therefore, is enabled to steer a better course in this world. For this cause, men having only partial reason or mere opinion of their own ought to follow the guidance of the saints, according to the text, "O believers, enter not upon any affair ere God and his Apostle lead the way."[1]

Then follows another anecdote of an Egyptian who asked an Israelite to draw water for him from the Nile, because the water of the Nile turned to blood when drawn by an Egyptian. Afterwards the Egyptian asked the

[1] Koran xlix. 1.

Israelite to pray for him, and the Israelite admonished him to renounce his egotism and conceit of his own existence, which blinded his eyes to divine verities. In illustration of this he tells the same story of an adulterous woman, which is known as the "Merchant's Tale" in Chaucer. This woman, desiring to carry on an intrigue with her paramour, climbed up a pear-tree to gather the fruit, and when she had reached the top she looked down, and pretended that she saw her husband misconducting himself with another woman. The husband assured her there was no one but himself there, and desired her to come down and see for herself. She came down and admitted there was no one there. Her husband then, at her request, ascended the tree, and she at once called her paramour, and began to amuse herself with him. Her husband saw her from his post in the tree, and began to abuse her; but she declared there was no man with her, and that the pear-tree made her husband see double, just as it had made her see double previously.

The evolution of man (p. 385).

First he appeared in the class of inorganic things,[1]
Next he passed therefrom into that of plants.
For years he lived as one of the plants,
Remembering naught of his inorganic state so different;
And when he passed from the vegetive to the animal state
He had no remembrance of his state as a plant,
Except the inclination he felt to the world of plants,
Especially at the time of spring and sweet flowers.
Like the inclination of infants towards their mothers,
Which know not the cause of their inclination to the breast,
Or the excessive inclination of young disciples
Towards their noble and illustrious teachers.
The disciple's partial reason comes from *that* Reason,
The disciple's shadow is from *that* bough.
When the shadows in the disciples cease,
They know the reason of their attachment to the teachers.
For, O fortunate one, how can the shadow move,
Unless the tree that casts the shadow move as well?
Again, the great Creator, as you know,
Drew man out of the animal into the human state.
Thus man passed from one order of nature to another,
Till he became wise and knowing and strong as he is now.
Of his first souls he has now no remembrance,
And he will be again changed from his present soul.
In order to escape from his present soul full of lusts
He must behold thousands of reasonable souls.
Though man fell asleep and forgot his previous states,
Yet God will not leave him in this self-forgetfulness;
And then he will laugh at his own former state,
Saying, "What mattered my experiences when asleep?
When I had forgotten my prosperous condition,
And knew not that the grief and ills I experienced
Were the effect of sleep and illusion and fancy?
In like manner this world, which is only a dream,
Seems to the sleeper as a thing enduring for ever
But when the morn of the last day shall dawn,
The sleeper will escape from the cloud of illusion;
Laughter will overpower him at his own fancied griefs
When he beholds his abiding home and place.
Whatever you see in this sleep, both good and evil,
Will all be exposed to view on the resurrection day.
Whatever you have done during your sleep in the world
Will be displayed to you clearly when you awake.
Imagine not that these ill deeds of yours exist not
In this sleep of yours, and will not be revealed to you.
But your present laughter will turn to weeping and woe
On the day of revealing, O you who oppress captives!
Your present wailing and sorrow and griefs,
On the other hand, will be joy when you awake.

[1] See the parallel passage in Gulshan i Raz, l. 317, and the note. It is based on the Aristotelian doctrine of the ascending grades of the soul, or vital principle.

O you, who have rent the garments of many Josephs,
You will rise from your heavy sleep as a wolf.
Your bad qualities will rise in the shape of wolves
And rend you limb from limb in vengeance.
By the law of retaliation blood sleeps not after death;
Say not, "I shall die and obtain pardon."
The retaliation of this world is illusive,
It is mere sport compared to the retaliation to come.
Therefore God calls the world "a pastime and a sport," [1]
For punishment in this world is sport compared to that.
Here punishment is as the repression of quarrels,
There it is as castration or circumcision.
But this discourse is endless, O Moses,
Go and leave these asses to their grazing!
Let them fatten themselves with the food they love,
For they are very wolves and objects of my wrath.

Zu'l Qarnain at Mount Qaf [2] (p. 387).

Zu'l Qarnain journeyed to Mount Qaf;
He saw it was formed of a bright emerald,
Forming as it were a ring round the world,
Whereat all people are filled with wonder.
He said, "Thou mighty hill, what are other hills?
Before thee they are mere playthings."
The Mount replied, "Those hills are my veins,
But they are not like me in beauty and importance.
A hidden vein from me runs to every city,
The quarters of the world are bound to my veins.
When God desires an earthquake under any city,
He bids me shake one of my veins.
Then in anger I shake that vein
Which is connected with that particular city.
When He says, 'Enough,' my vein remains still,
I remain still, and then haste to perform my work.
Now still like a plaster, and now operating;
Now still like thought, and then speaking my thought.
But they who are void of reason imagine
That these earthquakes proceed from earth's vapours."
Just so an ant, who saw a pen writing on paper,
Delivered himself to another ant in this way:—
'That pen is making very wonderful figures,
Like hyacinths and lilies and roses.'
The other said, 'The finger is the real worker,
The pen is only the instrument of its working.'
A third ant said, 'No; the action proceeds from the arm,
The weak finger writes with the arm's might.'
So it went on upwards, till at last
A prince of the ants, who had some wit,
Said, 'Ye regard only the outward form of this marvel,
Which form becomes senseless in sleep and death.
Form is only as a dress or a staff in the hand,
It is only from reason and mind these figures proceed.'
But he knew not that this reason and mind
Would be but lifeless things without God's impulsion.

The angel Gabriel appears to the Prophet Muhammad (p. 388).

Mustafa said to the angel Gabriel,
"O friend, show me thy form as it really is;
Show it to me openly and perceptibly,
That I may behold thee with my eyes."
Gabriel said, "Thou canst not do so, thou art too weak,
Thy senses are exceeding weak and frail."
Muhammad said, "Show it, that this body of mine may see
To what extent its senses are frail and impotent.
True, man's bodily senses are frail,

[1] Koran xxix. 64.
[2] Zu'l Qarnain, Chaucer's Dulkarn, means "He of the two horns," and here denotes Alexander the Great.

But he possesses within him a mighty property.[1]
This body resembles flint and steel,
But like them it has the power of kindling fire.
Flint and steel are able to generate fire,
From them springs fire which can destroy its parents."

. . . .

As he continued importuning him, Gabriel displayed
His awful form, whereat the mountains were rent asunder.
It occupied the sky from east to west.
And Mustafa swooned with fear.
When Gabriel beheld him swooning with fear,
He came and clasped him in his arms.

Address to Husamu-'d-Din (p. 389).

O light of God, Husamu-'d-Din, admit
This ass's head into that melon-garden!
For when this ass is killed in the slaughter-house
That kitchen will bestow upon him a new existence.
From me proceeds the form, from thee the spirit;
Nay, form and spirit both proceed from thee!
Thou art as Muhammad in heaven, O brilliant Sun!
Be also as Muhammad on earth for ever and ever!
So that earth and heaven on high may be united
With one heart, one worship, one aspiration!
And schism and polytheism and duality disappear,
And Unity abide in the Real Spiritual Being!
When my spirit recognises thy spirit,
We remember our essential union and origin.

[1] See the parallel passage in Gulshan i Ras, l. 431, and the note thereon. This property is the mystic "inner light" or spiritual intuition.

Book V.

Story I. *The Prophet and his Infidel Guest* (p. 393).

After the usual address to Husamu-'d-Din follows a comment on the precept addressed to Abraham, "Take four birds and draw them towards thee, and cut them in pieces."[1] The birds are explained to be the duck of gluttony, the cock of concupiscence, the peacock of ambition and ostentation, and the crow of bad desires, and this is made the text of several stories. Beginning with gluttony, the poet tells the following story to illustrate the occasion of the Prophet's uttering the saying, "Infidels eat with seven bellies, but the faithful with one." One day some infidels begged food and lodging of the Prophet. The Prophet was moved by their entreaties, and desired each of his disciples to take one of the infidels to his house and feed and lodge him, remarking that it was their duty to show kindness to strangers at his command, as much as to do battle with his foes. So each disciple selected one of the infidels and carried him off to his house; but there was one big and coarse man, a very giant Og, whom no one would receive, and the Prophet took him to his own house. In his house the Prophet had seven she-goats to supply his family with milk, and the hungry infidel devoured all the milk of those seven goats, to say nothing of bread and other viands. He left not a drop for the Prophet's family, who were therefore much annoyed with him, and when he retired to his chamber one of the servant-maids locked him in. During the night the infidel felt very unwell in consequence of having overeaten himself, and

[1] Koran ii. 262.

tried to get out into the open air, but was unable to do so, owing to the door being locked. Finally, he was very sick, and defiled his bedding. In the morning he was extremely ashamed, and the moment the door was opened he ran away. The Prophet was aware of what had happened, but let the man escape, so as not to put him to shame. After he had gone the servants saw the mess he had made, and informed the Prophet of it; but the Prophet made light of it, and said he would clean it up himself. His friends were shocked at the thought of the Prophet soiling his sacred hands with such filth, and tried to prevent him, but he persisted in doing it, calling to mind the text, "As thou livest, O Muhammad, they were bewildered by drunkenness,"[1] and being, in fact, urged to it by a divine command. While he was engaged in the work the infidel came back to look for a talisman which he had left behind him in his hurry to escape, and seeing the Prophet's occupation he burst into tears, and bewailed his own filthy conduct. The Prophet consoled him, saying that weeping and penitence would purge the offence, for God says, "Little let them laugh, and much let them weep;"[2] and again, "Lend God a liberal loan;"[3] and again, "God only desireth to put away filthiness from you as His household, and with cleansing to cleanse you."[4] The Prophet then urged him to bear witness that God was the Lord, even as was done by the sons of Adam,[5] and explained how the outward acts of prayer and fasting bear witness of the spiritual light within. After being nurtured on this spiritual food the infidel confessed the truth of Islam, and renounced his infidelity and gluttony. He returned thanks to the Prophet for bringing him to the knowledge of the true faith and regenerating him, even as 'Isa had regenerated Lazarus. The Prophet was satisfied of his sincerity, and asked him to sup with him again. At supper he drank only half the portion of milk yielded by one goat, and steadfastly refused to take more, saying he felt perfectly satisfied with the little he had already taken. The other guests marvelled much to see his gluttony so soon cured, and were led to reflect on the virtues of the spiritual food administered to him by the Prophet.

Outward acts bear witness of the state of the heart within (p. 396).

Prayer and fasting and pilgrimage and holy war
Bear witness of the faith of the heart.
Giving alms and offerings and quitting avarice
Also bear witness of the secret thoughts.
So, a table spread for guests serves as a plain sign,
Saying, "O guest, I am your sincere well-wisher."
So, offerings and presents and oblations
Bear witness, saying, "I am well pleased with you."
Each of these men lavishes his wealth or pains,—
What means it but to say, "I have a virtue within me,
Yea, a virtue of piety or liberality,
Whereof my oblations and fasting bear witness"?
Fasting proclaims that he abstains from lawful food,
And that therefore he doubtless avoids unlawful food.
And his alms say, "He gives away his own goods;
It is therefore plain that he does not rob others."
If he acts thus from fraud, his two witnesses
(Fasting and alms) are rejected in God's court;—
If the hunter scatters grain
Not out of mercy, but to catch game;—
If the cat keeps fast, and remains still
In fasting only to entrap unwary birds;—
Making hundreds of people suspicious,
And giving a bad name to men who fast and are liberal;—
Yet the grace of God, despite this fraud,
May ultimately purge him from all this hypocrisy.
Mercy may prevail over vengeance, and give the hypocrite

[1] Koran xv. 72.
[2] Koran ix. 33.
[3] Koran lxxiii. 20.
[4] Koran xxxiii. 33.
[5] Koran vii. 171.

Go on, walk into the fire, walk joyously into our pyre

Such light as is not possessed by the full moon.
God may purge his dealings from that hypocrisy,
And in mercy wash him clean of that defilement.
In order that the pardoning grace of God may be seen,
God pardons all sins that need pardon.
Wherefore God rains down water from the sign Pisces,
To purify the impure from their impurities.[1]

. . . .

Thus acts and words are witnesses of the mind within,
From these two deduce inferences as to the thoughts.
When your vision cannot penetrate within,
Inspect the water voided by the sick man.
Acts and words resemble the sick man's water,
Which serves as evidence to the physician of the body.
But the physician of the spirit penetrates the soul,
And thence ascertains the man's faith.
Such an one needs not the evidence of fair acts and words;
"Beware of such, they spy out the heart."
Require this evidence of act and word only from one
Who is not joined to the divine Ocean like a stream.
But the light of the traveller arrived at the goal,
Verily that light fills deserts and wastes.
That witness of his is exempt from bearing witness,
And from all trouble and risk and good works.
Since the brilliance of that jewel beams forth,
It is exempted from these obligations.
Wherefore require not from him act and word evidence,
Because both worlds through him bloom like roses.
What is this evidence but manifestation of hidden things,
Whether it be evidence in word, or deed, or otherwise?
Accidents serve only to manifest the secret essence;
The essential quality abides, and accidents pass away.
This mark of gold endures not the touchstone,
But only the gold itself, genuine and undoubted.
These prayers and holy war and fasting
Will not endure, only the noble soul endures.

[1] "Islam is the baptism of God" (Koran ii. 132).

The soul exhibits acts and words of this sort,
Then it rubs its substance on the touchstone of God's command,
Saying, "My faith is true, behold my witnesses!"
But witnesses are open to suspicion.
Know that witnesses must be purified,
And their purification is sincerity, on that you may depend.
The witness of word consists in speaking the truth,
The witness of acts in keeping one's promises.
If the witness of word lie, its evidence is rejected,
And if the witness of act play false, it is rejected.
Your words and acts must be without self-contradiction
In order to be accepted without question.
"Your aims are different,"[1] and you contradict yourselves,
You sew by day, and tear to pieces by night.
How can God listen to such contradictory witness,
Unless He be pleased to decide on it in mercy?
Act and word manifest the secret thoughts and mind,
Both of them expose to view the veiled secret.
When your witnesses are purified they are accepted,
Otherwise they are arrested and kept in durance.
They enter into conflict with you, O stiff-necked one;
"Stand aloof and wait for them, for they too wait."[2]

Prayers for spiritual enlightenment (p. 399).

O God, who hast no peer, bestow Thy favour upon me;
Since Thou hast with this discourse put a ring in my ear,
Take me by the ear, and draw me into that holy assembly
Where Thy saints in ecstasy drink of Thy pure wine!
Now that Thou hast caused me to smell its perfume,
Withhold not from me that musky wine, O Lord of faith!
Of Thy bounty all partake, both men and women,
Thou art ungrudging in bounties, O Hearer of prayer.
Prayers are granted by Thee before they are uttered,

[1] Koran xcii. 4.
[2] Koran xxxii. 30. *I.e.*, Wait thou for their punishment, as they wait for thy downfall (Rodwell).

Thou openest the door to admit hearts every moment!
How many letters Thou writest with Thy Almighty pen!
Through marvelling thereat stones become as wax.
Thou writest the *Nun* of the brow, the *Sad* of the eye,
And the *Jim* of the ear, to amaze reason and sense.
These letters exercise and perplex reason;
Write on, O skilful Fair-writer!
Imprinting every moment on Not-being the fair forms
Of the world of ideals, to confound all thought![1]
Yea, copying thereon the fair letters of the page of ideals,
To wit, eye and brow and moustache and mole!
For me, I will be a lover of Not-being, not of existence,
Because the beloved of Not-being is more blessed.[2]
God made reason a reader of all these letters,
To suggest to it reflections on that outpouring of grace.[3]
Reason, like Gabriel, learns day by day
Its daily portion from the "Indelible Tablet."[4]
Behold the letters written without hands on Not-being!
Behold the perplexity of mankind at those letters!
Every one is bewildered by these thoughts,
And digs for hidden treasure in hope to find it.

This bewilderment of mankind as to their true aims is compared to the bewilderment of men in the dark looking in all directions for the Qibla, and recalls the text, "O the misery that rests upon my servants."[5]

Then follow reflections on the sacrifice by Abraham of the peacock of ambition and ostentation. Next comes a discourse on the thesis that all men can recognise the mercies of God and the wrath of God; but God's mercies are often hidden in His chastisements, and *vice versâ*, and it is only men of deep spiritual discernment who can recognise acts of mercy and acts of wrath concealed in their opposites. The object of this concealment is to try and test men's dispositions; according to the text, "To prove which of you will be most righteous in deed."[1]

[1] Here we have another Platonic doctrine. "Some say the belief of the Sufis is the same as that of the Ishraqin (Platonists)." Dabistan i Muzahib, by Shea and Troyer, iii. 281.

[2] *I.e.*, I will recognise the nonentity of all this phenomenal being, and court self-annihilation.

[3] The Bulaq translator renders *An naward* thus.

[4] The "Indelible Tablet" (of God's decrees) is here applied to the Logos,—the channel through whom God renews the "world of creation" day by day.

[5] Koran xxxvi. 29.

Story II. *The Arab and his Dog* (p. 402).

The doctrine of the Mu'tazilites,[2] already mentioned, that all men's intellects are alike and equal at birth, is again controverted, and the poet dwells on the essential differences which characterise the intellects akin to Universal Reason or the Logos, and those swayed by partial or carnal reason; the former, like the children of Israel, seeking exaltation through self-abasement; and the others, like Pharaoh, running after worldly rank and power, to their own destruction. In order to make probation of men, as already explained, God fills the world with deceptions,[3]—making apparent blessings destructive to us, and apparent evils salutary. On the other hand, if men try to deceive God, they fail signally. Hypocritical weeping and wailing like that of Joseph's brethren is at once detected by God. Thus a certain Arab had a dog to which he was much attached; but one day the dog died of hunger. He at once began to weep and wail, and disturbed the whole neighbourhood by his ostentatious grief. One of the neighbours came and inquired into the matter, and on hearing that the dog had died of hunger, he asked the Arab why he had not fed him from the wallet of food which he had in his hand. The Arab said that he had collected this food to support himself, and made it a principle not to part with any of it to any one who could not pay for it; but that, as his tears cost him

[1] Koran lxvii. 2.

[2] The Mu'tazilites were one of the principal unorthodox sects. See Sale, Prelim. Disc., p. 112.

[3] "Of them who devise stratagems, God is best" (Koran iii. 47).

nothing, he was pouring them forth in token of the sorrow he felt for his dog's death. The neighbour, on hearing this, rebuked him for his hypocrisy, and went his way.

Then follows a commentary on the text, "Almost would the infidels strike thee down with their very looks when they hear the reading of the Koran."[1]

Story III. *The Sage and the Peacock* (p. 404).

A sage went out to till his field, and saw a peacock busily engaged in destroying his own plumage with his beak. At seeing this insane self-destruction the sage could not refrain himself, but cried out to the peacock to forbear from mutilating himself and spoiling his beauty in so wanton a manner. The peacock then explained to him that the bright plumage which he admired so much was a fruitful source of danger to its unfortunate owner, as it led to his being constantly pursued by hunters, whom he had no strength to contend against; and he had accordingly decided on ridding himself of it with his own beak, and making himself so ugly that no hunter would in future care to molest him. The poet proceeds to point out that worldly cleverness and accomplishments and wealth endanger man's spiritual life, like the peacock's plumage; but, nevertheless, they are appointed for our probation, and without such trials there can be no virtue.

"*There is no monkery in Islam*"[2] (p. 405).

Tear not thy plumage off, it cannot be replaced;
Disfigure not thy face in wantonness, O fair one!
That face which is bright as the forenoon sun,—
To disfigure it were a grievous sin.
'Twere paganism to mar such a face as thine!
The moon itself would weep to lose sight of it!

[1] Koran lxviii. 51.

[2] A *Hadis*.

Knowest thou not the beauty of thine own face?
Quit this temper that leads thee to war with thyself!
It is the claws of thine own foolish thoughts
That in spite wound the face of thy quiet soul.
Know such thoughts to be claws fraught with poison,
Which score deep wounds on the face of thy soul.

. . . .

Rend not thy plumage off, but avert thy heart from it,
For hostility between them is the law of this holy war.
Were there no hostility, that war would be impossible.
Hadst thou no lust, obedience to the law could not be.[1]
Hadst thou no concupiscence there could be no abstinence.
Where no antagonist exists, what need is there of armies?
Ah! make not thyself an eunuch,[2] become not a monk,
Because chastity is mortgaged to lust.
Without lust denial of lust is impossible;
No man can display bravery against the dead.
God says, "Expend;"[3] wherefore earn money.
Since expenditure is impossible without previous gain?
Although the passage contains only the word "Expend,"
Read "Acquire first, and then expend."
In like manner, when the King of kings says "Abstain,"[4]
It implies an object of desire wherefrom to abstain.
Again, "Eat ye," is said recognising the snares of lust,
And afterwards, "Exceed not," to enjoin temperance.
When there is no subject,
The existence of a predicate is not possible.[6]
When thou endurest not the pains of abstinence,
And fulfillest not the terms, thou gainest no reward.
How easy those terms! how abundant that reward!—
A reward that enchants the heart and charms the soul!

This is followed by the admonition that the only way

[1] Cp. Bp. Butler, "On a state of probation as implying trial and danger" (Analogy, Chap. iv. Pt. 1).

[2] Probably referring to Origen.

[3] Koran ii. 264.

[4] Koran iii. 200.

[5] Koran vi. 142: "Eat of their fruit, but be not prodigal, and exceed not."

[6] Or, "If there be no supporter, there can be nothing supported."

to be safe from one's internal enemies is to annihilate self, and to be absorbed in the eternity of God, as the light of the stars is lost in the light of the noonday sun. Everything but God is at once preyed on by others, and itself preys on others, like the fowl which, when catching a worm, was itself caught by a cat. Men are so intent on their own low objects of pursuit that they see not their foes who are trying to make them their prey. Thus it is said, "Before them have we set a barrier, and behind them a barrier, so that they shall not see."[1] Persons who lust after the vile pleasures of this world, and desire long life, not to serve God, but to satisfy their own carnal lusts, resemble the crow slain by Abraham, because he only lived for the sake of carrion; or Iblis, who prayed to be respited till the day of judgment, not for the purpose of reforming himself, but only to do mischief to mankind.[2]

Prayers to God to change our base inclinations and give us higher aspirations (p. 409).

O Thou that changest earth into gold,
And out of other earth madest the father of mankind,
Thy business is changing things and bestowing favours,
My business is mistakes and forgetfulness and error.
Change my mistakes and forgetfulness to knowledge;
I am altogether vile, make me temperate and meek.
O Thou that convertest salt earth into bread,
And bread again into the life of men;
Thou who madest the erring soul a guide to men,
And him that erred from the way a prophet;[3]
Thou makest some earth-born men as heaven,
And multipliest heaven-born saints on earth!
But whoso seeks his water of life in worldly joys,
To him comes death quicker than to the rest.
The eyes of the heart which behold the heavens
See that the Almighty Alchemist is ever working here.
Mankind are ever being changed, and God's elixir
Joins the body's garment without aid of needle.
On the day that you entered upon existence,
You were first fire, or earth, or air.
If you had continued in that, your original state,
How could you have arrived at this dignity of humanity?
But through change your first existence remained not;
In lieu thereof God gave you a better existence
In like manner He will give you thousands of existences,
One after another, the succeeding ones better than the former.
Regard your original state, not the mean states,
For these mean states remove you from your origin.
As these mean states increase, union recedes;
As they decrease, the unction of union increases.
From knowing means and causes holy bewilderment fails;
Yea, the bewilderment that leads you to God's presence.
You have obtained these existences after annihilations;
Wherefore, then, do you shrink from annihilation?
What harm have these annihilations done you
That you cling so to present existence, O simpleton?
Since the latter of your states were better than the former,
Seek annihilation and adore change of state.
You have already seen hundreds of resurrections
Occur every moment from your origin till now;
One from the inorganic state to the vegetive state,
From the vegetive state to the animal state of trial;
Thence again to rationality and good discernment;
Again you will rise from this world of sense and form.

. . . .

Ah! O crow, give up this life and live anew!
In view of God's changes cast away your life!
Choose the new, give up the old,
For each single present year is better than three past.

This is followed by a commentary on the saying of the Prophet, "Pity the pious man who falls into sin, and the

[1] Koran xxxvi. 8. [2] Koran vii. 13. [3] Koran xciii. 7.

rich man who falls into poverty, and the wise man who falls into the company of fools." This is illustrated by an anecdote of a young deer who was placed in the asses' stable, and jeered at and maltreated by them. This suggests—

STORY IV. *Muhammad Khwarazm Shah and the Ráfizis of Sabzawar* (p. 411).

Muhammad Shah was the last prince but one of the Khwarazm dynasty of Balkh, to which family both the poet's mother and grandmother belonged. He was the reigning prince in A.D. 1209, the year in which the poet's father fled from Balkh, and was defeated by Chingiz Khan a year or two later. In one of his campaigns Muhammad Shah captured the city of Sabzawar, in Khorasan, which city was inhabited by Ráfizis or rank Shi'as, naturally most obnoxious to a Sunni prince claiming descent from the first Khalif Abu Bakr. After the city was taken the inhabitants came out, and proceeded with all humility to beg their lives, offering to pay any amount of ransom and tribute that he might impose upon them. But the prince replied that he would spare their lives only on one condition, viz., that they produced from Sabzawar a man bearing the name Abu Bakr. They represented to him that it would be impossible to find in the whole city a single man bearing a name so hateful to the Shi'as; but the prince was inexorable, and refused to alter the conditions. So they went and searched all the neighbourhood, and at last found a traveller lying at the roadside at the point of death, who bore the name of Abu Bakr. As he was unable to walk, they placed him on a bier and carried him into the king's presence. The king reproached them for their contempt and neglect of this pious Sunni, the only true heart amongst them, and reminded them of the saying of the Prophet, "God regards not your outward show and your wealth, but your hearts and your deeds." In this parable, says the poet, Sabzawar is the world, the poor Sunni the man of God, despised and rejected of men, and the king is God Almighty, who seeks a true heart amongst evil men.

Satan's snares for mankind (p. 413).

Thus spake cursed Iblis to the Almighty,
"I want a mighty trap to catch human game withal."
God gave him gold and silver and troops of horses,
Saying, "You can catch my creatures with these."
Iblis said, "Bravo!" but at the same time hung his lip,
And frowned sourly like a bitter orange.
Then God offered gold and jewels from precious mines
To that laggard in the faith,
Saying, "Take these other traps, O cursed one."
But Iblis said, "Give me more, O blessed Defender."
God gave him succulent and sweet and costly wines,
And also store of silken garments.
But Iblis said, "O Lord, I want more aids than these,
In order to bind men in my twisted rope
So firmly that Thy adorers, who are valiant men,
May not, man-like, break my bonds asunder."

. . . .

When at last God showed him the beauty of women,
Which bereaves men of reason and self-control,
Then Iblis clapped his hands and began to dance,
Saying, "Give me these; I shall quickly prevail with these!"

This is followed by comments on the text, "Of goodliest fabric we created man, and then brought him down to the lowest of the low, saving those who believe and do the things that are right;"[1] and on the verses,—

"If thou goest the road, they will show thee the road;
If thou becomest naught, they will turn thee to being."

[1] Koran xcv. 4.

Story V. *The Man who claimed to be a Prophet* (p. 417).

A man cried out to the people, "I am a prophet; yea, the most excellent of the prophets." The people seized him by the collar, saying, "How are you any more a prophet than we are?" He replied, "Ye came to earth from the spirit-world as sleeping children, seeing nothing of the way; but I came hither with my eyes open, and marked all the stages of the way like a guide." On this they led him before the king, and begged the king to punish him. The king, seeing that he was very infirm, took pity on him, and led him apart and asked him where his home was. The man replied, "O king, my home is in the house of peace (heaven), and I am come thence into this house of reproach." The king then asked him what he had been eating to make him rave as he did, and he said if he lived on mere earthly bread he should not have claimed to be a prophet. His preaching was entirely thrown away on worldly men, who only desire to hear news of gold or women,[1] and are annoyed with all who speak to them of the eternal life to come. They cleave to the present life so fast that they hate those who tell them of another. They say, "Ye are telling us old fables and raving idly;" and when they see pious men prospering they envy them, and, like Satan, become more opposed to them. God said, "What thinkest thou of him who holdeth back a servant of God when he prayeth?"[2] The king then said to him, "What is this inspiration of yours, and what profit do you derive from it?" The man answered, "What profit is there that I do not derive from it? I grant I am not rich in worldly wealth, yet the inspiration God teaches me is surely as precious as that which He taught the bees.[3] God taught them to make wax and honey, and He teaches me nobler things than these. Whoso has his face reddened with celestial wine is a prophet of like disposition with Muhammad, and whoso is unaffected by that spiritual drink is to be accounted an enemy to God and man."

[1] Koran iii. 12. [2] Koran xcvi. 9. [3] Koran xvi. 70.

The Prophet's prayer for the envious people (p. 419).

O Thou that givest aliment and power and stability,
Set free the people from their instability.
To the soul that is bent double by envy
Give uprightness in the path of duty,
Give them self-control, "weigh down their scales,"[1]
Release them from the arts of deceivers.
Redeem them from envying, O gracious One,
That through envy they be not stoned like Iblis.[2]
Even in their fleeting prosperity, see how the people
Burn up wealth and men through envy!
See the kings who lead forth their armies
To slay their own people from envy!
Lovers of sweethearts have conceived jealousy,
And attempted one another's lives,
Read "Wais and Rámin" and "Khosrau and Shirin,"
To see what these fools have done to one another.
Lovers and beloved have both perished;
And not themselves only, but their love as well.
'Tis God alone who agitates these nonentities,
Making one nonentity fall in love with another.
In the heart that is no heart envy comes to a head,
Thus Being troubles nonentity.

This is followed by an anecdote of a lover who recounted to his mistress all the services he had done, and all the toils he had undergone for her sake, and inquired if there was anything else he could do to testify the sincerity of his love. His mistress replied, "All these things you have done are but the branches of love; you have not

[1] Koran ci. 5.
[2] Koran xv. 17. The sin of Iblis was his envy of Adam.

yet attained to the root, which is to give up life itself for the sake of your beloved." The lover accordingly gave up his life, and enjoyed eternal fruition of his love, according to the text, "O thou soul which art at rest, return to thy Lord, pleased, and pleasing Him."[1]

This is followed by a statement of the doctrine of the jurist Abu Hanífa, to whose school the poet belonged, that weeping, even aloud, during prayer does not render the prayers void, provided that the weeping be caused by thoughts of the world to come, and not by thoughts of this present world.[2] And, apparently in allusion to the name Abu Hanífa, the poet recalls the text, "They followed the faith of Abraham, the orthodox" (*Hanífun*).[3]

Story VI. *The Disciple who blindly imitated his Shaikh* (p. 421).

An ignorant youth entered an assembly of pious persons who were being addressed by a holy Shaikh. He saw the Shaikh weeping copiously, and in mere blind and senseless imitation he copied the Shaikh's behaviour, and wept as copiously himself, though he understood not a word of the discourse. In fact, he behaved just like a deaf man who sees those around him laughing, and laughs himself out of compliment to them, though he knows not the subject of their merriment, and is obliged to have it explained to him before he can laugh again with real perception of the joke. After he had wept in this ignorant way for some time he made due obeisance to the Shaikh, and took his departure. But one of the Shaikh's true disciples, being jealous for the honour of his master, followed him, and thus addressed him, "I adjure you by Allah that you go not and say, 'I saw the Shaikh weeping, and I too wept like him.' Your ignorant and mere imitative weeping is totally unlike the weeping of that holy saint. Such weeping as his is only possible to one who has, like him, waged the spiritual war for thirty years. His weeping is not caused by worldly griefs, but by the deep concerns of the spirit. You cannot perceive by reason or sense the spiritual mysteries that are open and plain to his enlightened vision, any more than the darkness can behold the light. His breathings are as those of 'Isa, and not like mere human sighs raised by worldly sorrows. His tears and his smiles and his speeches are not his own, but proceed from Allah. Fools like you are ignorant of the motive and design of saints' actions, and therefore only harm themselves if they try to imitate them, without understanding their meaning." To illustrate this a curious story is told of a foolish lady who copied a trick of her clever slave-girl, without understanding the *modus operandi*, and by so doing caused her own death. In like manner parrots are taught to speak without understanding the words. The method is to place a mirror between the parrot and the trainer. The trainer, hidden by the mirror, utters the words, and the parrot, seeing his own reflection in the mirror, fancies another parrot is speaking, and imitates all that is said by the trainer behind the mirror. So God uses prophets and saints as mirrors whereby to instruct men, being Himself all the time hidden behind these mirrors, viz., the bodies of these saints and prophets; and men, when they hear the words proceeding from these mirrors, are utterly ignorant that they are really being spoken by "Universal Reason" or the "Word of God" behind the mirrors of the saints.

The worthlessness of mere blind imitation (*taqlid*) *of religious exercises* (p. 421).

When a friend tells a joke to his friend,
The deaf man who listens laughs twice over;—
The first time from imitation and foolishness,
Because he sees all the party laughing;—
Yet, though he laughs like the others,

[1] Koran lxxxix. 27.
[2] Mishkat ul Masabih, i. p. 209, note.
[3] Koran iv. 124.

He is then ignorant of the subject of their laughter ;—
Then he inquires what the laughter was about,
And, on hearing it, proceeds to laugh a second time.
Wherefore the blind imitator is like a deaf man,
In regard to the joy he feigns to feel.
The light is the Shaikh's, the fountain the Shaikh's,
And the outpouring of joy is also the Shaikh's, not his.
'Tis like water in a vessel, or light through a glass;
If they think they come from themselves, they are wrong.
When the vessel leaves the fountain, it sees its error;
It sees the water in it comes from the fountain.
The glass also learns, when the moon sets,
That its light proceeded from the shining of the moon.
When his eyes are opened by the command, "Arise!"[1]
Then that disciple smiles a second time, like the dawn.
He laughs also at his own previous laughter,
Which overtook him out of mere blind imitation.
When he returns from his long and distant wanderings
He says, "Lo! this was the truth, this the secret!
With what blindness and misconception did I pretend.
To experience joy in that distant valley?
What a delusion I was under! what a mistake!
My feeble wit conjured up vain imaginations."
How can an infant on the road know the thoughts of men?
How far its fancies are removed from true knowledge!
The thoughts of infants run on the nurse and milk,
Or on raisins or nuts, or on crying and wailing.
The blind imitator is like a feeble infant,
Even though he possesses fine arguments and proofs.
His preoccupation with obscure arguments and proofs
Drags him away from insight into truth.
His stock of lore, which is the salve of his eyes,
Bears him off and plunges him in difficult questions.
Ah! man of imitation, come out of Bokhara![2]

[1] Koran lxxiv. 2. Dawn smiles first as "false dawn," and the second time as "true dawn."
[2] Alluding to Bokhari, the author of the "*Sahih Bokhari,*" the first and most esteemed collection of traditions.

And humble yourself in order to be exalted.
Then you will behold another Bokhara within you,
Whereof the heroes ignore these questions of law.
Though a footman may be swift of foot on land,
Yet on the sea he is as one with ruptured tendons.
That footman is only "carried by land,"[1]
But he who is "carried by sea" is the truly learned one.
The King of kings showers special favours upon him;
Know this, O man pledged to vain illusions!

The mere legal theologian is impotent to behold the light of the Spirit (p. 422).

When the day dawns from heaven night flees away;
What, then, can its darkness know of the nature of light?
The gnat scuds away before the blast of the winds;
What, then, knows the gnat of the savour of the winds?
When the Eternal appears the transitory is annulled;
What, then, knows the transitory of the Eternal?
When He sets foot on the transitory He bewilders it;
When it is become naught He sheds his light upon it.[2]
If you wish, you can adduce hundreds of precedents,
But I take no heed of them, O man poor in spirit!
The letters *Lam*, *Mim*, and *Ha*, *Mim* prefixed to some Suras
Resemble the staff of Moses, when fully understood.[3]
Ordinary letters resemble these to outward view,
But are far beneath them in signification.
If an ordinary man take a staff and try it,
Will it prove like the staff of Moses in the test?
This breath of 'Isa is not like every ordinary breath,
Which proceeds from mere human joy or sorrow.
These *Alif*, *Mim*, *Ha* and *Mim*, O father,

[1] Koran xvii. 72. The man of "external knowledge" is "carried only by land," but the mystic is led over sea as well.
[2] When reason is annihilated, the "Truth" is reflected in the resulting *caput mortuum* or Not-being, as in a mirror (Gulshan i Raz, l. 125).
[3] These letters were supposed to have mysterious meanings. See Rodwell, Koran, p. 17, note.

Proceed from the Lord of mankind.
If you have sense, regard not in the same way as these
Every ordinary *Alif* and *Lam* which resembles these;
Although these sacred letters consist of common ones,
And resemble common ones in their composition.
Muhammad himself was formed of flesh and skin,
Although no man is of the same genus as he.
He had flesh and skin and bones,
Although no man resembles him in composition;
Because in his composition were contained divine powers,
Whereby all human flesh was confounded.
In like manner the composition of the letters *Ha, Mim*
Is far exalted above ordinary compounds of letters;
Because from these mysterious compositions comes life,
Even as utter confusion follows the last trump.
That staff becomes a serpent and divides the Nile,
Like the staff of *Ha, Mim*, by the grace of God.
Its outward form resembles the outward forms of others,
Yet the disk of a cake differs much from the moon's disk.
The saint's weeping and laughter and speech
Are not his own, but proceed from God.
Whereas fools look only to outward appearances,
These mysteries are totally hidden from them;
Of necessity the real meaning is veiled from them,
For the mystery is lost in the intervening medium.

. . . .

Then follows an anecdote of a man who heard whelps barking in their mother's womb. A voice came from heaven and explained that these whelps were like the men who have not emerged into the light of truth, but are still veiled in spiritual darkness, and, though they make pretensions to spiritual sight, their discourses are useless, both to procure spiritual food for themselves, and to warn their hearers of spiritual dangers.

Next comes an anecdote of a pious man of Zarwán, who made a point of giving to the poor four times the legal amount of alms due from his growing crops. Thus, instead of paying one-tenth on each crop, which is the legal amount enjoined by the Prophet,[1] he was wont to pay one-tenth of the green ears of corn, another tenth of the ripe wheat, a third tenth of the threshed grain, and a fourth of the bread made therefrom, and so on with grapes and other produce of his garden. In recognition of his piety God blessed his garden and made it bear fruit abundantly. But his sons, who were blind to spiritual matters, saw only his lavish expenditure upon the poor, and could not see the divine blessing upon the garden, called down by his liberality, and rebuked him for his extravagance. There is no limit to the divine bounty, because God's ability to bestow bounties, unlike human ability, is unbounded and infinite.

Story VII. *How Adam was created out of a handful of earth brought by an Angel* (p. 428).

When the Almighty determined to create mankind to be proved by good and evil, He deputed the angel Gabriel to bring a handful of earth for the purpose of forming Adam's body. Gabriel accordingly girded his loins and proceeded to the Earth to execute the divine commands. But the Earth, being apprehensive that the man so created would rebel against God and draw down God's curse upon her, remonstrated with Gabriel, and besought him to forbear. She represented that Gabriel would at the last day be pre-eminent over all the eight angels who would then support the throne,[2] and that it therefore was only right that he should prefer mercy to judgment. At last Gabriel granted her prayer, and returned to heaven without taking the handful of earth. Then God deputed Michael on the same errand, and the Earth made similar excuses to him, and he also listened to her crying, and returned to heaven without taking a handful. He excused

[1] Miskat ul Masabih, i. 417.

[2] Koran lxix. 17.

himself to the Almighty by citing the example of the people to whom the prophet Jonah was sent, who were delivered from the threatened penalty in consequence of their lamentation for their sins;[1]—and the text, "If He please, He will deliver you from that which ye shall cry to Him to avert."[2] Then God sent the angel Israfil on the same errand, and he also was diverted from the execution of it by a divine intimation. At last God sent 'Izrail, the angel of death, who, being of sterner disposition than the others, resolutely shut his ears to the Earth's entreaties, and brought back the required handful of earth. The Earth pressed him with the argument that God's command to bear away a handful of her substance against her will did not override the other divine command to take pity on suppliants; but 'Izrail would not listen to her, remarking that, according to the canons of theological interpretation, it was not allowable to have recourse to analogical reasoning to evade a plain and categorical injunction. He added, that in executing this injunction, painful though it might be, he was to be regarded only as a spear in the hand of the Almighty. The moral is, that when any of God's creatures do us a harm, we ought to regard them only as instruments of God, who is the Only Real Agent.

God the Only Real Agent (p. 431).

Do not, like fools, crave mercy from the spear,
But from the King in whose hand the spear is held.
Wherefore do you cry to spear and sword,
Seeing they are captives in the hand of that Noble One?
He is as Azar, maker of idols; I am only the idol;
Whatever instrument He makes me, that I am.
If He makes of me a cup, a cup am I;
If He makes of me a dagger, a dagger am I.
If He makes me a fountain, I pour forth water;
If He makes me fire, I give forth heat.
If He makes me rain, I produce rich crops;
If He makes me a dart, I pierce bodies.
If He makes me a snake, I dart forth poison;
If He makes me a friend, I serve my friends.
I am as the pen in the fingers of the writer,
I am not in a position to obey or not at will.

On the return of 'Izrail to heaven with the handful of earth, God said he would make him the angel of death. 'Izrail represented that this would make him very hateful to men; but God said 'Izrail would operate by disease and sickness, and men would not look for any cause beyond these diseases, according to the text, "He is nearer to you than ye are; yet ye see Him not."[1] Moreover, death is in reality a boon to the spiritual, and it is only fools who cry, "Would that this world might endure for ever, and that there were no such thing as death!"

Death is gain, for "God will change their evil things into good things"[2] (p. 432).

One said, "The world would be a pleasant place
If death never set foot within it."
Another answered, "If there were no death,
The complicated world would be worth not a jot.
It would be a crop raised in a desert,
Left neglected and never threshed out.
Thou fanciest that to be death, which is life,
Thou sowest thy seed in salt ground.
Carnal reason deceives us; do thou contradict it,
For that fool takes what is really death to be life.
O God, show us all things in this house of deception,—
Show them all as they really are!"[3]

. . . .

It is said in the *Hadis* that on the last day

[1] Koran x. 98.

[2] Koran vi 41.

[1] Koran lvi. 84.

[2] Koran xxv. 70. The "final restitution" of all by free grace.

[3] Cp. the *Hadis*: "Inspiration is a light that shines in the heart, and shows the nature of all things as they really are."

The command, "Arise," will come to every single body.
The blast of the last trump will be God's command
To every atom to lift its head from the earth.
The souls, also, of each will return to their bodies,
Even as sense returns to bodies awaking from sleep.
On that morn each soul will recognise its own body,
And return to its own ruin like hidden treasure.
It will recognise its own body and enter it.
The soul of the goldsmith will not enter the tailor;
The soul of the wise will enter the body of the wise,
The soul of the unjust the body of the unjust.

. . . .

In like manner as the souls will fly into their clay,
So will the books fly into their right hands and left.[1]
God will place in their hands their books of greed and liberality,
Of sin and piety, and whatever they have practised.
When they shall awake from sleep on that morning,
All the evil and good they have done will recur to them.

. . . .

Every thought which has dwelt in them during life
Will appear as a form visible to all,[2]
Like the thought of an architect realised in a house,
Or the perfect plant issuing from the seed in the ground.

. . . .

From onion and saffron and poppy
The hand of spring will unfold the secret of winter.
This one will be verdant and flourish, saying, "We are the pious;"
That other will hang his head like the violet,—
With tears starting from his eyes through deadly fear;
Yea, tens of founts of tears through terrible dread;
With eyes wide opened in deadly apprehension
Lest his book may be placed in his left hand.

. . . .

Then will the evildoer be sent to the fiery prison,

[1] See Koran lxix. 18.
[2] See the parallel passage in Gulshan i Raz, l. 690.

For thorn can in no wise escape the flame.
When his guardian angels behind and before,
Who before were unseen, shall appear like patrols,
They will hurry him off, pricking him with their spears,
And saying, "O dog, begone to thy kennel!"

. . . .

Then the prisoner will cry, "O Lord, I am a hundred,
Yea, a hundred times as wicked as Thou sayest.
But in mercy Thou veilest my sins,
Otherwise my vileness were known to Thy all-seeing eye.
But, independently of my own works and warfare,—
Independently of my faith or unfaith, good or evil,—
Independently of my poor devotion to Thee,
And of my thoughts and the thoughts of hundreds like me,—
I fix my hopes on Thy mercy alone.
Whether Thou adjudge me upright or rebellious,
I sue for free pardon from Thy unbought justice.
O Lord, who art gracious without thought of consequence,
I set my face towards that free grace of Thine;
I have no regard to my own acts.
I set my face towards this hope,
Seeing that Thou gavest me my being first of all;
Thou gavest me the garment of being unasked,
Wherefore I firmly trust in Thy free grace."
When he thus enumerates his sins and faults,
God at last will grant him pardon as a free gift,
Saying, "O angels, bring him back to me,
Since the eyes of his heart were set on hope,
Without care for consequences I set him free,
And draw the pen through the record of his sins!"

STORY VIII. *Mahmud and Ayáz*[1] (p. 434).

Mahmud, the celebrated king of Ghazni, had a favourite named Ayaz, who was greatly envied by the other courtiers. One day they came to the king and informed him that

[1] All the latter part of this story is a parable of the last judgment.

Ayaz was in the habit of retiring to a secret chamber, and locking himself in, and that they suspected he had there concealed coin stolen from the treasury, or else wine and forbidden drink. The fact was, that Ayaz had placed in that chamber his old shoes and the ragged dress which he used to wear before the king had promoted him to honour, and used to retire there every day and wear them for a time, in order to remind himself of his lowly origin, and to prevent himself from being puffed up with pride. This he did in accordance with the text, "Let man reflect out of what he was created."[1] The intoxication of the present life puffs up many with false pride, even as Iblis, who refused to worship Adam, saying, "Who is Adam, that he should be lord over me?" This he said because he was one of the Jinn, who are all created of fire.[2] Adam, on the other hand, confessed his own vileness, saying, "Thou hast formed me out of clay." The king was well assured of the fidelity of Ayaz; but in order to confute those who suspected him, he ordered them to go by night and break open that chamber and bring away all the treasure and other things hidden in it. It is a characteristic of evildoers to think evil of the saints, because they judge of their conduct by the light of their own evil natures, as the crooked foot makes a crooked footprint, and as the spider sees things distorted through the web he has spun himself. The king's conduct in this did not betoken any diminution of his love for Ayaz, because lover and beloved are always as one soul, though they may be opposed to outward view. Accordingly the courtiers proceeded to the chamber of Ayaz at night, and broke open the door, and searched the floor and the walls, but found only the old shoes and the ragged dress. They then returned to the king discomfited and shamefaced, even as the wicked who have slandered the saints will be on the day of judgment, according to the text, "On the resurrection day thou shalt see those who have lied

[1] Koran lxxxvi. 5. [2] Koran xviii. 48 and lv. 14.

of God with their faces black."[1] Then they besought the king to pardon their offence, but he refused, saying that their offence had been committed against Ayaz, and that he would leave it to Ayaz to decide whether they should be punished or pardoned. If Ayaz showed mercy it would be well; and if he punished it would be well also, for "the law of retaliation is the security for life."[2] Only he enjoined him to pronounce his sentence without delay, because "Waiting is punishment."

A description of genuine union with God (p. 438).

A loved one said to her lover to try him,
Early one morning, "O such an one, son of such an one,
I marvel whether you hold me more dear,
Or yourself; tell me truly, O ardent suitor!"
He answered, "I am so entirely absorbed in you,
That I am full of you from head to foot.
Of my own existence nothing but the name remains,
In my being is nothing besides you, O Object of desire!
Therefore am I thus lost in you,
Just as vinegar is absorbed in honey;
Or as a stone, which is changed into a pure ruby,
Is filled with the bright light of the sun.
In that stone its own properties abide not,
It is filled with the sun's properties altogether;
So that, if afterwards it holds itself dear,
'Tis the same as holding the sun dear, O beloved!
And if it hold the sun dear in its heart,
'Tis clearly the same as holding itself dear.
Whether that pure ruby hold itself dear,
Or hold the sun dear,
There is no difference between the two preterences;
On either hand is naught but the light of dawn.
But till that stone becomes a ruby it hates itself,
For till it becomes one 'I,' it is two separate 'I's,'

[1] Koran xxxix. 61. [2] Koran ii. 175.

When no result was gained from the coordinates on the map. The shah was most dissatisfied:

For 'tis then darkened and purblind,
And darkness is the essential enemy of light.
If it *then* hold itself dear, it is an infidel;
Because that self is an opponent of the mighty Sun.
Wherefore 'tis unlawful for the stone then to say 'I,
Because it is entirely in darkness and nothingness."

Pharaoh said, "I am the Truth," and was laid low.
Mansur Hallaj said, "I am the Truth," and escaped free.[1]
Pharaoh's "I" was followed by the curse of God;
Mansur's "I" was followed by the mercy of God, O beloved!
Because Pharaoh was a stone, Mansur a ruby;
Pharaoh an enemy of light, Mansur a friend.
O prattler, Mansur's "I am He" was a deep mystic saying,
Expressing union with the light, not mere incarnation.[2]

STORY IX. *The sincere repentance of Nasúh* (p. 443).

Ayaz, in weighing the pros and cons in regard to pardoning the courtiers, remarks that professions of faith and penitence when contradicted by acts are worthless, according to the text, "If ye ask them who hath created the heavens and the earth, they will say 'God;' yet they devise lies."[3] And in illustration of this he tells a story of a faithless husband who retired to a secret chamber ostensibly to say his prayers, but really to carry on an intrigue with a slave-girl, and the falsity of whose pretences was demonstrated by ocular proof of his condition. In like manner, on the day of resurrection man's hands and eyes and feet will bear witness against him of the evil actions done by him, thus confuting his pretences to piety. The test of a sincere repentance is abhorrence of past sins and utter abandonment of all pleasure in them,—the old love for sin being superseded by the new love for holiness.

[1] See Gulshan i Raz, Answer vii. p. 45. Mansur Hallaj (woolcarder), the celebrated Sufi who was put to death at Bagdad in 309 (A. H.)

[2] See Gulshan i Raz, l. 454, and note. The doctrine of the descent of the Deity into man (*Halúl*), or incarnation, is rejected both by Rumi and Shabistari in favour of the doctrine of intimate union (*Ittihad* or *Wahdat*).

[3] Koran xxix. 61.

Such a repentance was that of Nasúh. Nasúh in his youth disguised himself in female attire and obtained employment as attendant at the women's baths, where he used to carry on shameful intrigues with some of the women who frequented the bath. At last, however, his eyes were opened to the wickedness of his conduct, and he went to a holy man and besought him to pray for him. The holy man, imitating the long-suffering of the "Veiler of sins," did not so much as name his sin, but prayed, saying, "God give thee repentance of the sin thou knowest!" The prayer of that holy man was accepted, because the prayers of such an one are the same as God's own will, according to the tradition, "My servant draws nigh to me by pious works till I love him; and when I love him I am his ear, his eye, his tongue, his foot, his hand; and by me he hears, sees, talks, walks, and feels." Nasúh then returned to the bath a truly repentant man; but soon afterwards one of the women frequenting the bath lost a valuable jewel, and the king gave order that all persons connected with the bath should be stripped and searched. When the officers came to the bath to execute this order Nasúh was overwhelmed with fear, for he knew that if his sex were discovered he would certainly be put to death. In his fear he called upon God for deliverance, and swooned with fear and became beside himself, so that his natural self was annihilated, and he became a new creature, even as a corpse rising from the grave. When he came to himself he found that the lost jewel had been found, and those who had suspected him came and begged his pardon. Shortly afterwards the king's daughter sent for him to come and wash her head; but, in spite of her imperative commands, he refused to place himself again in the way of temptation, lest he might fall again, and God might "make easy to him the path to destruction."[1]

[1] Koran xcii. 10.

Man's members will bear witness against him on the day of judgment, and confute his claims to piety (p. 443).

On the resurrection day all secrets will be disclosed;
Yea, every guilty one will be convicted by himself.
Hand and foot will bear testimony openly
Before the Almighty concerning their owner's sins.
Hand will say, "I stole such and such things;"
Lip will say, "I asked for such and such things."
Foot will say, "I went after my own desires;"
Arm will say, "I embraced the harlot."
Eye will say, "I looked after forbidden things;"
Ear will say, "I listened to evil talk."
Thus the man will be shown to be a liar from head to foot,
Since his own members will prove him to be a liar.

STORY X. *The Lion, the Fox, and the Ass* (p. 445).

As an instance of false and insincere repentance, a story is next told, which is also found in the fifth chapter of the *Anwar i Suhaili*. A lion had been wounded in fight with a male elephant, and was unable to hunt game for himself. In this strait he called a fox who was wont to attend upon him, and to live on the meat that was left from his repasts, just as disciples attending on a saint subsist on the heavenly food dropping from his lips. He called this fox, and bade him go and entice some animal to come near his lair, so that he might kill it and make a meal of it. The fox went and searched the neighbourhood, and at last found a lean and hungry ass who was grazing in a stony place where there was little or no grass. The fox, after making due salutations, condoled with the ass on his unfortunate condition; but the ass replied that it was his divinely appointed lot, and that it would be impious to complain of the dispensations of Providence. He also instanced the case of the ass of a water-carrier, which, after having starved and worked hard in its master's service, by chance found admittance to the king's stables, where it was struck by the sleek appearance of the horses. But one day the horses were taken out to battle, and returned in a most miserable plight, some grievously wounded, and others dying. After seeing this sight it determined that its own hard life was preferable, and returned to its master. The fox replied that the ass was wrong in carrying passive resignation to such an extent as to refuse to try to better his condition when the opportunity of doing so presented itself, because God says, "Go in quest of the bounties of God."[1] He added, if the ass would come with him, he would take him to a delightful meadow, where he would never lack plenty of grass all the year round. The ass rejoined that the command to strive for sustenance was only issued on account of the weakness of man's faith. The fox replied that this exalted faith was only vouchsafed to a few great saints, because the Prophet describes contentment as a treasure, and treasure is not found by every one. The ass rejoined that the fox was perverting the Scripture, as no pious man who trusted in God was ever forsaken. In illustration of this he told an anecdote of a devotee who determined to put the matter to the test, and went out into the desert, trusting only to God to supply his wants, and resolved to seek no aid of man, and not to exert himself in any way to gain food. He lay down on a stone and went to sleep; and God sent a caravan of travellers that way, who found him, and forced him to take food in spite of himself. The fox again pressed the ass to try to better his condition, saying that God had given men hands to use, and not to do nothing with. The ass answered that he knew of no occupation and exertion better than trust in God, as worldly occupations often lead to ruin, according to the text, "Throw not yourselves with your own hands into ruin."[2] But though the ass repeated all these excellent precepts, yet it was only so much cant on his part, because he was not firmly

[1] Koran lxii. 10. [2] Koran ii. 191.

rooted in the faith. He had all the time a carnal hankering after the pleasant grazing-ground the fox told him of, and the objections he made were only a parrot-like repetition of precepts heard, but not thoroughly understood and taken to heart. To illustrate the worthless nature of mere imitated religion and profession divorced from practice, a story is told of an infamous fellow who used to carry a dagger to protect as he said, his honour, though his every action showed that he had neither honour to protect nor manliness to protect it. The ass, though like Abraham, he had broken his idols, had not a sufficiently rooted faith to leap, like Abraham, into the fire, and thus prove his faith. [Here the poet apologises for the trivial illustrations he uses by citing the text, "Verily God is not ashamed to set forth as well the instance of a gnat as of any nobler object"[1].] Finally the ass yielded to the fox's enticement, and accompanied him to the lion's lair. The lion, being famished with hunger, sprang upon him the moment he appeared. Being, however, weak with sickness and fasting, he missed his aim, and the ass escaped with a slight wound. Then the fox blamed the lion for his precipitation, and the lion, after excusing himself as best he could, persuaded the fox to try to allure the ass a second time into his lair. The fox consented to try, observing that experience would probably have been thrown away on an ass, and his vows of repentance forgotten. Those who lapse from repentance, in forgetfulness of their former experience, may be compared to the Jews changed into apes and swine by 'Isa.[2] The fox was received by the ass with many reproaches for having deceived him; but he at last managed to persuade the ass that what he had seen was not a real lion, but only a harmless talisman; and the silly ass allowed himself to be again deluded, and forgot his vows of repentance, and again followed the fox to the lion's lair, where he speedily met his doom.

[1] Koran ii. 24. [2] Koran v. 65.

Men who make professions of holiness merely from blind imitation of others are detected and confuted by the opposition between their words and their deeds (p. 449).

A man asked a camel, saying, "Ho! whence comest thou,
Thou beast of auspicious footstep?"
He replied, "From the hot bath of thy street."
The man said, "That is proved false by thy dirty legs!"
So, when stubborn Pharaoh saw Moses' staff a serpent,
And begged for a delay (to fetch magicians)[1] and relented,
Wise men said, "He ought to have become harsher,
If He really be, as He says, the Lord Supreme.[2]
What could miracles such as these of serpents,
Or even dragons, matter to the majesty of His divinity?
If He be really Lord Supreme, seated on His throne,
What need has He to wheedle a worm like Moses?"
O babbler, while thy soul is drunk with mere date wine,
Thy spirit hath not tasted the genuine grapes.
For the token of thy having seen that divine light
Is this, to withdraw thyself from the house of pride.
When a fowl flies to the salt water,
It has never beheld the blessing of sweet water;
But its faith is mere imitation of other fowl,
And its soul has never seen the face of real faith.
Wherefore the blind imitator encounters great perils,—
Perils of the road, of robbers, of cursed Satans.
But when he has seen the light of God, he is safe
From the agitation of doubt, and is firm in the faith.
Till the foam has landed on the shore and dry land,
Which is its home, it is ever tossed to and fro.
'Tis at home on the land, but a stranger on the water.
While it remains a stranger, it must be tossed about.
When its eyes are opened, and it sees the vision of land,
Satan has no longer any domination over it.
Although the ass repeated verities to the fox,

[1] Koran xx. 25. [2] Koran xxviii. 38.

He spoke them idly and in the way of cant.
He praised the water, but was not eager to drink;
He rent his garments and his hair, but was no real lover.
The excuse of a hypocrite is rejected, not approved,
Because it comes only from the lips, not from the heart.
He has the scent of the apple, but not a piece of it,
And the scent only for the purpose of misleading others.
Thus a woman's onset in the midst of a battle array,—
She keeps in line, and forms part of the battle array,
Yet, though she looks a very lion as she stands in line,
Her hand begins to tremble as soon as she takes a sword.
Woe to him whose reason is like a woman
While his lust is like a resolute man!
Of a certainty his reason will be worsted in the fight,
And his imitation of a man will only lead him to ruin.
Happy is he whose reason is masculine,
And his ugly lust feminine and under subjection!

. . . .

Though the mere imitator quotes a hundred proofs,
They are all based on opinion, not on conviction.
He is only scented with musk, he is not himself musk;
He smells of musk, but is really naught but dung.
For his dung to become musk, O disciple,
He must graze year after year in the divine pasture.
For he who, like the musk-deer, feeds on saffron of Khoten
Must not eat grass and oats like asses.

. . . .

That man of cant has at his tongue's end
A hundred proofs and precepts, but there is no life in him.
When the preacher has himself no light or life,
How can his words yield leaves and fruit?
He impudently preaches to others to walk aright,
While himself he is unsteady as a reed shaken by wind.
Thus, though his preaching is very eloquent,
It hides within it unsteadiness in the faith.

In order to gain true wisdom man must shake off worldly illusions (p. 453).

The fox said, "In my pure wine there are no dregs;
These vain suspicions are not becoming.
All this is only baseless suspicion, O simple one,
Else you would know I am not plotting against you.
You repudiate me on account of your own bad fancies;
Why do you thus suspect your true friends?
Think well of the 'Brothers of purity,' [1]
Even though they show harshness toward you;
For when evil suspicion takes hold of you,
It severs you from hundreds of friends.
If a tender friend treats you roughly to try you,
'Tis contrary to reason to distrust him.
Though I bear a bad name, my nature is not malevolent;
What you saw was not dangerous, it was only a talisman.
But even if there were danger in that object of suspicion,
Friends always pardon an offence."
This world of illusions, fancies, desires, and fears,
Is a mighty obstacle in the traveller's path.
Thus, when these forms of delusive imaginations
Misled Abraham, who was a very mountain of wisdom,
He said of the star, "This is my Lord," [2]
Having fallen into the midst of the world of illusion.
He thus interpreted the meaning of sun and stars,—
Yea, he, that great man who threaded jewels of interpretation,
Seeing then that this world of eye-fascinating illusion
Seduced from the right path such a mountain as Abraham,
So that he said of the star, "This is my Lord,"—
What will not its illusions effect on a stupid ass?
Human reason is drowned, like the high mountains,
In the flood of illusion and vain imaginations.
The very mountains are overwhelmed by this flood,

[1] A society at Basra, who wrote, about 980 A.D., an encyclopædia of philosophy (trans. by Dieterici).
[2] Koran vi. 76.

Where is safety to be found save in Noah's ark?
By illusions that plunder the road of faith
The faithful have been split into seventy-two sects.
But the man of conviction escapes illusion;
He does not mistake his eyelash for the new moon.
He who is divorced from 'Omar's light
Is deceived by his own crooked eyelash.[1]
Thousands of ships, in all their majesty and pomp,
Have gone to pieces in this sea of illusion.

Then follows an anecdote of Shaikh Muhammad of Ghazni, who was named "*Sar i Razi*," because he used to take only a vine-leaf to break his fast. He dwelt a long time in the desert, and was there miraculously preserved from death, and directed by divine intimation to proceed to Ghazni, and beg money of the rich and distribute it to the poor. After he had done this some time a second intimation came to him to beg no longer, as the money for his charities would be supplied to him miraculously. He at last attained to such a degree of spiritual insight that he knew the wants of those who came to him for aid before they uttered them. He said the reason of this preternatural discernment was, that he had purified his heart of all but the love of God, and thus, whenever thoughts of anything besides God occurred to his mind, he knew they did not appertain to him, but must have been in some way suggested to him by the person asking aid of him.

Then follow some reflections on the power of fasting and abstinence to subdue the carnal lusts which lead man to destruction; and two short anecdotes to illustrate the thesis that God never fails to provide sustenance for those who take no thought for the morrow, but place absolute trust in Him.

The fate of the ass then suggests to the poet another train of reflections. After the lion had slain the ass, he went to the river to quench his thirst, telling the fox to watch the dead body till he returned; but the moment the lion's back was turned the fox ate up the heart and liver, which are the daintiest parts. When the lion returned and inquired for them, the fox assured him that the ass had possessed neither a heart nor a liver, for if he had he would never have shown himself so stupid. Men without understanding are not really men at all, but only *simulacra* or forms of men. For lack of understanding many will cry in the world to come, "Had we but hearkened or understood, we had not been among the dwellers in the flame."[1] Then follows a story of a monk (Diogenes) who took a lantern and searched all through a bazaar crowded with men to find, as he said, a man.

[1] Alluding to the first anecdote in Book ii.

The monk's search for a man (p. 459).

The monk said, "I am searching everywhere for a man
Who lives by the life of the breath of God."
The other said, "Here are men; the bazaar is full;
These are surely men, O enlightened sage!"
The monk said, "I seek a man who walks straight
As well in the road of anger as in that of lust.
Where is one who shows himself a man in anger and lust?
In search of such an one I run from street to street.
If there be one who is a true man in these two states,
I will yield up my life for him this day!"
The other, who was a fatalist, said, "What you seek is rare.
But you are ignorant of the force of the divine decree;
You see the branches, but ignore the root.
We men are but branches, God's eternal decree the root.
That decree turns from its course the revolving sky,
And makes foolish hundreds of planets like Mercury.
It reduces to helplessness the world of devices;
It turns steel and stone to water.

[1] Koran lxxvii. 10.

O you who attribute stability to these steps on the road,
You are one of the raw ones; yea, raw, raw!
When you have seen the millstone turning round,
Then, prithee, go and see the stream that turns it.
When you have seen the dust rising up into the air,
Go and mark the air in the midst of the dust.
You see the kettles of thought boiling over,
Look with intelligence at the fire beneath them.
God said to Job, 'Out of my clemency
I have given a grain of patience to every hair of thine.'
Look not, then, so much at your own patience;
After seeing patience, look to the Giver of patience.
How long will you confine your view to the waterwheel?
Lift up your head and view also the water."

STORY XI. *The Musulman who tried to convert a Magian* (p. 460).

A Musulman pressed a Magian to embrace the true faith. The Magian replied, "If God wills it, no doubt I shall do so."[1] The Musulman replied, "God certainly wills it, that your soul may be saved from hell; but your own evil lusts and the Devil hold you back." The Magian retorted, using the arguments of the *Jabriyan* or "Compulsionists," that on earth God is sole sovereign, and that Satan and lust exist and act only in furtherance of God's will. To hold that God is pulling men one way and Satan another is to derogate from God's sovereignty. Man cannot help moving in the direction he is most strongly impelled to go; if he is impelled wrongly he is no more to blame than a building designed for a mosque but degraded into a fire-temple, or a piece of cloth designed for a coat but altered into a pair of trousers. The truth is, that whatever occurs is according to God's will, and Satan himself is only one of His agents. Satan resembles the Turkoman's dog who sits at the door of the tent, and is "vehement against aliens, but full of tenderness to friends."[1] The Musulman then replied with the arguments of the *Qadarians* and *Mu'tazilites,* to prove the freedom of the will and consequent responsibility of man for his actions. He urged that man's free agency and consequent responsibility are recognised in common parlance, as when we order a man to act in a certain way,—that God expressly assumes man to be a free agent by addressing commands and prohibitions to him, and by specially exempting some, such as the blind,[2] from responsibility for certain acts,—that our internal consciousness assures us of our power of choice, just as outward sense assures us of properties in material objects, —and that it is just as sophistical to disbelieve the declarations of the interior consciousness, as those of the outward senses as to the reality of the material world. He then told an anecdote of a man caught robbing a garden and defending himself with the fatalist plea of irresponsibility, to whom the owner of the garden replied by administering a very severe beating, and assuring him that this beating was also predestined, and that he therefore could not help administering it. He concluded his argument by repeating that the traditions, "Whatever God wills is," and "The pen is dry, and alters not its writing," are not inconsistent with the existence of freewill in man. They are not intended to reduce good action and evil to the same level, but good actions will always entail good consequences, and bad actions the reverse. A devotee admired the splendid apparel of the slaves of the Chief of Herat, and cried to Heaven, "Ah! learn from this Chief how to treat faithful slaves!" Shortly after the Chief was deposed, and his slaves were put to the torture to make them reveal where the Chief had hidden his treasure, but not one would betray the secret. Then a voice from heaven came to the devotee, saying, "Learn from them how to be a faithful

[1] Note the true believer is here represented as using the arguments of the *Qadarians* or *Mu'tazilites* for free will, as against the *Jabriyan* or fatalist argument put into the mouth of the Magian.

[1] Koran xlviii. 29.

[2] Koran xxiv. 60.

slave, and then look for recompense." The Magian, unconvinced by the arguments of the Musulman, again plied him with "Compulsionist" arguments, and the discussion was protracted, with the usual result of leaving both the disputants of the same opinion as when they began. The poet remarks that the contest of the "Compulsionists" and the advocates of man's free agency will endure till the day of judgment; for nothing can resolve these difficulties[1] but the true love which is "a gift imparted by God to whom He will."[2]

Love puts reason to silence (p. 467).

Love is a perfect muzzle of evil suggestions;
Without love who ever succeeded in stopping them?
Be a lover, and seek that fair Beauty,
Hunt for that Waterfowl in every stream!
How can you get water from that which cuts it off?
How gain understanding from what destroys understanding?
Apart from principles of reason are other principles
Of light and great price to be gained by love of God.
Besides this reason of yours God has other reasons
Which will procure for you heavenly nourishment.
By your carnal reason you may procure earthly food,
By God-given reason you may mount the heavens.
When, to win enduring love of God, you sacrifice reason,
God gives you "a tenfold recompense;"[3] yea, seven hundred fold.
When those Egyptian women sacrificed their reason,[4]
They penetrated the mansion of Joseph's love;
The Cup-bearer of life bore away their reason,
They were filled with wisdom of the world without end.
Joseph's beauty was only an offshoot of God's beauty;
Be lost, then, in God's beauty more than those women.

[1] The Prophet said, "Sit not with a disputer about fate, nor converse with him."
[2] Koran iii. 66.
[3] Koran vi. 161.
[4] "And when they saw him they were amazed at him, and cut their hands" (Koran xii. 31).

Love of God cuts short reasonings, O beloved,
For it is a present refuge from perplexities.
Through love bewilderment befalls the power of speech,
It no longer dares to utter what passes;
For if it sets forth an answer, it fears greatly
That its secret treasure may escape its lips.
Therefore it closes lips from saying good or bad,
So that its treasure may not escape it.
In like manner the Prophet's companions tell us,
"When the Prophet used to tell us deep sayings,
That chosen one, while scattering pearls of speech,
Would bid us preserve perfect quiet and silence."
So, when the mighty phœnix hovers over your head,[1]
Causing your soul to tremble at the motion of its wings,
You venture not to stir from your place,
Lest that bird of good fortune should take wing.
You hold your breath and repress your coughs,
So as not to scare that phœnix into flying away.
And if one say a word to you, whether good or bad,
You place finger on lip, as much as to say, "Be silent."
That phœnix is bewilderment,[2] it makes you silent;
The kettle is silent, though it is boiling all the while.

STORY VIII. (*continued*). *Mahmud and Ayáz* (p. 467).

The poet now returns to the story of Mahmud and Ayaz, which is continued at intervals till the end of the book. The king inquired of Ayáz what made him continually visit his old shoes and garments, as Majnun used to visit his Laila, or as a Christian regularly visits his priest to obtain absolution for his sins. Why should he call to these dead things, like a fond mother calling to her dead infant, were it not that faith and love made them, as it were, living beings to him? The eye sees what it brings

[1] It is supposed to bring good fortune.
[2] Bewilderment is the "truly mystical darkness of ignorance" which falls upon the mystic when the light of absolute Being draws near to him, and "blinds him with excess of light." See Gulshan i Raz, p. 13, and notes.

with it to see ; it can see nothing but what it has gained the faculty of seeing. Thus the face of Laila, which seemed so lovely to the eyes of Majnun, made *clairvoyant* by love, seemed to strangers to have no claims to beauty. The earthly forms which here surround us are, as it were, vessels fraught with spiritual wine, only visible to those who have learnt to discern the deep things of the Spirit.

Love and faith are a mighty spell (p. 467).

O Ayáz, what is this love of yours for your old shoes,
Which resembles the love of a lover for his mistress?
You have made these old shoes your object of devotion,
Just as Majnun made an idol of his Laila!
You have bound the affection of your soul to them,
And hung them up in your secret chamber.
How long will you say orisons to this old pair of shoes?
And breathe your oft-told secrets into inanimate ears?
Like the Arab lover to the house of his dead mistress,
You address to them long invocations of love.
Of what great Asaf were your shoes the house?
Is your old garment, think you, the coat of Yusuf?
Like a Christian who confesses to a priest
His past year's sins of fornication, fraud, and deceit;
In order that the priest may absolve him of those sins;
He thinks the priest's absolution the same as God's!
That priest is unable to condemn or to absolve;—
But faith and love are a mighty enchantment!

God's dealings visible to the spiritual (p. 468).

The wine is from *that* world, the vessels from *this;*
The vessels are seen, but the wine is hidden!—
Hidden indeed from the sight of the carnal,
But open and manifest to the spiritual!
O God, our eyes are blinded!
O pardon us, our sins are a heavy burden!
Thou art hidden from us, though the heavens are filled
With Thy light, which is brighter than sun and moon!
Thou art hidden, yet revealest our hidden secrets!
Thou art the source that causes our rivers to flow.
Thou art hidden in Thy essence, but seen by Thy bounties.
Thou art like the water, and we like the millstone.
Thou art like the wind, and we like the dust;
The wind is unseen, but the dust is seen by all.
Thou art the spring, and we the sweet green garden;
Spring is not seen, though its gifts are seen.
Thou art as the soul, we as hand and foot;
Soul instructs hand and foot to hold and take.
Thou art as reason, we like the tongue;
'Tis reason that teaches the tongue to speak.
Thou art as joy, and we are laughing;
The laughter is the consequence of the joy.
Our every motion every moment testifies,
For it proves the presence of the Everlasting God.
So the revolution of the millstone, so violent,
Testifies to the existence of a stream of water.
O Thou who art above our conceptions and descriptions,
Dust be on our heads, and upon our similitudes of Thee!
Yet Thy slaves never cease devising images of Thee;
They cry to Thee alway, "My life is Thy footstool!"
Like that shepherd who cried, "O Lord![1]
Come nigh to thy faithful shepherd,
That he may cleanse thy garment of vermin,
And mend thy shoes, and kiss the hem of thy robe!"
No one equalled that shepherd in love and devotion,
Though his manner of expressing it was most faulty.
His love pitched its tent on the heavens,
He himself was as the dog at the tent-door.
When the sea of love to God boiled up,
It touched his heart, but it touches your ears only.

The thesis that silence may indicate emotions too deep

[1] Alluding to Story vii. Book II.

for expression, while eloquent expressions may indicate that the ears only, and not the heart, have been touched, is next illustrated by a ludicrous anecdote of a dwarf who disguised himself as a woman, and presented himself at a sermon addressed to women. This dwarf played a trick on a woman sitting next him, which made her cry out, and the preacher fancied that his sermon had touched her heart; but the dwarf said that if her heart had been touched she would not have betrayed her feelings by publishing them to the whole congregation.

The king then again pressed Ayáz to explain the mystery of his regard for the old shoes and rags, in order to admonish the courtiers, for he said that the beauty of true holiness is such that it attracts even infidels. To illustrate this he told an anecdote of a Musulman who tried to convert a Gueber in the time of Bayazid. The Gueber said that he admired and envied the faith of Bayazid, though he had no power to imitate it; but as for the faith of the missionary who was trying to convert him, it only inspired him with aversion, because it was plainly insincere and hypocritical. And he told an anecdote of a harsh-voiced *Mu'azzin* who went into a heathen country and there uttered the call to prayer. It happened that there was a girl in that place who had long been inclined to embrace Islam, much to the grief of her parents; but when she heard this harsh call she was at once cured of her wish to forsake her own religion. Her father was so delighted at this that he ran out and loaded the *Mu'azzin* with gifts. The Gueber said the missionary had cured him of the wish to embrace Islam, just as the girl was cured by the *Mu'azzin's* harsh voice. But he said he still retained his reverence for the faith of Bayazid, though he failed to understand how so much spirituality as was seen in Bayazid could be contained in an earthly body. He gave a curious illustration of his meaning. A man brought home a piece of meat weighing over half a *man*, to provide a meal for a guest; but his wife, who was very greedy, ate it all up secretly. When the man missed his meat he asked his wife for it, and she said the cat had eaten it. The man took the cat and weighed her, and found she weighed only half a *man*. Then he said to his wife, "If this half-*man* is all cat, where is the meat?—and if it is meat, where is the cat?" The Gueber said this was exactly the difficulty he felt about the spirit and the body of Bayazid. He concluded by saying, in the words of the *Hadis*, "The true believer is attached to others, and others are attached to him, but the hypocrite inspires affection in no one."

Story XII. *The Devotee who broke the noble's wine-jar* (p. 471).

A certain noble, who lived under the Christian dispensation when wine was allowed, sent his servant to a monastery to fetch some wine. The servant went and bought the wine, and was returning with it, when he passed the house of a very austere and testy devotee. This devotee called out to him, "What have you got there?" The servant said, "Wine, belonging to such a noble." The devotee said, "What! does a follower of God indulge in wine? Followers of God should have naught to do with pleasure and drinking; for wine is a very Satan, and steals men's wits. Your wits are not too bright already, so you have no need to render them still duller by drink." In illustration of this, he told the story of one Ziáyi Dalaq, a very tall man, who had a dwarfish brother. This brother one day received him very ungraciously, only half rising from his seat in answer to his salutation, and Ziáyi Dalaq said to him, "You seem to think yourself so tall that it is necessary to clip off somewhat of your height." Finally the devotee broke the wine-jar with a stone, and the servant went and told his master. The noble was very wrathful at the presumption of the devotee in taking upon himself to prohibit wine, as condemned by the law of nature, when it had not been prohibited by the Gospel, and he took a thick stick and went to the devotee's house to chastise him. The devotee heard of his approach and hid himself under some wool, which belonged to the ropemakers of the village. He said to himself, "To tell an angry man of his faults one needs to have a face as hard as a mirror, which reflects his ugliness without fear or favour." Just so the Prince of Tirmid was once playing chess with a courtier, and being checkmated, got into a rage and threw the chessboard at his courtier's head. So before playing the next game the courtier protected his head by wrappings of felt. Then the neighbours of the devotee, hearing the noise, came out and interceded for him with the noble, telling him that the devotee was half-witted, and could not be held responsible for his actions; and moreover, that as he was a favourite of God,[1] it was useless to attempt to slay him before his time, for the Prophet and other saints had been miraculously preserved in circumstances fatal to ordinary persons. The noble refused to be pacified; but the neighbours redoubled their entreaties, urging that he had so much pleasure in his sovereignty that he could well dispense with the pleasure of wine. The noble strenuously denied this, saying that no other pleasure of sovereignty, or what not, could compensate him for the loss of wine, which made him sway from side to side like the jessamine. The prophets themselves had rejected all other pleasures for that of spiritual intoxication, and he who has once embraced a living mistress will never put up with a dead one. The moral is, that spiritual pleasures, typified by wine, are not to be bartered away for earthly pleasures. The Prophet said, "The world is carrion, and they who seek it are dogs;" and the Koran says, "The present life is no other than a pastime and a sport; but the future mansion is life indeed."[2]

[1] Half-witted persons are supposed to be divinely protected.
[2] Koran xxix. 64.

Description of a devotee who trusted to the light of nature (p. 473).

His brain is dried up; and as for his reason,
It is now less than that of a child.
Age and abstinence have added infirmity to infirmity,
And his abstinence has yielded him no rejoicing.
He has endured toils, but gained no reward from his Friend;
He has done the work, but has not been paid.
Either his work has lacked value,
Or the time of recompense is not decreed as yet.
Either his works are as the works of the Jews,[1]
Or his reward is held back till the appointed time.
This grief and sorrow are enough for him,
That in this valley of pain he is utterly friendless.
With sad eyes he sits in his corner,
With frowning face and downcast looks.
There is no oculist who cares to open his eyes,[2]
Nor has he reason enough to discover the eye-salve.
He strives earnestly with firm resolve and in hope,
His work is done on the chance of being right.
The vision of "The Friend" is far from his course,
For he loses the kernel in his love for the shell.

STORY VIII. (*continued*). *Mahmud and Ayáz* (p. 476).

Mahmud again presses Ayáz to reveal his secrets, remarking that even if they suggest sad thoughts, they will benefit the hearers. The wise man is as a guest-house, and he admits all the thoughts that occur to him, whether of joy or of sorrow, with the same welcome, knowing that, like Abraham, he may entertain angels unawares. This is illustrated by the story of a woman who drove away a valued guest by a petulant remark, which he was not

[1] "But as to the infidels, their works are like the mirage in the desert" (Koran xxiv. 39).
[2] *I.e.*, he has no director (*Murshid i kámil*) to instruct him in the right course.

intended to hear, and afterwards repented her discourtesy so deeply that she put on mourning and turned her house into an inn. Let grief as well as joy lodge in the heart, for grief is sent for our benefit as well as joy. Endure woe patiently, like Joseph and Job, and regard it as a blessing, saying with Solomon, "Stir me up, O Lord, to be thankful for Thy favour which Thou hast showed upon me!"[1] Mahmud then praises Ayáz for being a true man who can control both lust and anger. Those who are carried away by anger or lust, like the girl of whom an anecdote is told, do not deserve the name of men. When anger or lust takes hold of a man reason departs from him. Then comes an anecdote of a cowardly Sufi who boasted of his bravery, but had not courage enough even to slay a captive infidel. Verily, the "greater warfare," viz., that against one's own lusts and passions, demands as much courage as the "lesser warfare" against the infidels. This is illustrated by a story of a saint named 'Iyázi, who, after having been a great warrior against the infidels, renounced the world and applied himself to wage the "greater warfare" against his own lusts. One day, while sitting in his cell, he heard the noise of the army going out to fight, and his carnal passion urged him to go and join in the fight, but he thus rebuked it:—

'Iyázi's rebuke to his passion, which lusted to join in the "lesser warfare" (p. 480).

I said, "O foul and faithless passion,
Whence have you derived this inclination to war?
Tell me truly, O passion, is this your trickery?
Or else is it stubbornness shunning obedience to God?
If you say not truly I will attack you,
And will afflict you more severely with discipline."
Passion then heaved a cry from its breast,
And without mouth vented the following complaints:—

[1] Koran xxvii. 19.

"In this cell you slay me every day;
You slay my life like the life of a Gueber.
Not a soul is aware of my condition;
You drag me along without food or sleep.
In the fight with one wound I shall quit the body,
And the people will admire my valour and self-devotion."
I said, "O bad passion, you live as an infidel,
And as an infidel you will die; shame be upon you!
In both worlds you are naught but a hypocrite;
In the two worlds only an unprofitable servant.
I have vowed to God never to quit this cell
While life remains in this body;
Because whatever the body does in this privacy
Is not done to make a fair show before men.
Its movements and its rest in the privacy of this cell
Are not intended for the sight of any besides God.
This is the 'greater warfare,' that the 'lesser;'
Both these warfares have their Rustams and Haidars.
They are not to be fought by one whose reason and sense
Flee away as soon as a mouse wags its tail.
Such persons must shun the array of battle,
And keep aloof from it even as women do."

This is followed by an anecdote of another brave warrior who "was among the faithful, and made good what he had promised to God."[1] Then comes a long story of a prince of Egypt who saw the portrait of a damsel belonging to the Chief of Mausil, and conceived an ardent passion for her, and sent an army to take her by force. The army succeeded in capturing her, and set out on the return march; but on the way the captain of the army fell in love with the damsel, and she returned his affection. When they reached Egypt she was made over to the prince, but at once took a dislike to him, as he was not nearly so manly as her beloved captain. The prince discovered her secret, and though he might justly have

[1] Koran xxxiii. 23.

resented the treachery of the captain, he refrained, and showed true manliness in the "greater warfare" by pardoning his fault and uniting him with the damsel to whom he was so much attached.

Ideas gained from hearing a thing lead to seeing it (p. 483).

A person put this question to a philosopher,
"O sage, what is true and what is false?"
The sage touched his ear and said, "This is false,
But the eye is true and its report is certain."
The ear is false in relation to the eye,
And most assertions are related to the ear.[1]
If a bat turn away its eyes from the sun,
Still it is not veiled from some idea of the sun;
Its very dread of the sun frames an idea of the sun,
And that idea scares it away to the darkness.
That idea of light terrifies it,
And makes it cling to the murky night.
Just so 'tis your idea of your terrible foe
Which makes you cling to your friends and allies.
O Moses, thy revelations shed glory on the mount,
But that frightened one endured not thy realities.[2]
Be not too proud, but know that you must first endure
The idea of the Truth, and thence come to the reality.
No one is frightened by the mere idea of fighting,
For "no courage is needed before fighting begins."[3]
In the mere idea of fighting a coward can imagine
Himself as attacking and retreating like a Rustam.
The pictures of Rustam on the wall of a bath
Are similar to a coward's ideas of fighting.
But when these ideas are tested by actual sight,
What of the coward then? His bravery is gone!
Strive, then, from mere hearing to press on to seeing;[1]
What ear has told you falsely eye will tell truly.
Then ear too will acquire the properties of an eye;
Your ears, now worthless as wool, will become gems;
Yea, your whole body will become a mirror,
It will be as an eye or a bright gem in your bosom.
First the hearing of the ear enables you to form ideas,
Then these ideas guide you to the Beloved.
Strive, then, to increase the number of these ideas,
That they may guide you, like Majnun, to the Beloved.

[1] *I.e.*, are based on hearsay.
[2] "When God manifested Himself to the mount He turned it to dust, and Moses fell in a swoon" (Koran vii. 139). As the bat cannot endure the sight of the sun, men cannot at once endure the full blaze of the beatific vision.
[3] A proverb not given by Freytag.

Concerning the unbelievers who say, "There is only this our present life; we live and we die, and naught but time destroyeth us"[2] (p. 483).

To return; that prince played the fool,
And took delight in the society of the damsel.
O prince, suppose your dominion extend from east to west,
Yet, as it endures not, esteem it transitory as lightning;
Yea, O sleeping heart, know the kingdom that endures not
For ever and ever is only a mere dream.
I marvel how long you will indulge in vain illusion,
Which has seized you by the throat like a headsman.
Know that even in this world there is a place of refuge;[3]
Hearken not to the unbeliever who denies it.
His argument is this: he says again and again,
"If there were aught beyond this life we should see it."
But if the child sees not the state of reason,
Does the man of reason therefore forsake reason?
And if the man of reason sees not the state of love,
Is the blessed moon of love thereby eclipsed?

[1] Ideas and types lead men on to actual sight when they are strong enough to bear it. Job xlii. 5.
[2] Koran xlv. 23.
[3] Place of refuge, *i.e.*, heavenly visions;—a foretaste of the world to come (Gulshan i Raz, l. 679).

Moses came upon a shephered along the way
Who was talking to God in his solitude

The beauty of Joseph was not visible to his brethren ;
Was it therefore hidden from the eyes of Jacob ?
The eyes of Moses regarded his staff as a stick,
But the divine eye saw it to be a deadly serpent.
The eye of the head was at issue with the divine eye,
But the latter prevailed and gave convincing proof.
To the eyes of Moses his hand looked a mere hand,
But to the divine eye it appeared a flashing light.
This subject in its entirety is endless,
But to the unbeliever it is a mere fanciful idea.
The only realities to him are lust and gluttony ;
Speak not then to him of the mysteries of the Beloved.
To us believers lust and gluttony are only ideas,
Therefore we behold alway the beauty of the Beloved.
To all men whose creed is lust and gluttony
Applies the text, "To you be your creed, to me mine." [1]
In the face of negations like these cut short speech,
"O Ahmad, say little to an old Fire-worshipper!"

"*We distribute among them*," [2] *to some carnal lusts, and to others angelic qualities* (p. 486).

If the prince lacked the animal manliness of asses,
Yet he possessed the true manliness of the prophets.
He renounced lust and anger and concupiscence,
And showed himself a man of the lineage of the prophets.
Grant that he lacked the virility of asses,
Yet God esteemed him a lord of lords.
Let me be dead, so long as God regards me with favour!
I am better off than the living who are rejected of God ;
The former is the kernel of manliness, the latter only the rind ;
The former is borne to Paradise, the latter to hell.
The Prophet says, "Paradise is annexed to tribulation,
But hell-fire follows indulgence in lust." [3]
O Ayaz, who slayest demons like a male lion,
Manliness of asses is naught, manliness of mind much.
What sort of man dost thou think him who sports as a boy,
But who has no comprehension of these chief matters?
O thou who hast seen the delight of my commandments,
And risked thy life to perform them faithfully,
Hear a tale of the sweetness of my commandments,
That the meaning of this sweetness may be made plain.

[1] Koran cix. 6.
[2] Koran xliii. 31.
[3] Cp. Freytag, Arabum Proverbia, vol ii. p. 165.

The story which follows is one in which Ayáz is himself the chief actor, and hence it may perhaps be inferred that this part of the poem had not received its final revision when the poet died. The king showed to all his courtiers in turn a valuable jewel, and asked them its value. Each declared it to be priceless. He thereupon ordered each of them to break it to pieces, but they refused, one after the other; on which he praised them highly and gave them presents. Finally the jewel came into the hands of Ayáz, and he, not being a mere imitator like the rest, nor being tempted by the rewards given to the rest, decided that the king's command ought to be obeyed at all costs, and therefore broke the jewel to pieces. Blind imitation of current fashions and ruling "public opinion" is the way of the world, but its worthlessness is at once manifested when it is put to the test. True faith is a reasonable faith, not one adopted and held in mechanical and parrot-like fashion. The king then commanded that those courtiers whose faith had been shown to be mere "*taqlid*" or imitation, and not vital and intelligent, should be put to death; but Ayáz interceded for them, saying, "O Lord, punish them not if they forget or fall into sin ;" [1] although their plea that they sinned through forgetfulness is of no more weight than the plea of having sinned through drunkenness, seeing that both forgetfulness and drunkenness are wilfully incurred. Those who die in amity with God have no cause to fear death,—"It cannot harm them,

[1] Koran ii. 286.

for to their Lord will they return;"[1] but those who die at enmity with God are in a very different position, and have therefore a very strong claim for mercy. The Egyptian magicians, when threatened by Pharaoh with death for believing in Moses, recognised the truth that death in such a cause would unite them with God, and that extinction of the phenomenal self, on which Pharaoh prided himself, would bring them to the real Self from whom they had been estranged by life on earth. Like Habib, the carpenter of Antioch, who was martyred for taking the part of 'Isa's two apostles in that city, they said, "O that my people knew how gracious God hath been to me, and that He hath made me one of His honoured ones!"[2] A man can only say "I" with truth when he has mortified self, and unlearnt to say "I" in the sense in which Pharaoh said it. Fakhru-'d-Din Razi[3] discoursed learnedly on this point, saying much of "incarnation" and "union" as the modes in which the real "I" of the Deity indwells in the human soul; but as he lacked the true mystic unction, his words only serve to darken counsel.[4] But here Ayáz breaks off, saying, "Who am I that I should say to the Almighty, 'Grant pardon to these offenders'?" The Omniscient God needs not to be informed of their case, for He knows all; nor to be reminded of it, for He forgets nothing; nor to be urged to act mercifully, for He created men "for their own benefit, and not to derive benefit from them." Such intercession, therefore, implies ignorance of God, and "such only of His servants as are possessed of knowledge of God truly fear God."[5] God is at once centre and circumference of the universe, and the only true wisdom consists in absolute self-surrender to His will, and this surrender of self will bring with it its own exceeding great reward.

[1] Koran xxvi. 50.
[2] Koran xxxvi. 25.
[3] A great theologian of Khorasan who lived from A.D. 1150 to 1210. De Slane's Ibn Khallikan, ii. 652.
[4] See Gulshan i Raz, l. 453, note.
[5] Koran xxxv. 25.

Book VI.

PROLOGUE (p. 492).

O LIFE of the heart, Husamu-'d-Din,
My zeal burnt within me to write this sixth part!
The Masnavi became a standard through thy influence,
Thy sword (*Husam*) has made it an exemplar to the world
O spiritual one, I now offer it to thee,—
This sixth part of the entire Masnavi.
Enlighten the world's six sides with its six parts,
That it may illuminate him who is not illuminated!
Love has naught to do with five senses or six sides,
Its only aim is to be attracted to the Beloved!
But haply leave may be given me hereafter
To tell those mysteries so far as they can be told,
In a discourse more closely approximating to the facts
Than these faint indications of those abstruse matters.
Mysteries are not communicable, save to those who know;
Mystery in the ear of infidels is no mystery.
Nevertheless, this is a call to you from God;
It matters not to Him whether ye accept or reject it.
Noah repeated His call for nine hundred years,
But his people only increased in rebellion.
Never did he draw back from admonishing them,
Never did he retire into the cave of silence.
He said, "At the barking and howling of the dogs
No caravan ever turned back in its road.
Nor does the full moon on a bright night cease shining
Because of the howling of dogs on earth.
The moon sheds her light, and the dogs howl;
Every one acts according to his nature.

To each one his office is allotted by the divine decree,
And he acts agreeably to his nature."

. . . .

Art thou thirsting for the Ocean of spirituality?
Disport thyself on this island of the Masnavi!
Disport thyself, so long as thou seest every moment
Spiritual verities revealed in this Masnavi.
When the wind blows the grass off the water,
The water then shows forth its own purity.
Behold the bright and fresh sprays of coral,
And the princely fruits growing in the water of life!
So, when the Masnavi is purged of letters and words,
It drops all these, and appears as the sea of Unity.
Then speaker and hearer and spoken words
All three give up the ghost in that consummation.
Bread-giver and bread-eater and bread itself
Are purified of their forms and turn to dust.
But their essences in each of these three grades
Are distinguished, as in those states, so eternally.[1]
Their form turns to dust, but their essence not;
If one says it does, tell him it does not.
In the world of spirits all three await judgment,
Sometimes wearing their earthly forms, sometimes not.

The worth of a man depends on the objects of his aspiration (p. 495).

One day a student asked a preacher,
Saying, "O most orthodox ornament of the pulpit,
I have a question to ask, O lord of learning;
Tell me the answer to it in this congregation.
A bird sat on the top of a wall;
Which was best, its head or its tail?"
He replied, "If its face was towards the town,
And its tail to the villages, then its face was best.
But if its tail was towards the town, and its face
Towards the villages, then prefer its tail to its face."
A bird flies with its wings towards its nest,
The wings of a man are his aspiration and aim.
If a lover be befouled with good and evil,
Yet regard not these; regard rather his aspiration.
Though a falcon be all white and unmatched in form,
If he hunts mice he is contemptible and worthless.
And if an owl fixes his affection on the king,
He is a falcon in reality; regard not his outward form.
Adam's clay was kneaded in the limits of a trough,
Yet was he exalted above heaven and stars.
"We have honoured Adam"[1] was not addressed to the sky,
But to Adam himself, full of defects as he was.
Did one ever propose to earth or heaven to receive
Beauty, reason, and speech and aspiration?[2]
Would you ever offer to the heavens
Beauty of face and acuteness of thought?
O son, did you ever present your silver body
As an offering to the damsels pictured on bath walls?
Nay, you pass by those pictures though fair as Huris,
And offer yourself sooner to half-blind old women.
What is there in the old women which the pictures lack,
Which draws you from the pictures to the old women?
Say not, for I will say it in plain words,—
'Tis reason, sense, perception, thought, and life.
In the old woman life is infused,
While the pictures of the bath have no life.
If the pictures of the bath should stir with life (soul),
They would uproot your love to all the old women.
What is soul? 'Tis acquainted with good and evil,—
Rejoicing at pleasant things, grieving at ills.
Since, then, the principle of soul is knowledge,
He who knows most is most full of soul.
Knowledge is the effect flowing from soul;

[1] Koran xxxvi. 32: "But all gathered together shall be set before us."

[1] Koran xvii. 72.

[2] "We proposed to the heavens and to the earth to receive the deposit, but they refused the burden. Man undertook to bear it, but hath proved unjust and senseless" (Koran xxxiii. 72).

He who has most of it is most godlike.
Seeing then, beloved, that knowledge is the mark of soul,
He who knows most has the strongest soul.
The world of souls is itself entirely knowledge,
And he who is void of knowledge is void of soul.
When knowledge is lacking in a man's nature,
His soul is like a stone on the plain.
Primal Soul is the theatre of God's court,
Soul of souls the exhibition of God Himself.
All the angels were pure reason and soul,
Yet when the new soul of Adam came, they were as its body.
When in joy they crowded round that new soul,[1]
They bowed before it as body does before soul.

Fear of men's censure the greatest obstacle to acceptance of the true faith (p. 496).

O Husamu-'d-Din, I might tell some of thy many virtues,
Were it not for the fear of the evil eyes.
From evil eyes and malice-empoisoned breaths
Already have I suffered fatal wounds.
Therefore I cannot relate thy ecstatic states,
Save by hints of the ecstatic states of others.
This manœuvre is one of the devices of the heart,
Whereby the heart's feet wend their way to the truth.
Many hearts and souls would become lovers of God
Did not evil eyes or evil ears hold them back.
Of these Abu Talib, the Prophet's uncle, was one;
The malice of the Arabs scared him from the faith.
He said, "What will the Arabs say of me?
That my own nephew has perverted me from my religion!"
Muhammad said, "O uncle, confess the faith to me,
That I may strive with God for thee!"
He said, "Nay; it will be published by them that hear;
'A secret known to more than two is known to every one.'[1]
As I live in the midst of these Arabs,
It will cause me to lose caste with them."
Yet, had the mighty grace of God led the way,
How could this fear have vied with God's attraction?
O Granter of aid, lend us aid
In this dilemma of the feeble will.

Prayers for right guidance in the use of free will, which gift was refused by heavens and earth, but accepted by man to his own peril[2] (p. 497).

This flux and reflux of resolves came to me from Thee,
Else these tides of will had rested still, O God!
By the same *fiat* whereby Thou madest me thus irresolute,
Of Thy mercy deliver me from this irresolution!
Thou triest me; O give me aid!
For men are as women through this trial.
How long, O Lord, is this trial to last?
Give me one ruling principle, not ten principles!
. . . . . .
The whole world flees away from its own will and being
Towards self-abandonment and intoxication.
In order to escape a while from self-consciousness,
Men incur the reproach of wine and strong drink;
For all know well this existence is a snare,
This thought and memory and will only a hell.
Therefore they flee from self to being beside themselves,
Call it intoxication or call it preoccupation, O guided one.
. . . .
Ere it is annihilated, no single soul
Finds admittance to the divine hall of audience.
What is "ascension" to heaven? Annihilation of self;
Self-abandonment is the creed and religion of lovers.

[1] "We said unto the angels, 'Prostrate yourselves before Adam,' and they prostrated themselves, except Iblis" (Koran vi. 10).

[1] Freytag, Arabum Proverbia, iii. 222.
[2] Koran xxxiii. 72, quoted above. "Deposit" is here interpreted of the will, the ability to go right or wrong.

STORY I. *The Hindu Slave who loved his Master's Daughter* (p. 498).

A certain man had a Hindu slave, whom he had brought up along with his children, one of whom was a daughter. When the time came for giving the girl in marriage many suitors presented themselves, and offered large marriage portions to gain her alliance. At last her father selected one who was by no means the richest or noblest of the number, but pious and well-mannered. The women of the family would have preferred one of the richer youths, but the father insisted on having his own way, and the marriage was settled according to his wishes. As soon as the Hindu slave heard of this he fell sick, and the mistress of the family discovered that he was in love with her daughter, and aspired to the honour of marrying her. She was much discomposed at this unfortunate accident, and consulted her husband as to what was best to be done. He said, "Keep the affair quiet, and I will cure the slave of his presumption, in such a way that, according to the proverb, 'The Shaikh shall not be burnt, yet the meat shall be well roasted.'" He directed his wife to flatter the slave with the hope that his wish would be granted, and the girl given to him in marriage. He then celebrated a mock marriage between the slave and the girl, but at night substituted for the girl a boy dressed in female attire, with the result that the bridegroom passed the night in quarrelling with his supposed bride. Next morning he had an interview with the girl and her mother, and said he would have no more to do with her, as, though her appearance was very seductive at a distance, closer acquaintance with her had altogether destroyed the charm. Just so the pleasures of the world seem sweet till they are tried, and then they are found to be very bitter and repulsive. The Prophet has declared that "Patience is the key of joy;"[1] in other words, that he who controls and restrains himself from grasping at worldly pleasures will find true happiness; but this precept makes no lasting impression on the bulk of mankind. When bitter experience overtakes them, as the pain of burning afflicts children, or moths sporting with fire, or the pain of amputation a thief, they curse the delusive temptations which brought this pain upon them; but no sooner is the pain abated than they run after the same pleasures as eagerly as ever. This is divinely ordained, that "God may bring to naught the craft of the infidels."[2] Their hearts have, as it were, been kindled on the tinder-box of bitter experience, but God has put out the sparks of good resolution, and caused them to forget their experience and vows of abstinence, according to the text, "Often as they kindle a beacon-fire for war doth God quench it."[3] This is illustrated by an anecdote of a man who heard a footstep in his house at night, and at once struck a light; but the thief put it out without being observed, and the man remained under the impression that it had gone out of itself. This leads the poet again to dwell on his favourite theme of the sole agency of Allah.

Then, to supply the necessary corrective of this doctrine, another anecdote is told concerning Mahmud and Ayáz. The courtiers grumbled because Ayáz received the stipend of thirty courtiers, and Mahmud by a practical test convinced them that the talents of Ayáz equalled those of thirty men. The courtiers replied that this was due to God's grace, not to any merit on the part of Ayáz; and the king confuted them by pointing out that man's responsibility and merit, or demerit, for his actions are recognised in the Koran. Iblis was condemned for saying to God, "Thou hast caused me to err,"[4] and Adam was commended

[1] Freytag, Arabum Proverbia, iii. 270.
[2] Koran viii. 18.
[3] Koran v. 69.
[4] Koran vii. 15 and 22.

for saying, "We have blackened ourselves."[1] And elsewhere it is said, "Whosoever shall have wrought an atom's weight of good shall behold it; and whoso shall have wrought an atom's weight of evil shall behold it."[2]

STORY II. *The Fowler and the Bird* (p. 502).

A fowler went out to catch birds, and disguised himself by wrapping his head up in leaves and grass, so as to avoid frightening the birds away from his snare. A bird of some sagacity came near him, and suspected something wrong, but foolishly lingered near, and began to question him as to his business. The fowler said he was a hermit who had retired from the world and dressed himself in weeds for the health of his soul. The bird said he was surprised to see a Musulman doing this in contravention of the Prophet's precept, "There is no monkery in Islam," and his repeated declarations that Islam involves association with the faithful and avoidance of a solitary life. The fowler replied that a solitary life was allowed in heathen countries for the soul's health.[3] The bird then asked what the grains of wheat were that were strewed on the trap. The fowler replied that they were the property of an orphan, which had been deposited with him in consequence of his known probity. The bird then asked permission to eat some, as he was very hungry, and the fowler, with much pretended reluctance, allowed him to do so. The moment he touched the grain the trap closed upon him, and he found himself a prisoner. He then abused the fowler for his trickery, but the fowler said he had only himself to blame for his greediness in eating the food which belonged to an orphan. The moral is, that it is not destiny which leads people into afflictions, but their own errors and vices.

[1] Koran vii. 15 and 22. [2] Koran xcix. 7.
[1] See Miskkat ul Masabih, ii. 541.

The bird's cries to God for aid (p. 505).

When he had eaten the grain he was caught in the trap,
And began to recite the chapters "*Yásín*" and "*An'am.*"
. . . .
Then he began to wail and cry loudly,
So that the very fowler and his trap shook with grief.
He said, "My back is broken by the conflict of my thoughts;
O Beloved One, come and stroke my head in mercy!
The palm of Thy hand on my head gives me rest,
Thy hand is a sign of Thy bounteous providence.
Remove not Thy shadow from my head,
I am afflicted, afflicted, afflicted!
Sleep has deserted my eyes
Through my longing for Thee, O Envy of cypresses!
Though I be unworthy of Thy favour, how were it
If thou shouldst regard the griefs of unworthy me?
What claim of right can a non-existent thing make
To have the doors of Thy bounty opened to it?
Yet Thy bounty had regard to my senseless dust,
And endued it with the ten jewels of the senses;—
Five external senses and five internal senses,
Whereby inanimate seed became a living man.
O Light on high! what is repentance without Thy grace
But a mere mockery of the beard of repentance;
Thou rootest up the hairs of such repentance,
Repentance is the shadow, Thou the shining Moon.
Alas! Thou hast ruined my house and home;
How can I cease wailing while Thou oppressest me?
How can I flee away when there is no living away?
Without Thy sustaining lordship there is no slave.
O take my life, Thou that art the source of life!
For apart from Thee I am wearied of my life.
I am a lover well versed in lovers' madness,
I am weary of learning and sense.

Since my bashfulness is destroyed, I will publish secrets;
How long must I bear this trepidation and anxiety?
Formerly I was covered by modesty as by a veil,
Now I will leap from it under Thy coverlet!
O comrades, our Beloved has closed up all paths;
We are as lame deer, and He as a raging lion.
Say what remedy is there but resignation[1]
When one is fallen into the hands of the raging lion?"

The poet then passes on to the subject of the need for constant watchfulness, in order to avoid the snares of the world, and not to miss the divine blessing whenever it may appear. There is a tradition, "When half the night has passed Allah will descend to earth, and cry, 'Ho, ye that ask, it shall be answered to you; and ye that crave pardon, it shall be pardoned to you; and ye that petition, your petitions shall be granted.'" But all who sleep the sleep of negligence will miss the promised blessing. This is illustrated by the story of a lover who obtained an assignation with his mistress, but when she came, was found asleep, and was accordingly rejected.

STORY III. *The Drunken Turkish Amír and the Minstrel* (p. 507).

Then follow exhortations to undergo "the pains of negation," as they are called in the *Gulshan i Raz,—i.e.*, even as the great saint and poet Faridu-'d-Din 'Attar cast away his drugs, to cast one's own will, knowledge, power, and "self" into the unique river of "annihilation,"[2] and from that state to rise to the higher state of eternal existence in God. The end and object of all negation is to attain to subsequent affirmation, as the negation in the creed, "There is no God," finds its complement and purpose in the affirmation "but God." Just so the purpose of negation of self is to clear the way for the apprehension of the fact that there is no existence but The One. The intoxication of life and its pleasures and occupations veils the Truth from men's eyes, and they ought to pass on to the spiritual intoxication which makes men beside themselves and lifts them to the beatific vision of eternal Truth. This is the same thing as saying they must pass on from negation to affirmation, from ignorance to the highest knowledge. This is illustrated by the story of the Turkish noble and the minstrel, which is given with an apology for using illustrations derived from drunkenness. A Turkish noble awoke from his drunken sleep, and called his minstrel to enliven him. The minstrel was a spiritual man, and proceeded to improve the occasion by singing a song with a deep spiritual meaning:—

"I know not if thou art a moon or an idol,
I know not what thou requirest of me.
I know not what service to pay thee,
Whether to keep silence or to speak.
Thou art not apart from me, yet, strange to say,
I know not where I am, or where thou art.
I know not wherefore thou art dragging me,
Now embracing me, and now wounding me!"

Thus the whole of his song consisted of repetitions of the words, "I know not." At last the noble could endure it no longer, and he took a stick and threatened to beat the minstrel, saying, "O wretch, tell us something you do know, and do not repeat what you do not know. If I ask you whence you come or what you have eaten, and you answer only by negations, your answer is a waste of time. Say what you mean by all these negations." The minstrel replied, "My meaning is a concealed one. I fear to make affirmations in opposition to your negations, so I state negations that you may get a hint of the corresponding affirmations from them. I now hint the truth to you in my song; and when death comes to you, you

[1] "To God I commit my case" (Koran xl. 47).
[2] Koran cxii. 4.

will learn the mysteries which at present I can only hint."

Spiritual mysteries set forth in the Masnavi under similes of intoxication (p. 507).

That wine of God is gained from *that* minstrel,[1]
This bodily wine from *this* minstrel.
Both of these have one and the same name in speech,
But the difference between their worth is great.

. . . .

Men's bodies are like pitchers with closed mouths;
Beware, till you see what is inside them.
The pitcher of this body holds the water of life,
Whilst that one holds deadly poison.
If you look at the contents you are wise;
If you look only at the vessel you are misguided.
Know words resemble these bodies,
And the meaning resembles the soul.
The body's eyes are ever intent on bodies,
The soul's eyes on the reasonable soul;
Wherefore, in the figures of the words of the Masnavi,
The form misleads, but the inner meaning guides.
In the Koran it is declared that its parables
"Mislead some and guide some."[2]
O God! when a spiritual man talks of wine,
How can a fellow spiritual man mistake his meaning?

. . . .

Thus that minstrel began his intoxicating song,
"O give me Thy cup, Thou whom I see not!
Thou art my face; what wonder if I see it not?
Extreme nearness acts as an obscuring veil.[3]

[1] "A wine-cup tempered at the camphor fountain shall the just quaff" (Koran lxxvi. 5).

[2] Koran ii. 24.

[3] See couplet 122 of the Gulshan i Raz:—

"When the object looked at is very close to the eye,
The eye is darkened so that it cannot see it."

I.e., When man is united with God he can no longer behold Him, for he is dwelling in Him.

Thou art my reason; what wonder if I see Thee not
Through the multitude of intervening obstacles?
Thou art 'nearer to me than my neck vein,'[1]
How can I call to Thee, 'Ho,' as if thou wert far off?
Nay, but I will mislead some by calling in the desert,
To hide my Beloved from those of whom I am jealous!"

This is illustrated by an anecdote of the Prophet and 'Ayísha. 'Ayísha was once sitting with the Prophet without her veil, when a blind man came in. 'Ayísha, knowing well the jealous disposition of her husband, at once prepared to retire, on which the Prophet said, "The man is blind and cannot see you." 'Ayísha replied by signs that though the man could not see her she could see him. Just so the spiritual man is jealous of exposing his mysteries to the gaze of the profane, and from excess of caution veils them in signs and hints.

Then comes a commentary on the tradition, "Die before you die," *i.e.*, mortify your carnal passions and lusts, and deny and annihilate your carnal "self" before the death of the body overtakes you. Men who put off repentance till they are at the point of death are likened to the Shi'as of Aleppo, who every year on the *'Ashura*, or tenth day of *Muharram*, meet at the Antioch gate to bewail the martyrdom of Hasan and Husain. Once, while they were thus engaged, a Sunni poet arrived at the city, and inquired the reason of this excessive grief and mourning. The Shi'as rebuked him for his ignorance of sacred history, and he said, "This martyrdom happened a long time ago; but it would seem, from your excessive grief, that the news of it has only just reached you. You must have been sleeping all this time not to have heard it before, and now you are mourning for your own sleepiness!" To the truly spiritual, who have drunk of God's wine and bear the "tokens of it on their foreheads,"[2] death is an occasion for rejoicing, not for wailing. The man who is engrossed

[1] Koran l. 15.

[2] Koran xlviii. 29.

with the trifling pleasures of the world and blind to the ample provision made for the soul is like an ant in a barn of wheat, toiling to carry off a single grain, when ample stores of wheat are already at its disposal. Spiritual men must continue urging the worldly to repent and avail themselves of this heavenly provision for their souls, careless, like Noah, whether their preaching is listened to or not. This is illustrated by an anecdote of a man who knocked at the door of an empty house at midnight, in order to give notice that it was time to prepare the meal taken at dawn in *Ramazan*.

Reasons for knocking at the empty house (p. 512).

You have said your say; now hear my answer,
So as not to remain in astonishment and bewilderment.
Though to you this time seems midnight,
To me the dawn of joyful morn seems nigh.

. . . . . .

To the vulgar all parts of the world seem dead,
But to God they are instinct with sense and love.
And as to your saying that "this house is empty,
Why then should I beat a drum before it?"
Know that the people of God expend money,
And build many mosques and holy places,
And spend health and wealth in distant pilgrimages,
In ecstatic delight, like intoxicated lovers;
And none of them ever say, "The Ka'ba is empty;"
How can one who knows the truth say that?

. . . . . .

These people are ranged in battle array,
And risk their lives to gain God's favour;
One plunged in calamities like Job himself,
Another exhibiting patience like Jacob.
Thousands of them are thirsty and afflicted,
Striving in earnest desire to do God's will.
I likewise, in order to please the merciful God,
Beat my drum at every door in hope of dawn.
Seek ye a purchaser who will pay you gold;
Where will you find one more liberal than God?
He buys the worthless rubbish which is your wealth,
He pays you the light that illumines your heart.
He accepts these frozen and lifeless bodies of yours,
And gives you a kingdom beyond what you dream of.
He takes a few drops of your tears,
And gives you the divine fount sweeter than sugar.
He takes your sighs fraught with grief and sadness,
And for each sigh gives rank in heaven as interest.
In return for the sigh-wind that raised tear-clouds,
God gave Abraham the title of "Father of the faithful."
Come! in this incomparable and crowded mart
Sell your old goods and take a kingdom in payment!

STORY IV. *The Purchase of Bilál* (p. 513).

To illustrate the rich recompense that is awarded to those who are faithful in tribulation, the story of Bilál is next recounted at length. Bilál was an Abyssinian slave belonging to a Jew of Mecca, and had incurred his master's displeasure in consequence of having embraced Islam. For this offence his master tortured him by exposing him to the heat of the midday sun, and beating him with thorns. But, notwithstanding his anguish, Bilál would not recant his faith, and uttered only the cry, "*Ahad, Ahad!*" "The One, the One God!" At this moment Abu Bakr, the "Faithful witness," happened to pass by, and was so struck by his constancy that he resolved to buy him of the Jew. After much higgling and attempts at cheating on the Jew's part he succeeded in doing so, and at once set him free. When the Prophet heard of this purchase he said to Abu Bakr, "Give me a share in him;" but Abu Bakr told him, somewhat to his annoyance, that he had already set him free. Notwithstanding this Bilál attached himself to the Prophet, and was afterwards promoted to the honourable post of the Prophet's *Mu'azzin.*

This is followed by the story of Hilal, another holy man who, like Bilál and Luqman and Joseph, served a noble in the capacity of groom. His affections were set on things above, and he was ever pressing upwards towards the high mark of spiritual exaltation, and saying, like Moses, "I will not stop till I reach the confluence of the two seas, and for years will I journey on."[1] Herein he presented a great contrast to ordinary men, who are ever giving way to their lusts, and so being dragged down into the state of mere animals, or even lower. Hilal's master was a Musulman, yet one whose eyes were only partially open to the truth. He was in the habit of asking his guests their age; and if they answered doubtfully, saying, "Perhaps eighteen, or seventeen, or sixteen, or even fifteen," he would rebuke them, saying, "As you seem to be putting yourself lower and lower, you had better go back at once to your mother's womb." These guests are a type of men who lower themselves from the rank of humanity to that of animals. This master, however, was blind to Hilal's spiritual excellence, and allowed him to drag on a miserable existence in his stables. At last Hilal fell sick; but no one cared for him, till the Prophet himself, warned by a divine intimation, came to visit him, and commiserated his wretched condition. Hilal proved himself to be faithful through tribulation; for, instead of grumbling at his lot, he replied, "How is that sleep wretched which is broken by the advent of the Sun of prophecy? or how can he be called athirst on whose head is poured the water of life?" In truth, Hilal had by degrees become purified from the stain of earthly existence and earthly qualities, and washed in the fountain of the water of life, *i.e.*, the holy revelations of the Prophet, till he had attained the exalted grade of purity enjoined on those who would study God's Word aright.[2]

[1] Koran xviii. 59.

[2] Koran lvi. 79.

Growth in grace is accomplished by slow degrees, and not per saltum (p. 519).

Since you have told the story of Hilal (the new moon)
Now set forth the story of Badr (the full moon).
That new moon and that full moon are now united,
Removed from duality and defect and shortcomings.
That Hilal is now exalted above inward defect;
His outward defects served as degrees of ascension.
Night after night that mentor taught him grades of ascent
And through his patient waiting gave him happiness.
The mentor says, "O raw hastener, through patient waiting,
You must climb to the summit step by step.
Boil your pot by degrees and in a masterly way;
Food boiled in mad haste is spoiled.
Doubtless God could have created the universe
By the *fiat* 'Be!' in one moment of time;
Why, then, did He protract His work over six days,
Each of which equalled a thousand years, O disciple?
Why does the formation of an infant take nine months?
Because God's method is to work by slow degrees,
Why did the formation of Adam take forty days?
Because his clay was kneaded by slow degrees.
Not hurrying on like you, O raw one,
Who claim to be a Shaikh whilst yet only a child!
You run up like a gourd higher than all plants,
But where is your power of resistance or combat?
You have leant on trees or on walls,
And so mounted up like a gourd, O little dog rose;
Even though your prop may be a lofty cypress,
At last you are seen to be dry and hollow.
O gourd, your bright green hue soon turns yellow,
For it is not a natural but an artificial colour."

This is illustrated by an anecdote of an ugly old hag who painted her face to make it look pretty, but was detected and exposed to scorn.

STORY V. *The Sufi and the Qázi* (p. 521).

A sick man labouring under an incurable disease went to a physician for advice. The physician felt his pulse, and perceived that no treatment would cure him, and therefore told him to go away and do whatever he had a fancy for. This was the advice given by God to the Israelites when they were seen to be incurable by the admonitions of the prophets. "Do what you will, but God's eye is on all your doings."[1] The sick man blessed the physician for his agreeable prescription, and at once went to a stream, where he saw a Sufi bathing his feet. He was seized with a desire to hit the Sufi on the back, and, calling to mind the physician's advice, at once carried his wish into effect. The Sufi jumped up, and was about to return the blow, but when he saw the weakly and infirm condition of his assailant he restrained himself. He disregarded his present angry impulse, and had regard to the future, so that the non-existent future became to him more really existent than the existing present. Here the poet digresses to point out that when wise men recognise the true relative importance of the present and the future they cease to shrink from death and annihilation, which lifts them to a higher and nobler life. This is illustrated by an anecdote of Mahmud of Ghazni, quoted from Faridu-'d-Din 'Attar. Mahmud, in one of his campaigns, took prisoner a Hindu boy, who at first regarded him with the greatest dread, in consequence of the stories he had heard of him from his mother, but afterwards experienced Mahmud's kindness and tenderness, and came to know him and love him. So it is with death. According to the *Hadis* "Those who have passed away do not grieve because of death, but because of wasted opportunities in life." The Masnavi is "a shop of poverty and self-abnegation," and a treasury containing only the doctrines of "Unity;" and if its stories suggest aught else, that is due to the evil promptings of Iblis, who also misled the Prophet himself to attribute undue power to the idols Lat and 'Uzza and Manat, in a verse which was afterwards cancelled.[1] The Sufi, being full of the spirit of self-abnegation, did not retaliate on his weak, assailant but led him before the Qázi. On learning the facts of the case the Qázi said, "This Faqir is sick to death, and you, being a Sufi, are, according to your profession, dead to the world. How, then, can I award a penalty against him in your favour? I am a judge, not of the dead, but of the living." The Sufi was dissatisfied with this view of the case, and again pressed the Qázi to do him justice. On this the Qázi asked the sick Faqir how much money he had, and on his replying, "Six dirhams," took pity on him, and let him off with a fine of three dirhams only. The moment the sentence was pronounced the sick Faqir went up to the Qázi and struck him a blow on the back, and cried out, "Now take the other three dirhams and let me go!" The Sufi then pointed out to the Qázi that by his ill-timed leniency to the Faqir he had brought this blow upon himself, and urged him to apply in his own case those principles of mercy and forgiveness which he had proposed in the case of another. The Qázi said that, for his part, he recognised every blow and misfortune that might befall him as divinely ordained, and sent for his good, according to the text, "Laugh little and weep much,"[2] and that his judgment in the matter of the Faqir had not been dictated by impulse, but by inspiration.[3] The Sufi again asked him how evils and misfortunes could proceed from the divine fount of good, and the Qázi replied that what seems good and evil to us has no absolute existence, but is merely as the foam on the surface of the vast ocean. Moreover, every misfortune occurring to the faithful in this life will be amply compensated for in the life to come. The Sufi asked why this world should not be so arranged that only good should be experienced in it, and the Qázi

[1] Koran xli. 40.

[1] Koran liii. 19, and Rodwell's note.

[2] Koran ix. 84.

[3] Koran liii. 3.

eplied by telling him an anecdote of a Turk and a tailor. The Turk, who typifies the careless pleasure-seeker, was so intent on listening to the jokes and amusing stories of the tailor, typifying the seductive world, that he allowed himself to be robbed of the silk which was to furnish him with a vesture for eternity. The Sufi again retorted that he did not see why the world would not get on better without the evil in it, and the Qázi replied with the poet's favourite argument that there would be no possibility of being virtuous if there were no temptations to be vicious. As Bishop Butler says, this life is a state of probation, and such a state necessarily involves trials and difficulties and dangers to be resisted and overcome.

The dead regret not dying, but having lost opportunities in life (p. 525).

Well said that Leader of mankind,
That whosoever passes away from the world
Does not grieve and lament over his death,
But grieves ever over lost opportunities.
He says, "Why did I not keep death always in view,
Which is the treasury of wealth and sustenance?
Why did I blindly all my life set my affections
On vain shadows which perish at death?
My regret is not that I have died,
But that I rested on these vain shadows in life.
I saw not that my body was a mere shadow or foam,
Which foam rises out of and lives on the Ocean (God).
When the Ocean casts its foam-drops to land,
Go to the graveyard and behold them,
And ask them, "Where is your motion and activity?
The Ocean has cast you into a mortal sickness!"
They will answer by their condition, if not with words,
"Put this question to the Ocean, not to us!"
How can mere foam move unless moved by the waves?
How can dust mount on high unless raised by wind?
When you see the dust-cloud, see the wind too!
When you see the foam, see the ocean that heaves it!
Ah! look till you see your own real final cause,
The rest of you is only fat and flesh, warp and woof.
Your fat kindles no light or flame in a lamp;
Your kneaded flesh is not good for roasting.
Burn up, then, all this body of yours with discernment;
Rise to sight, to sight, to sight!

Virtue cannot exist without temptation and difficulties to be overcome (p. 531).

The Sufi said, "The Great Helper is able
To procure for us profit without loss.
He who casts into the fire roses and trees
Can accomplish good without injury to any.
He who extracts the rose from the thorn
Can also turn this winter into spring.
He who exalts the heads of the cypresses
Is able also out of sadness to bring joy.
He by whose *fiat* all non-existent things exist,
What harm to Him were it if He made them eternal?
He who gave to the body a soul and made it live,
What loss to Him were it if He never caused it to die?
How would it be if That Liberal One were to give
Their hearts' desire to his slaves without toil,
And keep away from these feeble ones
The ambushed snares of lust and temptations of Iblis?"
The Qázi said, "If there were no bitter things,
And no opposition of fair and foul, stone and pearl,
And no lust or Satan or concupiscence,
And no wounds or war or fraud,
Pray, O destroyer of virtue, by what name and title
Could the King of kings address His slaves?
How could He say, 'O temperate or O meek one!'
Or, 'O courageous one, or O wise one?'
How could there be temperate, gentle, or liberal men

If there were no cursed Satan to tempt them astray?
Rustam and Hamza would be all the same as cowards;
Wisdom and knowledge would be useless and vain.
Wisdom and knowledge serve to guide the wanderers;
Were there but one road wisdom would be needless.
To pamper the house of your body fleeting as water,
Do you think it right to ruin both worlds?
I know you are pure of guile and ripe,
And ask this only to edify the ignorant.
The ills of fortune and all troubles soever
Are better than exile from God and neglect of Him;
For the former pass away, but the latter abide;
He is happy who carries a wary heart before God."[1]

This is illustrated by an anecdote of a woman who complained of the hard life she had to lead with her husband owing to his poverty, and was silenced by being asked whether she would prefer to be divorced. No troubles are so hard to bear as separation from the Beloved. Fasting and holy war bring pains with them, but not so great as those incurred by banishment from God. In the midst of their troubles God is ever caring for His servants, and they must not let their tribulations blot out the memory of God's previous goodness to them.

To do this shows an entire absence of growth in grace. This is illustrated by an anecdote of a sage and a monk. The sage asked the monk which was the older, his white beard or himself. The monk replied that he himself was older by some years, whereupon the sage rebuked him for his ignorance, saying his beard had grown pure and white, but he was still black with sin, and had progressed not at all in goodness since he was born.

[1] Koran xxvi. 88.

Each of our members testifies to God's bounties towards us (p. 632).

Inquire now, I pray, of each one of your members;
These dumb members have a thousand tongues.
Inquire the detail of the bounties of the All-sustainer,
Which are recorded in the volume of the universe.
Day and night you are eagerly asking for news,
Whilst every member of your body is telling you news.
Since each member of your body issued from Not-being,
How much pleasure has it seen, and how much pain?
For no member grows and flourishes without pleasure,
And each member is weakened by every pain.[1]
The member endures, but that pleasure is forgotten,
Yet not all forgotten, but hidden from the senses.
Like summer wherein cotton is produced,—
The cotton remains, but the summer is forgotten.
Or like ice which is formed in great frost,—
The frost departs, but the ice is still before us.
The ice is mindful of that extreme cold,
And even in winter that crop is mindful of the summer.
In like manner, O son, every member of your body
Tells you tales of God's bounties to your body.
Even as a woman who has borne twenty children,—
Each child tells a tale of pleasure felt by her.
She became not pregnant save after sexual pleasure,
Can a garden bloom without the spring?
Pregnant women and their teeming wombs
Tell tales of love frolics in the spring.
So every tree which nurtures its fruits
Has been, like Mary, impregnated by the Unseen King.
Though fire's heat be hidden in the midst of water,
Yet a thousand boiling bubbles prove it present.
Though the heat of the fire be working unseen,
Yet its bubbles signify its presence plainly.

In like manner, the members of those enjoying "union"

[1] Cp. Nicom. Ethics, x., iv. 6.

Become big with child, viz., with forms of "states" and "words."[1]
Gazing on the beauty of these forms they stand agape,
And the forms of the world vanish from their sight.
These spiritual progenies are not born of the elements,
And are perforce invisible to the sensual eye.
These progenies are born of divine apparitions,
And are therefore hidden by veils without colour.
I said "born," but in reality they are not born;
I used this expression only by way of indication.
But keep silence till the King bids you speak,
Offer not your nightingale songs to these roses;
For they themselves are saying to you in loud tones,
"O nightingale, hold your peace, and listen to us!"
Those two kinds of fair forms (ecstatic states and words)
Are undeniable proofs of a previous "union;"
Yea, those two kinds of exalted manifestations
Are the evident fruits of a preceding wedlock.

. . . . . .

The ecstasy is past, but your members recall it;
Ask them about it, or call it to mind yourself.
When sorrow seizes you, if you are wise,
You will question that sorrow-fraught moment,
Saying to it, "O sorrow, who now deniest
Thy portion of bounty given thee by the Perfect One,
Even if each moment be not to thee a glad spring,
Yet of what is thy body, like a rose-heap, a storehouse?
Thy body is a heap of roses, thy thought rosewater;
'Twere strange if rosewater ignored the rose-heap!"

STORY VI. *The Faqir and the Hidden Treasure* (p. 533).

Notwithstanding the clear evidence of God's bounty, engendering these spiritual states in men, philosophers and learned men, wise in their own conceit, obstinately shut their eyes to it, and look afar off for what is really close to them, so that they incur the penalty of "being branded on the nostrils,"[1] adjudged against unbelievers. This is illustrated by the story of a poor Faqir who prayed to God that he might be fed without being obliged to work for his food. A divine voice came to him in his sleep and directed him to go to the house of a certain scribe and take a certain writing that he should find there. He did so, and on reading the writing found that it contained directions for finding a hidden treasure. The directions were as follows:—"Go outside the city to the dome which covers the tomb of the martyr; turn your back to the tomb and your face towards Mecca, place an arrow in your bow, and where the arrow falls there dig for the treasure." But before the Faqir had time to commence the search the rumour of the writing and its contents had reached the king, who at once sent and took it away from the Faqir, and began to search for the treasure on his own account. After shooting many arrows and digging in all directions the king failed to find the treasure, and got weary of searching, and returned the writing to the Faqir. Then the Faqir tried what he could do, but failed altogether to hit the spot where the treasure was buried. At last, despairing of success by his own unaided efforts, he cast his care upon God, and implored the divine assistance. Then a voice from heaven came to him, saying, "You were directed to fix an arrow on your bow, but not to draw your bow with all your might, as you have been doing. Shoot as gently as possible, that the arrow may fall close to you, for the hidden treasure is indeed 'nearer to you than your neck-vein.'"[2] Men overlook the spiritual treasures close to them, and for this reason it is that prophets have no honour in their own countries, as is illustrated by the cases of the saint Abu-'l-Hasan Khirqáni and the Prophet Hud or Heber.

[1] Compare Gulshan i Raz, l. 624. Ecstatic words and states are the offspring of communion with God.

[1] Koran lxviii. 16.

[2] Koran l. 15.

God rules men by alternations of hope and fear (p. 533).

This sad Faqir too put up his cries for aid,
And bore off the ball of acceptance from the field.
But at times he distrusted the efficacy of his prayers,
On account of the delay in answering them.
Again, hope of the mercy of the Lord
Arose in his heart as an earnest of rejoicing.
When he was hopeless and ceasing to pray in weariness
He heard from God the word "Ascend!"
God is an Abaser and an Exalter;
Without these two processes nothing comes into being.
Behold the abasement of earth and uplifting of heaven;
Without these two heaven would not revolve, O man!
The abasement and exaltation of earth is otherwise,
Half the year is barren, half green and verdant.
The abasement and exaltation of weary time
Is otherwise again,—half day and half night.
The abasement and exaltation of this compound body
Is now health and now grievous sickness.
Know all the conditions of the world are in this wise,—
Drought, famine, peace, war, and trials.
This world flies, as it were, with these two wings;
Through these all souls are homes of hope and fear;
So that the world keeps trembling like leaves,
In the cold and hot winds of death and resurrection.
Till the jar of pure wine of our 'Isa (Unity)
Shall supersede the jar of many-coloured wine (plurality),
For that world (of unity) is as a saltpan;
Whatever enters it loses its varied hues.

On the text, "Verily I am about to place a Khalifa or Vicegerent on earth" [1] (p. 540).

Whereas the aim and will of the Merciful God
Inclined to the revelation and manifestation of Himself,
And one opposite cannot be shown but by its opposite,

[1] Koran ii. 28.

And that Unique King of kings has no opposite or peer,[1]
Therefore that Lord of the heart set up a Khalifa,
To serve as a mirror to reflect His own sovereignty.
Therefore He gave him unlimited purity and light,
And on the other side He set darkness opposing the light.[2]
God set up two standards, a white and a black one,
The one Adam and the other Iblis;
And between these two mighty armies
Ensued war and battle and all we have witnessed.
Thus, too, in the second generation lived pure Abel;
Cain was the opposite of his pure light.
In like manner these two standards of right and wrong
Were borne aloft till the age of Nimrod.
Nimrod was the opponent and adversary of Abraham,
And their opposing camps warred and fought one another.
When God grew weary of the length of this war,
His fire was appointed to arbitrate between them.
He commanded fire and its flaming torment
To settle the matter in dispute between them.
Age after age these two parties contended,
Even till the time of Pharaoh and gentle Moses.
Between these two the war was waged for years,
And when it passed all bounds and affliction increased
God made the water of the Nile a judge between them,
That the one who deserved pre-eminence should endure.
In like manner it went on till the time of Mustafa
And Abu Jahl, that prince of iniquity.
Likewise did God ordain a punishment for the Thamud,
Namely, an earthquake which destroyed their lives.
Likewise a punishment for the Adites,
Namely, a swiftly rising and violent wind.
Likewise God ordained acute punishment for Qarun;
For the earth concealed wrath under its mildness,
Till all its mildness was converted into wrath,

[1] Because, as Sir T. Browne says, "God is all things."

[2] See Gulshan i Raz, l. 265, and note.

And it swallowed up Qarun and his wealth in its depth.
So with the mouthful which nourishes your body
And wards off the darts of hunger like a cuirass,
When God instils wrath into this mouthful of bread,
That same bread will choke you like a halter.
This same garment which protects you from the cold,
God may give it the quality of intense cold,
So that this warm vest may become to your body
Cold as ice and biting as frost;
So that you will cast off these furs and silks,
And seek for a refuge from cold with cold itself.
You have only one eye, not two (for these two possibilities).
You have forgotten the story of the "shadowing cloud."[1]
God's command came to city and village,
And to house and wall, saying, "Afford no shade!
Ward not off the pouring rain and the sun's heat;"
Till those men hasted to listen to the prophet Shu'aib,
Saying, 'O king, have pity; most of us are dead!'
But read the rest of the tale in the commentaries.
When that Omnipotent hand made the staff a serpent,
If you have reason, that portent should suffice.
You have sight indeed, but fail to mark carefully;
Your eyes are dimmed and closed with fat.

The heavenly treasure lies "nearer to us than our neck-vein" (p. 544).

The Faqir was in this state when a divine voice came,
And God thus solved his difficulties,
Saying, "The voice told you to place an arrow on the bow,—
It did not bid you draw the bowstring to the utmost;
It did not bid you draw the bow with all your might;
It said, 'Adjust an arrow,' not 'Draw the bow fully.'

[1] Koran xxvi. 189. The cloud emitted heat instead of rain, to punish those who disregarded Shu'aib, or Jethro.

You elevated the bow to excess,
You magnified unduly the bowman's art,
Go! abandon this strong bowmanship,
Fix an arrow on the string, but make it not fly far.
When it falls, dig in that spot and search,
Abandon force and seek the treasure with humility."
God is "what is nearer to you than your neck-vein,"
You have cast the arrow of speculation afar off.
O you, who have made ready your bow and arrows,
The game is close to you, and you shoot too far off.
The further a man shoots, the further off he is,
And the more removed from the treasure he seeks.
The philosopher kills himself with thinking,
Tell him that his back is turned to that treasure;
Tell him that the more he runs to and fro,
The further he is removed from his heart's desire.
The Almighty says, "Make efforts in *our* ways,"[1]
Not "Make efforts away from us," O restless one.
Like Canaan, who went away, from shame to follow Noah,
Up to the top of that lofty mountain,
The more he sought safety on that mountain,
The further was he removed from the safe asylum.
So this Faqir, in search of that hidden treasure,
Day after day drew his bow stronger and stronger;
And the harder he drew his bow,
The further was he from the seat of that treasure.
This parable applies to all times,
For the soul of the ignorant is pledged to misfortune.
Because the ignorant man is ashamed of a master,
Perforce he goes and opens a new school for himself.
That school is higher than your true master, O beloved,
And hard of access, and full of scorpions and snakes.
Straightway overthrow it, and turn back again
To the green garden and sweet watered meadows.
Not like Canaan, who, through pride and ignorance,
Sought his ark of safety on a protecting mountain.

[1] Koran xxix. 69.

His far-shooting learning veiled his eyes,
While his heart's desire was all the while in his grasp.
Ah! oftentimes have learning and genius and wit
Proved to the traveller to be *Ghouls* and highwaymen!
"The majority of those in Paradise are the simple," [1]
Who have escaped the snares of philosophy.
Strip yourself bare of overweening intellect,
That grace may ever be shed upon you from above.
Cleverness is the opposite of humility and submission,
Quit cleverness, and consort with simple-mindedness!

STORY VII. *The Three Travellers* (p. 545).

A Musulman was travelling with two unbelievers, a Jew and a Christian, like wisdom linked with the flesh and the devil. God was "nigh unto His faithful servant," [2] and when the first stage was completed He caused a present of sweetmeats to be laid before the travellers. As the Jew and the Christian had already eaten their evening meal when the sweetmeats arrived, they proposed to lay them aside till the morrow; but the Musulman, who was keeping fast, and therefore could not eat before nightfall, proposed to eat them that night. To this the other two refused to consent, alleging that the Musulman wanted to eat the whole of the sweetmeats himself. Then the Musulman proposed to divide them into three portions, so that each might eat his own portion when he pleased; but this also was objected to by the others, who quoted the proverb, "The divider is in hell." The Musulman explained to them that this proverb meant the man who divides his allegiance between God and lust; but they still refused to give way, and the Musulman therefore submitted, and lay down to sleep in the endurance of the pangs of hunger. Next morning, when they awoke, it was agreed between them that each should relate his dreams, and that the sweetmeats should be awarded to him whose dream was the best. The Jew said that he had dreamed that Moses had carried him to the top of Mount Sinai, and shown him marvellous visions of the glory of heaven and the angels. The Christian said he had dreamed that 'Isa had carried him up to the fourth heaven and shown him all the glories of the heavens. Finally the Musulman said that the Prophet Muhammad had appeared to him in person, and after commending him for his piety in saying his prayers and keeping fast so strictly on the previous night, had commanded him to eat up those divinely provided sweetmeats as a reward, and he had accordingly done so. The Jew and the Christian were at first annoyed with him for thus stealing a march upon them; but on his pointing out that he had no option but to obey the Prophet's commands, they admitted that he had done right, and that his dream was the best, as he had been awake, while they were asleep. The moral is, that the divine treasure is revealed as an immediate intuition to those who seek it with prayer and humble obedience, and not to those who seek to infer and deduce its nature and quality from the lofty abstractions of philosophy.

Lofty philosophical speculation does not lead to the knowledge of God (p. 547).

The Musulman said, "O my friends,
My lord, the Prophet Muhammad, appeared to me,
And said, 'The Jew has hurried to the top of Sinai,
And plays a game of love with God's interlocutor;
The Christian has been carried by 'Isa, Lord of bliss
Up to the summit of the fourth heaven;
Thou who art left behind and hast endured anguish,
Arise quickly and eat the sweetmeats and confections!
Those two clever and learned men have ascended,
And read their titles of dignity and exaltation;

[1] A *Hadis*. Cp. 1 Cor. i. 25, 26.

[2] Koran ii. 182.

Those two exalted ones have found exalted science,
And rivalled the very angels in intellect;
O humble and simple and despised one,
Arise and eat of the banquet of the divine sweets!"
They said to him, "Then you have been gluttonous;
Well indeed! you have eaten all the sweets!"
He answered, "When my sovereign lord commanded me,
Who am I that I should abstain from obeying?
Would you, O Jew, resist the commands of Moses
If he bade you do something, either pleasant or not?
Would you, O Christian, rebel against 'Isa's commands,
Whether those commands were agreeable or the reverse?
How could I rebel against the 'Glory of the prophets'?
Nay, I ate the sweets, and am now happy."
They replied, "By Ållah, you have seen a true vision;
Your vision is better than a hundred like ours.
Your dream was seen by you when awake, O happy one,
For it was seen to be real by your being awake."
Quit excessive speculation and inordinate science,
'Tis service of God and good conduct that gains its end.
'Tis for this that God created us,
"We created not mankind save to worship us."[1]
What profit did his science bring to Samiri?[2]
His science excluded him from God's portals.
Consider what Qarun gained by his alchemy;
He was swallowed up in the depths of the earth.
Abu-l Jahl, again, what gained he from his wit
Save to be hurled head-foremost into hell for infidelity?
Know real science is seeing the fire directly,
Not mere talk, inferring the fire from the smoke.
Your scientific proofs are more offensive to the wise
Than the urine and breath whence a physician infers.
If these be your only proofs, O son,
Smell foul breath and inspect urine like physicians.
Such proofs are as the staff of a blind man,

[1] Koran li. 56.
[2] Samiri, the maker of the golden calf. Qarun Korah.

Which prove only the blindness of the holder.
All your outcry and pompous claims and bustle
Only say, "I cannot see, hold me excused!"

This is illustrated be an anecdote of a peasant who, hearing a proclamation issued by the Prince of Tirmid, to the effect that a large reward would be given to him who should take a message to Samarcand in the space of four days, hurried to Tirmid by relays of post-horses in the utmost haste, and threw the whole city into alarm, as the people thought that his extreme haste and bustle must portend the approach of an enemy or some other calamity. But when he was admitted to the presence of the prince, all he had to say was, that he had hurried to inform him that he could not go to Samarcand so quickly. The prince was very angry with him for making all this disturbance about nothing, and threatened to punish him.

The uses of chastisements (p. 550).

He said, "Alms of mercy repel calamity,[1]
Alms cure thy sickness, O son!
'Tis not charitable to burn up the poor,
Or to put out the eyes of the meek."
The prince replied, "Kindness is good in its place,
Provided you do kindness in its proper place.
If at chess you put the king in the rook's place
That is wrong; and so if you put the knight in the king's,
The law prescribes both rewards and chastisements.
The king's place is the throne, the horse's the gate.
What is justice but putting each in his place?
What injustice but putting each in what is not his place?
Nothing is vain of all that God has created,
Whether vengeance or mercy, or plain dealing or snares.
Not one of all these is good absolutely,

[1] Freytag Arabum Proverbia, iii. 277.

Nor is any one of them absolutely bad.
Each is harmful or beneficial according to its place,
Wherefore knowledge of these points is proper and useful.
Ah! many are the chastisements sent to the poor
Which are more beneficial to him than bread and sweets;
Because sweets out of season excite biliousness,
While blows make him pure from impurity.
Strike the poor man timely blows,
Which may save him from being beheaded later."

The peasant, in reply, urged the prince not to be over hasty in punishing him, but to take counsel with suitable advisers, as enjoined in various texts,[1] and in the *Hadis* prohibiting monkery, and warned him that if he shunned the advice and society of his equals he would assuredly be led astray by wretched companions.[2] In illustration of this a story is told of a mouse who conceived a great affection for a frog living in a neighbouring pond.[3] That he might be able to communicate with his friend at all times, he fastened a string to the frog's leg, and the other end of it to his own. The proverb says, "Occasional intermission of visits augments love,"[4] but ardent lovers desire to be in communication with the object of their love without intermission. The frog was at first unwilling to enter into such close relations with an animal of another species, but at last allowed himself to be persuaded to do so, against his better judgment. Shortly afterwards a raven swooped down on the mouse and carried him off, and the frog, being fastened to the mouse, was dragged off and destroyed along with it. The raven's friends said to him, "How is it you managed to catch an animal that lives in the water?" and he replied, "Because it was so silly as to consort with one of another species that lived on dry land."

[1] Koran lxvii. 22, iii. 155, xlii. 36. [2] Koran xliii. 37.
[3] Anvari Suhaili, Chap. vii. Story III.
[4] Freytag, Arabum Proverbia, i. 287.

Comparison of the body to the mouse, and the soul to the frog (p. 553).

The two friends discussed the matter long,
And after discussion this plan was settled,
That they should fetch a long string,
By means of which to communicate with one another.
The mouse said, "One end must be tied to your leg,
And the other end to the leg of me, your double,
That by this contrivance we two may be united,
And be mingled together like soul and body."
Body is like a string tied to soul's foot,
That string drags soul down to earth.
The soul is the frog in the water of ecstatic bliss;
Escaping from the mouse of the body, it is in bliss.
The mouse of the body drags it back with that string;
Ah! what sorrow it tastes through being dragged back!
If it were not dragged down by that insolent mouse,
The frog would remain at peace in its water.
On the last day, when you shall awake from sleep,
You will learn the rest of this from the Sun of truth!

In illustration of the thesis that the sense which perceives the unseen and spiritual world is superior to the other senses, and is exempt from death and decay, the poet tells an anecdote of Sultan Mahmud of Ghazni and some robbers. One night, when walking about the city alone, he fell in with a band of robbers. He told them he was one of them, and proposed that each should tell his own special talent. Accordingly one said he could hear what the dogs said when they barked; another that his sight was so good that when he saw a man at night he could recognise him without fail next day; another said his talent lay in the strength of his arms, whereby he dug holes through the walls of houses; another said he could divine by his sense of smell where gold was hidden; another said his wrist was so strong that he could throw a rope farther than any one. At last it came to the turn of the king, and he told them that his talent lay in his beard, for when he wagged it he could deliver criminals from the executioner. The robbers then went to the king's palace, and, each of them co-operating by the exercise of his peculiar talent, they broke into it, and plundered a large sum of money. The king, after witnessing the burglary, withdrew from them secretly, and, having summoned his Vazir, gave orders for their apprehension. No sooner were the robbers brought before the king than the one whose talent lay in recognising by day those whom he had seen in the darkness of night at once knew him, and said to the others, "This is the man who said his talent lay in his beard!" Thus the only one whose talent profited him at the time of need was he who could recognise by day what he had previously seen by night; for he appealed to the king to exercise his talent of deliverance, and the king listened to his entreaty, and delivered him from the executioner.

He whose eyes discern God in the world is safe from destruction (p. 555).

He who, when he had once seen a person at night,
Recognised him without fail when he saw him by day,
Saw the king upon the throne, and straightway cried,
"This was he who accompanied us on our nightly walk;
This is he whose beard possessed such rare talent;
Our arrest is due to his sagacity."
He added, "'Yea, he was with you,'[1] this great king;
He beheld our actions and heard our secrets.
My eyes guided me to recognise that king at night,
And dwelt lovingly on his face, like the moon at night.

[1] Koran lvii. 4.

Now, therefore, I will implore his grace for myself,
For he will never avert his face from him that knew him."
Know the eye of the 'Knower' is a safeguard in both worlds,
For therein ye will find a very Bahram to aid you.
For this cause Muhammad was the intercessor for faults,
Because his eye 'did not wander'[1] from the King of kings.
In the night of this world, when the sun is hidden,
He beheld God, and placed his hopes on Him.
His eyes were anointed with the words, 'We opened thy heart,'[2]
He beheld what Gabriel himself had not power to see.[3]"

The story of the frog is concluded by the lamentations of the frog over his folly in consorting with an animal of a different genus to his own, on which Reason warns him that homogeneity lies in spirit, not in outward form; and this is illustrated by an anecdote of a man named 'Abdu'l Ghaus, who was the son of a fairy mother, and consequently homogeneous with the fairies, though only an ordinary man to outward appearance.

Story VIII. *The Man who received a Pension from the Prefect of Tabriz* (p. 559).

These reflections on the nothingness of outward form compared to spirit lead the poet to the corollary that often men whose outward forms are buried in the grave are greater benefactors to the poor and helpless than men still living in the body. This is illustrated by the story of the man who was maintained by the Prefect of Tabriz. This man incurred heavy debts on the credit of his pension, even as the Imam Ja'far Sadiq was able to capture a strong fort single-handed through the power of

[1] Koran liii. 17. [2] Koran xciv. 1. [3] Gulshan i Raz, l. 120.

God assisting him. When the creditors became pressing the man journeyed to Tabriz to seek further aid; but on arriving there he found the Prefect was dead. On learning this he was much cast down, but eventually recognised that he had erred in looking to a creature instead of his Creator for aid, according to the text, "The infidels equalise others with their Lord."[1] This obliquity of spiritual sight, causing him to see a mere human benefactor, where the real benefactor was God alone, is illustrated by anecdotes of a man buying bread at Kashan, of Sultan Khwarazm Shah deluded into misliking a fine horse by the interested advice of his Vazir, and of Joseph, who when imprisoned by Pharaoh was induced to trust for deliverance to the intercession of the chief butler rather than to God alone, for which cause "he remained several years in prison."[2] A charitable person of Tabriz endeavoured to raise funds for the poor man, and appealed to the citizens to aid him, but only succeeded in collecting a very small sum. He then visited the Prefect's tomb, and implored assistance from him; and the same night the Prefect appeared to him in a dream, and gave him directions where to find a great treasure, and directed him to make over this treasure to the poor man. Thus the dead Prefect proved a more liberal benefactor than the citizens of Tabriz who were still living.

The poor man's regrets for having placed his trust in man and not in God (p. 561).

When he recovered himself he said, "O God,
I have sinned in looking for aid to a creature!
Although the Prefect showed great liberality,
It was in no wise equal to Thy bounty.
He gave me a cap, but Thou my head full of sense;
He gave me a garment, but Thou my tall form.
He gave me gold, but Thou my hand which counts it;
He gave me a horse, but Thou my reason to guide it;
He gave me a lamp, but Thou my lucid eyes;
He gave me sweetmeats, but Thou my appetite for them;
He gave me a pension, but Thou my life and being;
His gift was gold, but Thine true blessings;
He gave me a house, but Thou heaven and earth;
In Thy house he and a hundred like him are nourished.
The gold was of Thy providing, he did not create it;
The bread of Thy providing, and furnished to him by Thee.
Thou also didst give him his liberality,
For thereby Thou didst augment his happiness.
I made him my *Qibla*, and directed my prayers to him;
I turned away my eyes from Thee, the *Qibla*-maker!
Where was he when the Supreme Dispenser of faith
Sowed reason in the water and clay of man,
And drew forth from Not-being this heavenly dome,
And spread out the carpet of the earth?
Of the stars He made torches to illumine the sky,
And of the four elements locks with keys (of reason).
Ah! many are the buildings visible and invisible
Which God has made between heaven's dome and earth.
Man is the astrolabe of those exalted attributes,
The attribute of man is to manifest God's signs.
Whatever is seen in man is the reflection of God,
Even as the reflection of the moon in water."

. . . . . .

Say not two, know not two, call not on two!
Know the slave is obliterated in his lord!
So the lord is obliterated in God that created him;
Yea, lost and dead and buried in his Creator!
When you regard this lord as separate from God,
You annihilate at once text and paraphrase.
With eyes and heart look beyond mere water and clay,
God alone is the *Qibla*; regard not two *Qiblas!*
If you regard two you lose the benefit of both;
A spark falls on the tinder and the tinder vanishes!

[1] Koran vi. 1. [2] Koran xii. 42.

Joseph kept in prison a long time for having placed his hopes of release in man and not in God (p. 567).

In like manner Joseph, in the prison,
With humble and earnest supplications
Begged aid, saying, "When you are released,
And are occupied with your ministrations to the king,
Remember me, and entreat the king
To release me too from this prison."
How can one prisoner fettered in the snare
Procure release for a fellow prisoner?
The people of the world are all prisoners,
Awaiting death on the stake of annihilation;
Except one or two rare exceptions,
Whose bodies are in prison but their souls in heaven.
Afterwards, because Joseph had looked to man for aid,
He remained in prison for many years.[1]
The Devil caused the man to forget Joseph,
And blotted Joseph's words from his remembrance;
And on account of this fault of that holy man
God left him in the prison for many years.

STORY IX. *The King and his Three Sons* (p. 571).

A certain king had three sons, who were the light of his eyes, and, as it were, a fountain whence the palm-tree of his heart drank the water of bliss. One day he called his sons before him and commanded them to travel through his realm, and to inspect the behaviour of the governors and the state of the administration; and he strictly charged them not to go near a particular fort which he named. But, according to the saying, "Man hankers after what is forbidden," the three princes disobeyed their father, and, before going anywhere else, proceeded to visit this fort. The result was, that they fell into calamities, and had occasion to repeat the text, "Had we but hearkened or understood, we had not been among the dwellers in the flame."[1] The fort was full of pictures, images and forms, and amongst them was a portrait of a beautiful damsel, the daughter of the King of China, which made such a deep impression on the three princes that they all became distracted with love, and determined to journey to the court of the King of China and sue for the hand of his daughter.

[1] Koran xii. 42.

The significance of forms[2] (p. 574).

Be not intoxicated with these goblets of forms,
Lest you become a maker and worshipper of idols.
Pass by these cups full of forms, linger not;
There is wine in the cups, but it proceeds not from them.
Look to the Giver of the wine with open mouth;
When His wine comes, is not cup too small to hold it?
O Adam, seek the reality of my love,
Quit the mere husk and form of the wheat.
When sand was made meal for "The Friend of God,"[3]
Know, O master, the form of wheat was dispensed with.
Form proceeds from the world that is without form,
Even as smoke arises from fire.

. . . . . .

The Divine art without form designs forms (ideals),[4]
Those forms fashion bodies with senses and instruments.
Whatever the form, it fashions in its own likeness
Those bodies either to good or to evil.

[1] Koran lxvii. 10.

[2] *Surat*, or "form," means picture, image, outward appearance as opposed to reality, conception or "form of thought," the "architypes" or "ideas" in the Divine mind, "the Substantial forms" of the Realist philosophy. Here the poet runs through nearly all these meanings.

[3] Sale's Koran, p. 75, note.

[4] *I.e.*, the architypes in the "Intellectual Presence" or "world of command," which are afterwards set forth in the "world of creation" or sensible objects.

If the form be blessing, the man is thankful;
If it be suffering, he is patient;
If it be cherishing, he is cheerful;
If it be bruising, he is full of lamentation!

. . . . . .

Since all these forms are slaves of Him without form,
Why do they deny their Lord and Master?
They exist only through Him that is without form;
What, then, means their disavowal of their Sustainer?
This very denial of Him proceeds from Him,
This act is naught but a reflection from Himself!
The forms of the walls and roofs of houses
Know to be shadows of the architect's thought;
Although stones and planks and bricks
Find no entrance into the sanctuary of thought,
Verily the Absolute Agent is without form,
Form is only a tool in His hands.
Sometimes that Formless One of His mercy
Shows His face to His forms from behind the veil of Not-being,
That every form may derive aid therefrom,—
From its perfect beauty and power.
Again, when that Formless One hides His face,
Those forms set forth their needs.
If one form sought perfection from another form,
That would be the height of error.
Why then, O simpleton, do you set forth your needs
To one who is as needy as yourself?
Since forms are slaves, apply them not to God,
Seek not to use a form as a similitude of God.[1]
Seek Him with humbleness and self-abasement,
For thought yields naught but forms of thought.
Still, if you are unable to dispense with forms,
Those occurring independently of your thought are best.[2]

[1] See Koran xlii. 9.

[2] *I.e.*, the similitudes used in the Koran.

The "Truth," which is our real self, lies hidden within our phenomenal and visible self, and the Prophets reveal it to us (p. 576).

"Now have we seen what the king saw at the first,
When that Incomparable One adjured us."
The prophets have many claims to our gratitude,
Because they forewarn us of our ultimate lot,
Saying, "What ye sow will yield only thorns;
If ye fly that way, ye will fly astray.
Take seed of us to yield you a good harvest,
Fly with our wings to hit the mark with your arrow.
Now ye know not the truth and nature of the 'Truth,'[1]
But at the last ye will cry, '*That* was the "Truth."'
The Truth is yourself, but not your mere bodily self,
Your real self is higher than 'you' and 'me.'
This visible 'you' which you fancy to be yourself
Is limited in place, the real 'you' is not limited.
Why, O pearl, linger you trembling in your shell?
Esteem not yourself mere sugar-cane, but real sugar.
This outward 'you' is foreign to your real 'you;'
Cling to your real self, quit this dual self.
Your last self attains to your first (real) self
Only through your attending earnestly to that union.
Your real self lies hid beneath your outward self,
For 'I am the servant of him who looks into himself.'"[2]
"What a youth sees only when reflected in a glass,
Our wise old fathers saw long ago though hid in stones.
But we disobeyed the advice of our father,
And rebelled against his affectionate counsels.
We made light of the king's exhortations,
And slighted his matchless intimations.
Now we have all fallen into the ditch,

[1] "The Truth," *Al Haqq*, the Divine Noumenon.

[2] See Gulshan i Raz, Answer III., and the *Hadis*, "Whoso knows himself knows his Lord."

Wounded and crushed in this fatal struggle.
We relied on our own reason and discernment,
And for that cause have fallen into this calamity.
We fancied ourselves free from defects of sight,
Even as those affected by colour-blindness.
Now at last our hidden disease has been revealed,
After we have been involved in these calamities."
"The shadow of a guide is better than directions to God,
To be satisfied is better than a hundred nice dishes.
A seeing eye is better than a hundred walking-sticks,
Eye discerns jewels from mere pebbles."

The princes ascertained the name of the lady depicted in the fort from an old Shaikh, who warned them of the perils they would encounter on their journey to China, and told them that the King of China would not bestow his favour on those who tried to gain it by tricks and clever stratagems, but solely on those who were prepared to yield up their lives to him, according to the saying, "Die before you die." This is illustrated by an anecdote of a Chief of Bokhara, who made it a rule never to bestow his bounty on beggars who asked for it, but only on those who awaited his pleasure in silence. A certain Faqir tried many stratagems to evade this rule, but his craft was at once seen through by the Chief, and turned to his own confusion. The thesis that the unbought free grace of God is superior to any blessing obtainable by human exertion and contrivance is further illustrated by an absurd anecdote of two youths, one of whom trusted for protection to his own contrivance, and found it a broken reed. The Prophet said, "Two there are who are never satisfied—the lover of the world and the lover of knowledge;" and he who loves knowledge will continue to trust in his knowledge, in spite of all exhortations and experience. But the eldest prince advised his brothers to risk the perils and persevere in the journey, reminding them that "Patience is the key of joy." Accordingly they abandoned their country and their parents, like Ibrahim Adham, who renounced the throne of Balkh, and like the old Arabian king Amru'l Qais, who fled from the pursuit of his female adorers to seek the Spiritual Beloved in a far country.

How the princes discoursed with one another in figurative language concerning their beloved mistress (p. 581).

They told their secrets to one another in dark sayings,
Speaking beneath their breath in fear and trembling.
None but God was privy to their secrets,
None but Heaven was partner in their sighs.
Yea, they used technical expressions one to another,
And possessed intelligence to extract the sense.
The vulgar learn the words of this "language of birds,"
And make boast of their mastery thereof;
But these words are only the outward form of the language,
The "raw" man is ignorant of the birds' meaning.
He is the true Solomon who knows the birds' language,
A demon, though he usurp his kingdom, is quite another.
The demon has taken upon him the form of Solomon,
His knowledge is fraud, not "what we have been taught."
When Solomon was blessed with inspiration from God,
He learned birds' language from "what we were taught."
But thou art only a bird of the air; understand then
That thou hast never seen the true spiritual birds!
The nest of the Simurgh is beyond Mount Qaf,[2]
Not every thought can attain thereto;
Save thoughts which catch a glimpse thereof,
And after the vision are again shut off.
Yet not all shut off, rather intermitted for a wise end,

[1] Koran xxvii. 16.
[2] Simurgh, "Oiseau extraordinaire qui réside au Caucase," as M. Garcin de Tassy calls it, means "thirty birds" (*Si murgh*), and is used as a type of the Divine Unity which embraces all plurality.

For the blessing abides, though shut off and hidden!
In order to preserve that body which is as a soul,
The Sun is veiled for a while behind a cloud;
In order not to melt that soul-like body,
The Sun withdraws itself as from ice.
For thy soul's sake seek counsel of these inspired ones.[1]
Ah! rob not their words of their technical meanings!
Zulaikha applied to Yusuf the names of all things,
Beginning with wild rue and ending with frankincense.
She veiled his name under all other names,
And imparted her secret meaning to her confidants.
When she said, "The wax is melted by the fire,"
She meant, "My lover is wroth with me."
So when she said, "See, the moon is risen!"
Or, "Lo! the willow-bough is putting forth leaves;"
Or if she said, "The leaves quiver in the wind,"
Or, "The wild rue yields perfume as it burns;"
Or if she said, "The rose tells her tale to the Bulbul,"
Or, "The king sings his love-strain;"
Or if she said, "Ah! what a blessed lot!"
Or, "Who hath disturbed my heart's repose?"
Or if she said, "The water-carrier hath brought water,"
Or, "Lo! the sun emerges from the clouds;"
Or if she said, "Last night the victuals were boiled,"
Or, "The food was perfectly cooked;"
Or if she said, "My bread is without savour,"
Or, "The heavens are revolving the wrong way;"
Or if she said, "My head aches with pain,"
Or, "My headache is now relieved;"—
If she gave thanks, 'twas for being united to Yusuf;
If she wailed, 'twas that she was separated from him.
Though she gave vent to thousands of names,
Her meaning and purport was only Yusuf;
Was she an hungred, when she pronounced his name,
She became filled and cheered by his nourishment.
Her thirst was quenched by Yusuf's name,
His name was spiritual water to her soul.
Was she in pain, by pronouncing his mighty name
At once her pain was turned into joy.
In the cold it was a warm garment;
Her lover's name accomplished all this through love.
Strangers may pronounce the "pure name" of God,
Yet it effects no such marvels, for they lack love.
All that 'Isa accomplished by the name of Jehovah,
Zulaikha attained through the name "Yusuf."
When the soul is intimately united with God,
To name the one is the same as naming the other.
Zulaikha was empty of self and filled with love of Yusuf,
And there flowed out of her jar what it contained.
The scent of the saffron of union made her smile,
The stench of the onion of separation made her weep.
Each to have in his heart a hundred meanings,—
Such is not the creed of true love and devotion.
"The Friend" is to the lover as day to the sun,
The material sun is a veil over the face of the real day.
Whoso distinguishes not the veil from "The Friend's" face
Is a worshipper of the sun; of such an one beware!
"The Friend" is the real day, and daily food of lovers,
The heart and the heart's torment of His lovers.

After enduring many toils and misfortunes the three princes at last arrived in the metropolis of China, and thereupon the eldest prince expressed his intention of presenting himself before the king, as he could wait no longer. His brothers tried to dissuade him from risking his life, pointing out that if he acted on blind impulse and vain conceit he would surely go astray, for "a conceit hath naught of truth;"[1] and they further urged him to listen to the counsels of the *Pir*, or Spiritual Director. But the eldest brother refused to be dissuaded from his purpose, saying he would no longer hide his passion for his beloved, like one who beats a drum under a blanket,

[1] *i.e.*, the prophets and saints.

[1] Koran x. 37.

but would proclaim it openly, and take the risk of whatever might ensue. He added that he was convinced that he should obtain his desire in some way or other, if not in the way that he expected;—according to the text, "Whoso feareth God, to him will he grant a prosperous issue, and will provide for him in a way he reckoned not."[1] Seekers after God fancy that He is far from them, and that they must travel far to reach Him; but these are both erroneous suppositions; and just as arithmeticians work out true answers to their problems by the "Method of Errors,"[2] so must the seekers of God from these errors work out the conviction that God is very nigh to them that call upon Him faithfully. To illustrate this an anecdote is told of a man of Bagdad who was in great distress, and who, after calling on God for aid, dreamt that a great treasure lay hid in a certain spot in Egypt. He accordingly journeyed to Egypt, and there fell into the hands of the patrol, who arrested him, and beat him severely on suspicion of being a thief. Calling to mind the proverb that "falsehood is a mischief but truth a remedy,"[3] he determined to confess the true reason of his coming to Egypt, and accordingly told them all the particulars of his dream. On hearing them they believed him, and one of them said, "You must be a fool to journey all this distance merely on the faith of a dream. I myself have many times dreamt of a treasure lying hid in a certain spot in Bagdad, but was never foolish enough to go there." Now the spot in Bagdad named by this person was none other than the house of the poor man of Bagdad, and he straightway returned home, and there found the treasure. And he gave thanks, and recognised how "God causes ease to follow troubles,"[4] and how "Men hate what is good for them,"[5] and how God delays the answer to prayer, and allows men to remain poor and hungry for a season, in order to make them call upon Him, even as the Prophet said, "My servant is a lute which sounds best when it is empty."

[1] Koran lxv. 2.
[2] *I.e.*, "The Rule of Position." *Khulásat ul Hisáb*, Book iv.
[3] Freytag, Arabum Proverbia, ii. 379.
[4] Koran ii. 213.
[5] Koran lxv. 7.

Why the answer to prayer is delayed (p. 586).

Ah! many earnest suppliants wail forth prayers,
Till the smoke of their wailing rises to heaven;
Yea, the perfume of the incense of sinners' groans
Mounts up above the lofty roof of heaven.
Then the angels supplicate God, saying,
"O Thou that hearest prayer and relievest pain,
Thy faithful slave is bowing down before Thee.
He knows of none on whom to rely save Thee;
Thou bestowest favours on the helpless.
Every suppliant obtains his desire from Thee."
God makes answer, "The delay in granting his prayer
Is intended to benefit him, not to harm him.
His pressing need draws him from his negligence to me;
Yea, drags him by the hair into my courts.
If I at once remove his need he will go away,
And will be destroyed in his idle sports.
Though he is wailing with heartfelt cry of 'O Aider!'
Bid him wail on with broken heart and contrite breast.
His voice sounds sweet in my ears,
And his wailing and cries of 'O God!'
In this way by supplication and lamentation
He prevails with me altogether."
It is on account of their sweet voices
That choice parrots and nightingales are prisoned in cages.
Ugly owls and crows[1] are never prisoned in cages;
Such a thing was never heard of in history.

. . . . . .

The disappointments of the pious, be sure,
Are appointed for this wise purpose.

[1] *i.e.*, hardened sinners like Pharaoh.

The eldest brother then delayed no longer, but rushed into the presence of the King and kissed his feet. The King, like a good shepherd, was well aware of the troubles and cravings of his sheep. He knew that the prince had abjured earthly rank and dignity through love for his daughter, even as a Sufi casts away his robe when overpowered by ecstatic rapture. The only reason why the prince had lagged behind in the race and not presented himself to the King before was that hitherto he had lacked the "inner eye" or spiritual sense which discerns spiritual verities, and had been consequently blind to the King's perfections. They who lack this inner spiritual sense can no more appreciate spiritual pleasures than a man lacking the sense of smell can enjoy the perfume of flowers, or a eunuch the society of fair women. But his eyes had now been opened by the King's grace, and he had escaped from the bondage of worldly lusts and illusions, and, taught by experience, had resolved never again to be led captive by them.

This is illustrated by the anecdote of the Qázi who was beguiled by the wife of a dwarf. The dwarf and his wife were very poor, and one day the dwarf said to his wife, "God has given you arched brows and arrowy glances and all manner of witchery; go and ensnare some rich man, so that we may extract money from him!" So the woman went to the court of the Qázi, pretending to have a grievance; and when she saw the Qázi she beguiled him, and induced him to pay her a visit at night. While the Qázi was sitting with her the dwarf returned home and knocked violently at the door, and the Qázi, in a great fright, hid himself in a large chest. The dwarf at once fetched a porter, and told him to take the chest to the bazar and sell it. On the way to the bazar the Qázi cried out to the porter to fetch the Deputy; and when the Deputy came he redeemed the chest for one hundred Dinars, and thus the Qázi escaped. Next year the woman went to the court and tried to seduce the Qázi a second time; but he said, "Begone; I have escaped from your toils once, and will not fall into them again." The action of the Deputy in freeing the Qázi reminds the poet of the saying of the Prophet, "Of him, of whom I am the master, 'Ali also is master," and is therefore able to free him from slavery.

The eldest prince at last fell sick of hope deferred, and gave up the ghost. But though he failed to obtain the King's daughter, the object of his earthly attachment, he obtained union with the King, the real spiritual object of his love, and the eternal fruition of dwelling in Him.

The joys of union with the Spiritual Beloved are inexpressible in speech (p. 595).

In short, the King cherished him lovingly,
And he like a moon waned in that sun.
That waning of lovers makes them wax stronger,
Just as the moon waxes brighter after waning.
Ordinary sick persons crave a remedy for sickness,
But the lovesick one cries, "Increase my waning!
I have never tasted wine sweeter than this poison,
No health can be sweeter than this sickness!
No devotion is better than this sin (of love),
Years are as a moment compared to this moment!"
Long time he dwelt with the King in this manner,
With burning heart, as a lively sacrifice.

. . . . . .

Thus his life passed, yet he gained not the union he wished.
Patient waiting consumed him, his soul could not bear it;
He dragged on life with pain and gnashing of teeth.
At last life ended before he had attained his desire.
The form of his earthly Beloved was hidden from him;
He departed, and found union with his Spiritual Beloved.
Then he said, "Though she lacks clothes of silk and wool,

'Tis sweeter to embrace her without those veils.
I have become naked of the body and its illusions,
I am admitted into the most intimate union."
The story admits of being told up to this point,
But what follows is hidden and inexpressible in words.
If you should speak and try a hundred ways to express it,
'Tis useless; the mystery becomes no clearer.
You can ride on saddle and horse up to the sea-coast,
But then you must use a horse of wood (*i.e.*, a boat).
A horse of wood is useless on dry land,
It is the special conveyance of voyagers by sea.
Silence is this horse of wood,
Silence is the guide and support of men at sea.
This Silence which causes you annoyance
Is uttering cries of love audible to the spiritual.
You say, "How strange the spiritual man is silent!"
He answers, "How strange you have no ears!
Though I utter cries, you hear them not;
Sensual ears, however sharp, are deaf to my cries."
The spiritual man, as it were, cries in his sleep,
Uttering thousands of words of comfort;
While the carnal man at his side hears nothing at all,
For he is asleep, and deaf to the other's voice.
But the perfect spiritualist who has broken his boat
Plunges into the sea as a fish of the sea (of Truth).
He is then neither silent nor speaking, but a mystery.
No words are available to express his condition.
That marvellous one is in neither of these states;
'Twould be irreverent to explain his state more fully.
These illustrations are weak and inappropriate,
But no fitter ones are obtainable from sensible objects.

When the eldest prince died, the youngest was sick and could not come; but the second brother came to the court to attend his funeral. There the King observed him, and took pity on him and entreated him kindly. He instilled into him spiritual knowledge of the verities hidden beneath phenomenal objects, and conveyed to him as deep a perception of spiritual truths as is not gained by a Sufi after years of fasting and retirement from the world. It is a fact, that when the pure spirit escapes from the bonds of the body, God gives it sight to behold the things of the spirit. The logician denies the possibility of this divine illumination of the heart, but he is confuted by the Prophet, who swore "by the star" that the Koran was revealed to him by divine illumination.[1] Those who cleave to their heresy (*Bid'at*) and obstinate unbelief are like to incur the punishment inflicted on the tribe of 'Ad for disbelieving the Prophet Hud.[2] Earthly forms are only shadows of the Sun of the Truth,—a cradle for babes, but too small to hold those who have grown to spiritual manhood. When the prince was thus nourished by the spiritual food given him by the King, which was such as the angels of heaven subsist upon, not the unspiritual food of Christians and those who give partners to God, he began to be puffed up with self-conceit, and forgot what he owed to the King, and rebelled against him. The King was cut to the heart by his ingratitude, which exactly resembled that of Nimrod. When Nimrod was an infant he was taken by his mother to sea, and the ship being wrecked, all that were in it perished, save only the infant Nimrod, who was saved through the pity of 'Izra'il, the Angel of Death. God spared him, and nurtured him without the aid of mother or nurse; but when he grew up he proved ungrateful, and was puffed up with self-conceit and egotism, and showed enmity against God and Abraham, His servant. When the prince found himself cast off by the King he came to himself, and repented and humbled himself with deep contrition. The King then pardoned him; but his doom had already been decreed by God, and he was slain by the King he had injured, acknowledging the King's goodness to him with his latest breath.

[1] Koran liii. 1. [2] Koran xlvi. 20.

The death of the second prince (p. 601).

In short, the vengeance of That Jealous One (God)
After one year bore him to the grave.
When the King awoke out of his trance to consciousness,
His Mars-like eyes shed tears of blood.
When that incomparable one looked into his quiver,
He saw that one of his arrow-shafts was missing.
He cried to God, "What has become of my arrow?"
God answered, "Thy arrow is fixed in his throat!"
That King, bountiful as the sea, had pardoned him;
Nevertheless his arrow had dealt him a mortal wound.
He was slain, and cried out with his last breath,
"The King is all in all, my slayer and my saviour.
If he is not both these, he is not all in all;
Nay, he is both my slayer and my mourner!"
That expiring martyr also gave thanks,
That the King had smitten his body, not his spirit;
For the visible body must perforce perish,
Ere the spirit can live in happiness for evermore.
Though he incurred chastisement, it affected his body only,
And as a friend he now goes, free of pain, to his Friend.
Thus at first he clung to the King's stirrup,
But at last went his way guided by perfect sight.

Finally the youngest brother, who was the weakest of all, succeeded where his brothers had failed, and obtained his earthly mistress, the king's daughter, as his bride, and the Spiritual Beloved as well.

Here the Masnavi breaks off; but, according to the Bulaq edition, the following conclusion was supplied by Jalalu-'d-Din's son, Baháu-'d-Din Sultan Valad:—

Part of the story remains untold; it was retained
In his mind and was not disclosed.
The story of the princes remains unfinished,
The pearl of the third brother remains unstrung.
Here speech, like a camel, breaks down on its road;
I will say no more, but guard my tongue from speech.
The rest is told without aid of tongue
To the heart of him whose spirit is alive.

Note on Apocryphal Supplements to the Masnavi.

In the Lucknow edition there follows an epilogue written by Muhammad Iláhi Bakhsh, giving a continuation of the story of the third brother, but nothing of the kind is found in any of the other editions.

The Bulaq edition adds a so-called Book VII., but this is known to be a comparatively recent forgery. Haji Khalfa says:—"It is notorious that the Masnavi is contained in six books, but a seventh book has made its appearance, put forth by Isma'il Dadah, the commentator. He also wrote a commentary on it, and therein replied with eloquence and strenuousness to those who denied its genuineness. He says in his commentary that when he came to write out his fifth volume in the year 1035 A.H., he met with Book VII. in a copy of the Masnavi dated 814 A.H. He bought it and read it through, and was satisfied that it was undoubtedly a composition of the author of the Masnavi. But the other Darveshes of the Maulavi order denied the genuineness of the Seventh Book."[1]

The contents of this Seventh Book consist of comments on various texts and traditions, illustrated by stories of no interest. They have nothing in common with the Epilogue of Muhammad Iláhi Bakhsh, found in the Lucknow edition.

[1] Haji Khalfa, v. 377. Ismá'il was a Darvesh of the Maulavi order, surnamed Anqúravi, from his native place Anguri, in Anatolia.

The End

(چلپی) منبعی از فیض و الهام پیدا کرد و نم او را به‌رمز و کنایه با اثر بزرگ خود، مثنوی، پیوند زد. اخی ترک آخرین مرید، محبوب و خلیفهٔ رومی در ده سال آخر عمر شاعر بود که پس از مرگ وی در سال ۶۹۴ هجری قمری به‌عنوان «پیشوای طریقهٔ مولوی» جانشین او شد.

باید خاطرنشان ساخت که سال‌ها قبل از آنکه رومی ادعا کند او و شمس تبریزی «جانی در دو تن» هستند صوفیان نوعی عشق عرفانی و افلاطونی به‌وجود آورده بودند. در این وحدت، اختلافات جان‌های عاشق از میان برخاسته و هیچ‌چیز جز ذات وحدت عشق که هستی عشق و معشوق در آن مستحیل می‌شود باقی نمی‌ماند. رومی غزلیات خود را «دیوان شمس» می‌خواند و از نام شمس به‌گونه‌ای یاد می‌کند که گویی او و شمس جانی واحد می‌باشند.

رومی فلسفهٔ اعتقادی خود را در قالب‌هایی می‌ریزد که قبلاً توسط دو شاعر بزرگ، یعنی عطار و سنایی، طراحی شده بودند. رومی دین خود را به‌این دو شاعر بزرگ پنهان نمی‌سازد، امّا در تخیلات شاعرانه بسی فراتر از آنها پرواز کرده و مضامین غنی‌تری ارائه می‌دهد. شیوهٔ رومی در پرداخت موضوع آنچنان اصیل است که گویی «سبکی تازه» در ادبیات به‌وجود آمده است. در زبان فارسی، ذوق و قریحهٔ ادبی با آثار جلال‌الدین رومی به‌اوج بیان عرفانی رسید. قول دانته در مورد «کمدی الهی» به‌خوبی در شرح مثنوی صدق می‌کند. دانته می‌گوید:

«این اثر مربوط به‌قسمت اخلاقی فلسفه شده و قابلیت تجربی، نه جدلی، پیدا می‌کند. هدف غایی شعر تأمین سعادت و خوشبختی انسان‌هایی است که حالیه زندگی فلاکت‌باری را می‌گذرانند.» در واقع عرفان رومی نیز تجربی است، نه نظری؛ یعنی او بیشتر جان را ندا می‌دهد تا اندیشه را.

جمال آل‌احمد

دیباچه

مقالهٔ حاضر شرحی است مختصر از وقایع مهمّ زندگی مولانا جلال‌الدین رومی و رویدادهای برجسته‌ای که سرچشمه فیض عارفانه و الهام شاعرانهٔ او محسوب می‌شدند.

مولانا جلال‌الدین رومی در سال ۶۲۸ هجری قمری در شهر بلخ (خراسان) به‌دنیا آمد. در آن زمان، شهر بلخ تحت حکومت محمّد خوارزمشاه توسعه یافت. خاندان این شاعر صوفی نسل‌ها قبل در بلخ رحل اقامت افکنده و از احترام فراوان برخوردار بودند. تذکره‌نویسان نقل کرده‌اند که روحانیون و فقهای برجسته‌ای در دامان این خانواده پرورش یافتند.

در سال ۶۴۰ هجری قمری، بهاءِالدین ولد، پدر جلال‌الدین رومی، همراه با خانوادهٔ خود ناگهان از بلخ عزیمت کرد و رهسپار غرب شد. هجرت بهاءِالدین ولد بی‌تردید قبل از حملهٔ وحشتناک و قریب‌الوقوع ترکان مغول به‌زادگاه وی صورت گرفت. زارنده (لارنده)، اولین منزلگاه آنها در روم (ترکیه) و قونیه، مرکز امپراطوری سلجوقیان، آخرین اقامتگاه آنها بود.

جلال‌الدین بر اثر ارادت به‌برهان‌الدین ترمذی سرشار از شور و علاقه به‌آئین و مکتب تصوف شد. وی عمر خود را وقف تقلید از پیر خود نمود و تمام مراحل طریقهٔ تصوف را تا زمان فوت برهان‌الدین (۶۶۱ هجری قمری) طی کرد؛ آنگاه، او خود به‌مقام «شیخی» نایل گشت و با شخصیّت فیاض خود شاگردان را در روم مجذوب خود ساخت.

در سال ۶۶۵ هجری قمری، درویشی دوره‌گرد، که بعدها به‌نام شمس تبریزی شهرت یافت، وارد قونیه شد. جلال‌الدین چهرهٔ کامل آن محبوب الهی را که سال‌ها در جستجویش بود در وجود این غریبه یافت و او را با خود به‌خانه برد. آنها دو سال از یکدیگر جدا نشدند. در این مدت، شاگردان رومی که از درس استاد خود محروم، و از شیفتگی عمیق او به‌شمس سخت آزرده‌خاطر شده بودند، با دشنام و رفتار خصمانه به‌میهمان ناخوانده حمله می‌کردند. سرانجام، درویش به‌دمشق گریخت. امّا، جلال‌الدین که از غیبت یار و همدم خود عمیقاً پریشان‌حال شده بود در فکر جستجوی او بر آمد و سلطان ولد، پسر خود را در پی او روانه کرد. سلطان ولد درویش را با تکریم و احترام به‌قونیه بازگرداند. شاگردان رومی نیز از رفتار خود توبه کردند و مورد عفو قرار گرفتند؛ امّا دیری نپائید که آتش حسد در وجود آنها دوباره زبانه کشید و شمس را راهی دمشق ساخت. این بار نیز سلطان ولد مأمور شد تا اوضاع را سامان بخشد. عاقبت، این سالک اسرار در سال ۶۶۸ هجری قمری بی‌آنکه نشانی از خود برجا گذارد ناپدید شد. در پی این غیبت، جلال‌الدین رومی مجموعهٔ عظیمی از غزلیات عارفانهٔ خود را به‌یاد شمس تصنیف کرد و آن را به‌نام «دیوان شمس تبریز» به‌او اختصاص داد.

حیات معنوی دورهٔ بعدی زندگی رومی (۶۸۲ - ۶۷۲) تقریباً مشابه دورهٔ قبل است. جلال‌الدین سال‌ها عمر خود را وقف صلاح‌الدین زرکوب نمود و او را به‌عنوان «خلیفه» مسئول ارشاد طالبان و پیروان خود نمود. پس از مرگ صلاح‌الدین، شاعر با ارادت به‌مریدی دیگر به‌نام حسام‌الدین ابن اخی ترک

مولوی، جلال الدین محمد بن محمد، ٦٠٤-٦١٢ ق.

[مثنوی . برگزیده (انگلیسی)]

مثنوی معنوی : د اسپیریچو ّل کوپلتس آو. . .).

Masanvi i Manavi: the Spiritual couplets of Maulana Jalalu - Din Muhammad i Rumi/ Treanslated and abridged by E. H. Whinfield.- Teheran: Farhangsara Yassavoli , ١٣٧٥ = ١٩٩٦.

[٤]، ١٦٥ ص . : مصور (رنگی).

ISBN 964-306-030-6

فهرستنویسی براساس اطلاعات فیپا.

ص.ع. به فارسی : مثنوی معنوی مولانا جلال الدین محمد بلخی " مولوی "

زبان انگلیسی و مقدمه به فارسی.

چاپ دوم: ١٣٧٨.

١. شعر فارسی-- قرن ٧ ق.-- ترجمه شده به انگلیسی. ٢. شعر انگلیسی-- ترجمه شده از فارسی . الف. وینفیلد ، ادوارد هنری ، ١٨٣٦- ١٩٢٢، Whinfield, Edward Henry ، مترجم.

ب . عنوان . ج . عنوان : مثنوی . برگزیده . انگلیسی . د. عنوان :

Masnavi i Manavi: the Spiritual couplets of . . .

٩و٣٨٢آ / PIR ٥٣٠٠ ٨ ١/٣١فا
١٣٧٥

کتابخانه ملی ایران ٧٨-٥١٧٩ م

عنوان : مثنوی معنوی (متن انگلیسی)

مولف : مولانا جلالالدین مولوی

ترجمه و تلخیص از : ای ، اچ ، وین فیلد E.H. Whinfield

مقدمه : جمال آل احمد

ترجمه مقدمه و شرح تصاویر: کریم امامی

خوشنویسی : استاد امیر فلسفی

لیتوگرافی : امین گرافیک

چاپ دوم : شادرنگ ١٣٧٨

تیراژ: ٣٥٠٠ نسخه

ناشر: انتشارات یساولی

تهران: نرسیده به میدان انقلاب، بازارچه کتاب، طبقه زیرین تلفن: ٦٤٦١٠٠٣ نمابر:٦٤١١٩١٣

تهران: خیابان کریم خان، نبش خردمند، پلاک ٨٠ ، تلفن: ٨٣٠٤١٥ نمابر: ٨٨٣٢٠٣٨

شابک : ٩٦٤-٣٠٦-٠٣٠-٦

آدرس اینترنت: www.yassavoliran.com

مثنوی معنوی

مولانا جلال الدّین محمّد بلخی

«مولوی»

ترجمه و تلخیص به زبان انگلیسی:

ئی. اِچ. وینفیلد

انتشارات یساولی